# The Crooked Mile:
## Through peak oil, biofuels, hybrid cars, and global climate change to reach a brighter future

By
**Kevin Clemens**

## ALSO BY KEVIN CLEMENS

*Motor Oil For a Car Guy's Soul*

*Motor Oil For a Car Guy's Soul, Volume II*

*Eat Free or Die*

*A Lap of the Globe*

*Thirty Years of the Volkswagen Golf and Rabbit*

# The Crooked Mile:
## Through peak oil, biofuels, hybrid cars, and global climate change to reach a brighter future

**By**

**Kevin Clemens**

**Foreword by**

**Thomas Gladwin, PhD**

DEMONTREVILLE PRESS, INC.

Lake Elmo, Minnesota

The Crooked Mile: Through peak oil, biofuels, hybrid cars,
and global climate change to reach a brighter future
By Kevin Clemens

Copyright © 2009 Kevin Clemens
ISBN 978-0-9789563-3-2
Cover Design by Michael Jekot

Published by:
Demontreville Press, Inc.
P.O. Box 835
Lake Elmo, Minnesota 55042-0835 USA
www.demontrevillepress.com

Manufactured in the United States of America
Printed on recycled paper (FSC Certified)
Library of Congress Control Number: 2008911896

*iunctus populi*

# TABLE OF CONTENTS

# Foreword by Thomas Gladwin

For the past two decades, a small group of scientists and researchers has been trying to warn the world's population that they are on a collision course with reality of a finite planet. The society we have created in the western world is using up our planet's resources at a rate that cannot be sustained into the future. Emerging economies are following our misguided lead toward catastrophic over-consumption. If something isn't done to curtail our extravagance, within the next century we face life on a dramatically different Earth than the one that we call our home today. We are running out of oil, we are changing our global climate, we are using up water and land resources, and we are indiscriminately forcing plants and animals into mass extinction. We must confront problems that not only cross international boundaries, but also must face up to our moral obligations toward the currently deprived, future generations and the rest of life.

Faced with such awesome challenges, some are ready to throw in the towel and give up on humanity. Not Kevin Clemens. In *The Crooked Mile*, Clemens has rolled up his sleeves and met with the men and women who are working on the front lines in the search for answers to the planet's most pressing problems. Some of the people he has encountered have names that are found in the front-page headlines— others have toiled for years in the relative obscurity

X

of their laboratories. Each has a story to tell, and *The Crooked Mile* weaves together their experiences into a compelling narrative.

Clemens is an engineer, journalist, and a car enthusiast, and his book focuses on the future of the automobile and the much larger question of personal mobility. His ability to explain the past, present and future of technology permits an understanding of how we can and will get out the deep mess that we are in. We can't shrink away from the fact that some of those solutions will require us to make sacrifices for the common good.

Thomas Jefferson said, "No nation is permitted to live in ignorance with impunity." Our nation has lived in ignorance for far too long. This book has ignorance in its sights. It examines history and science and debunks the myths disguised as science that have prevented real progress. Time is running out, and if we are to leave any chance of building a better world to our children and to their children, we must act now and decisively.

Surprisingly, given the potential for gloom and despair, *The Crooked Mile* manages to find optimism. The real hope is found in today's youth. They are the ones who will ultimately be charged with solving the problems that the extravagance of our and previous generations has helped to create. We have left them with huge task, but as Clemens says of the millennial generation, "We are expecting great things." This book is an excellent starting point for readers of any generation—it tells the story of where we are, how we got here, and provides guidance on where should we be going if we wish to have a brighter and sustainable human future.

Thomas Gladwin, PhD
Ann Arbor, Michigan
January, 2009

*Thomas N. Gladwin is the Max McGraw Professor of Sustainable Enterprise at the Ross Business School and School of Natural Resources and Environment at the University of Michigan, The Associate Director of the Erb Institute for Global Sustainable Enterprise, and the Director of the Sustainable Mobility & Accessibility Research and Transformation (SMART) project, University of Michigan. He is a Core Faculty Member in HRH The Prince of Wales's Business & The Environment Programme.*

# Introduction

I am addicted to carbon—the fossilized liquid carbon found deep in the Earth in the form of oil. Oil that is pumped out of the ground, shipped around the world, and refined into gasoline and diesel fuel. I share my addiction with almost 300 million other Americans. Blessed with an abundance of natural resources, America's transition from muscle power, to wood, coal, and to oil has fueled revolutions in agriculture, science, medicine, politics, and transportation. Cheap energy has been the cornerstone of America's economic growth and the major reason for its rise to technological prominence over the past 200 years.

Oil has had a bigger impact on American mobility than all other types of energy. From the start of, and throughout most of the twentieth century, oil was easy to find and pump out of a well. It has been distilled and processed into a variety of products: kerosene for lighting and heating, lubricating oil and grease that keep machines moving, and gasoline and diesel fuel to power cars, buses, trucks, trains, ships, and airplanes.

"Cheap energy" came at a cost, however. Oil and coal are old carbon. They are leftover from the decay of plants and animals that lived millions of years ago. These organisms captured carbon dioxide from the atmosphere and eventually became hydrocarbons trapped within the Earth's crust. Oil has long been a cheap, plentiful, and

portable source of energy, and every time a doomsayer has predicted
we would eventually run out of it, another big oil field has been
discovered. There seemed to be no end to our ability to pull oil out of
the ground and burn it in our machines, particularly in automobiles,
returning the carbon dioxide that had been captured millions of years
ago back to the atmosphere.

Now it turns out that we really are running out of this
seemingly inexhaustible resource. The consensus among most
geologists and energy experts is that the amount of oil remaining
in the earth is finite, and a sustainable energy source must be found
soon to meet our future energy needs. What's more, there is also a
consensus among the world's top scientists (the Nobel Prize-winning
Intergovernmental Panel on Global Climate Change, or IPCC) that the
carbon dioxide buildup in the atmosphere, released largely through the
burning of oil and coal, is causing climate change on a global scale.

Oil has proven to be critical to transportation. Burning railroad
cars full of coal in a stationary power plant generates plenty of
electricity, but it is difficult to burn a lump of coal in an automobile,
truck, or jet airplane. Each day in the United States, we use enough
gasoline in our cars to fill a row of standard forty-two gallon oil
barrels reaching from New York to Los Angeles. Battery-electric cars,
gasoline-electric hybrids, fuel-cells, bio-mass fuels, ethanol and other
alcohol fuels, hydrogen, liquefied coal, and synthetic diesel fuels have
all been proposed as solutions to the problems of petroleum depletion
and the need to reduce greenhouse gases (of which carbon dioxide is
a major one), but as of this writing our reliance on the long line of oil
barrels remains.

My own case of oil addiction has been chronic. For much of
my professional career I have written about cars. I've driven cars in

all fifty states, in more than fifty countries, and on five continents. I've driven Ferraris through Alpine passes in Europe, Land Rovers through swampy jungles in Central America, and Porsches at more than 160 mph on race tracks. I've traversed South America's infamous Highway of Death, driven across trackless deserts, and raced an array of modern and vintage racing cars at many of the major tracks in North America. Cars have been a big part of my life, both when I worked as an engineer and in the time since then as I've built an interesting and often exciting career writing magazine stories and books about them. Lately however, I have begun to realize that my beloved automobiles have been the cause of many of the social, environmental, and economic problems and challenges that the world faces. Global warming, energy dependence, urban and suburban sprawl, and national security are all tied to the primacy of the automobile in shaping our society in America and, more recently, in developing parts of the world.

I began to wonder where the energy will come from that will allow us to continue driving our automobiles and living our energy intensive and highly mobile way of life. How would global climate change determine what car I drove to work and where I went on my vacations? Is there anything I could do now to make a difference in the future? What would personal transportation in the world of 2030 or 2050 look like when compared to today?

I decided I needed to go on my own quest to find what was being done to solve America's growing transportation and energy problems. As an advocate for personal mobility and a lifelong "car guy," I needed to find out who was working on these problems and what they saw as the outlook for the automobile.

My initial goal seemed simple: to find out for myself and

write about what is coming next in the world of transportation and to put a human face on the technologies that we will use to meet the future challenges of personal mobility. Little did I know how crooked and convoluted the path for my quest would become. If I had known how many sleepless nights I was in for, I would have stayed in my workshop and tinkered with my old cars. Unfortunately, the deeper I got into it, the more I discovered that finding a way out of this mess, caused in large part by 100 years of cheap energy, is not going to be easy.

# Chapter 1
## Driving Down a Slippery Slope

On the June 10, 1907, the total population of automobiles in Peking, the ancient capital of China, was five. How do we know this? Each of them had been carefully shipped some months earlier from Europe to take part in an extraordinary adventure: a race from Peking to Paris! The Chinese had never seen an automobile before, but they quickly invented a name for it. They called it a *chi-cho*, which meant fuel-chariot, as opposed to *huo-cho*, or fire-chariot, the Chinese name for the railway, a technology with which they were already familiar. The Wai-wu-pu, or State Council of the Celestial Empire, nervous about European imperialism and possible designs on the Far East, was more than a little relieved when all cars left the next day and Peking's streets returned to normal.

In the early years of the twentieth century cars were still new and nobody was quite sure what they could do. Speeds in excess of 100 mph had already been attained, but travel more than fifty miles from home was a risky proposition. When the French newspaper *Le Matin* proposed a 1907 race across two continents—from Peking in China to Paris in France—at first blush it appeared to be an impossible task. The absence of roads, lack of gasoline stations, and the possibility of armed highwaymen were just some of the difficulties. Yet, the race was on.

The undisputed favorite was Italian Prince Scipione Borghese, accompanied by his personal mechanic Ettore Guizzardi and an Italian

*The winning Itala on the 1907 Peking to Paris Race (Luigi Barzini)*

journalist named Luigi Barzini. An accomplished sportsman and explorer, Borghese had carefully researched the route and had arranged for fuel depots along the way. His choice of motorcar, a forty horsepower Itala automobile was known as a robust machine and was well prepared and meticulously maintained by his mechanic Ettore. On August 10th, after traveling more than 8,000 miles across China, Mongolia, Siberia, Russia, and Europe, Borghese rolled into Paris, winner of this amazing race and an instant worldwide celebrity. It didn't hurt that he carried a journalist on the Itala. Barzini's book, "Peking to Paris," chronicling the adventure became an international bestseller and was published in more than a dozen languages. Four of the five cars that left Peking eventually made it to the finish in Paris, the last arriving many weeks after the Itala. The fifth was lost somewhere in the Gobi desert…

A hundred years have passed since Prince Borghese and his fellow adventurers left Peking (now called Beijing) on his epic drive.

Today there are perhaps as many as 3.5 million cars in the city. Rush hour in Beijing lasts eleven hours a day, and more than 1,000 new cars are added to the city's traffic problems during each twenty-four hour period. Driving across the city during midday is a nightmare, as on any given day more than 90 percent of Beijing's urban roads are in gridlock. It's going to get worse, as China is predicted to pass the U.S. in the number of yearly new car sales within the next five years.

In May 2007, I went to Beijing along with 129 other teams of old-car aficionados to commemorate the hundredth anniversary of the 1907 race. My goal was to drive a 1929 Chrysler Model 77 Roadster from Beijing to Paris, but I quickly found that the immediate challenge was just getting from one side of Beijing to the other through bumper-to-bumper traffic. Often, I could barely see more than one city block through the dense haze caused by the city's air pollution. Earlier, on my morning jog through the city streets, it had been as if I was breathing through a straw. There was so much carbon monoxide and other pollutants choking my lungs in the smog-charged atmosphere. Add to the toxic mix generated by cars, trucks, buses, mopeds, motorcycles, and scooters the smoke created from the burning of coal used to produce more than 70 percent of China's electricity, and it's easy to see why on some days the city's air is nearly opaque.

It was my second time in Beijing—I'd been there for a few days in 2000 during another far-flung adventure of driving around the world in a 1959 Mercedes-Benz. Back then, the pollution didn't strike me as bad. At that time I thought that China might be able to control its traffic problems and perhaps avoid the air pollution and congestion that cities like Los Angeles, Phoenix, and Houston have long fought. Traffic from private vehicles was light and bicycles were everywhere. With just 1.5 million cars on its roads, I thought Beijing might find alternatives to gasoline and diesel-powered vehicles and create a cleaner and environmentally sound personal mobility system. Sustainability wasn't the buzz word then that it has become now, but Beijing seemed to me to be the perfect crucible for electric cars, hybrids, alternative fuels, and the range of urban mobility concepts that the world's other major cities were studying. Here was a chance to build a utopian world of clean and sustainable personal transportation without traffic and pollution. Starting effectively from scratch, could China pull off what so many countries wanted to achieve?

Seven years later, I found the answer in Beijing's overstressed highways, barely breathable air, and rapidly diminishing bicycle fleets. China's newfound emphasis on the automobile is being replicated around the globe in other emerging economies. As the worldwide market grows, automobiles are no longer considered a sign of wealth or a luxury, but as a necessity. Automobiles are rapidly becoming the preferred method of personal mobility, even in regions that relied on animal power less than a generation ago. In the United States, of course, our love affair with the automobile has been studied and dissected and often vilified as the cause of a variety of societal ills.

More than merely a mode of transportation, the automobile has provided Americans with freedom, social equality, and entertainment, but the price we have paid for our infatuation with having our own set of four wheels has often been high. The unintended adverse consequences of our largely unrestricted mobility has included air pollution, global climate change, economic dependence on foreign energy sources, injury and death in collisions, and a sprawled and inefficient social infrastructure. On the other hand, the freedom and convenience to travel almost anywhere at any time has provided much of the quality of life that Americans enjoy and, increasingly, the world wants to emulate. This option to travel wherever and whenever we wish induces middle-class Americans to spend up to 15 percent of their income on their automobiles.

I shouldn't have been surprised that the same autonomy the car provides to American citizens would prove so enticing to the Chinese, but seeing it first hand made me realize from a global view how it really will fall to Americans to find and adopt the answers to the personal mobility questions before we can expect the world to follow.

My 2007 drive across China, Mongolia, Siberia, Russia, Europe, and finally into Paris was successful. I returned home to the U.S., but I couldn't get the image of Beijing's choked and choking city streets out of my mind. It would be easy to blame inadequate automotive pollution controls or a wholesale disregard for the environment by China's government, but this would be a lie. While tailpipe emissions from China's booming automotive fleet of cars do contribute to the country's appalling air pollution, new vehicles made in China must meet stringent air pollution requirements and its fuel economy regulations are actually higher than those of the U.S.

All of those idling cars on Beijing's gridlocked highways were burning up plenty of precious oil and producing air pollution, but more and more they were doing so with relative cleanliness. I did discover that, just as in the U.S., burning coal in massive power plants to produce electricity is China's biggest source of both air pollution and the greenhouse gases that are creating global climate change. Coal is China's most important fossil fuel and the country relies on it for two-thirds of its energy needs. The problems don't end at the Chinese border. Sulfur dioxide and nitrogen oxides from its coal-fired plants fall as acid rain on Seoul, South Korea and Tokyo, Japan, while a significant amount of the particulate pollution in the skies over Los

Angeles can be traced to China, according to a report in the *Journal of Geophysical Research*. China's need for electricity is acute and a new coal-fired plant comes online someplace in the country nearly every week. The need for cheap energy to fuel a growing economy overcomes almost every other need, including concerns for air quality and the environment. In fact, in 2007 China became the world's biggest emitter of greenhouse gases, surpassing the U.S. for that dubious distinction.

Beyond the 100th anniversary of the historic Peking to Paris race, 2007 was also the year in which the American public woke up to the problems presented by declining oil supplies and global warming. Former Vice-President Albert Gore was honored with an Academy Award and a portion of the Nobel Peace Prize for his film "An Inconvenient Truth" and his work to make the world aware of the realities and possible outcomes of global warming. The Intergovernmental Panel on Climate Change (IPCC), a United Nations group that shared the Nobel Prize with Mr. Gore, concluded a nine year study that stated categorically and undeniably that global warming was both real and that it was to a large extent caused by human activity. In 2007, nuclear power, although long decried by a generation of environmentalists for the dangers posed by long-term storage of nuclear waste, came back onto the table because it provides electricity without producing greenhouse gases. At the same time, corn farmers were enjoying robust commodity prices on a record harvest and at least 20 percent of the U.S. corn crop was converted to ethanol, a form of alcohol that many believe will help displace imports of foreign oil. Ethanol is new carbon—a combination of carbon, oxygen, and hydrogen atoms that does not come from deep within the earth.

The Energy Independence and Security Act of 2007, mandating

ever increasing alternative fuel production and a new Farm Bill that continued to provide incentives to farmers who grow corn, further boosted the business of producing ethanol from corn. The Energy Act also demanded an increase of Corporate Average Fuel Economy (CAFE) to thirty-five miles-per-gallon for both trucks and cars by the year 2020, the first statutory increase in U.S. fuel economy since 1976.

Early in 2007, General Motors showed a concept car called the "Volt" at the North American International Auto Show in Detroit. This plug-in battery-gasoline hybrid vehicle promised huge gains in "fuel economy" by electrifying a part of the daily commute. Public reaction to the Volt was so strong that GM's executives, perhaps with visions of Toyota's successful Prius Hybrid in their heads and a short memory of the less than successful GM EV-1 electric car from less than a decade earlier, promised they would build a version of the Volt by 2010. Meanwhile, all through 2007, Toyota ran neck and neck with GM for the title of the world's largest automaker, partially on the halo image by vehicles like its Prius Hybrid.

In the decidedly third world, India's Tata truck manufacturer announced in 2007 a $2,500 gasoline-powered car, designed to replace the motorbike as the average Indian family's primary means of transportation, virtually guaranteeing a new and unprecedented level of congestion on India's already overcrowded streets. All the while worldwide oil prices flirted with $100 per barrel, finally breaking that barrier in the first few days of 2008. It seemed as though everyone was talking about oil, climate change, and future energy options, with the problems of the clean generation of electricity and the future of the automobile topping many lists.

Some have suggested that the best solution is to abandon the automobile, moving to alternative forms of public transportation. This will not happen. In just over 100 years, the automobile has become too heavily integrated into the fabric of American society to allow it to be easily replaced by less convenient systems. Further, the rapid emergence of the automobile in China, India, and other parts of the world ensures that the private automobile will expand its role as the primary means of transportation worldwide. Solutions must be found that allow the current levels of personal mobility that an automobile affords with a responsible attitude toward the environment, energy use, safety, and national security.

Meanwhile, ExxonMobil's profits during 2007 set a record at more than $40 billion, with a single quarter record of more than $11 billion. And 2008 ended up being even better for the oil giant with a third quarter of 2008 profit of $14.83 billion, the highest-ever quarterly profit for any company in any industry. After topping out at more than $140 a barrel, oil prices took a nose dive in late 2008, along with the rest of the world economy. Gasoline was cheap again in the U.S., going from more than $4.00 a gallon in July to less than half that in November, and when gasoline prices are low, many people don't think about alternative energy. During the 1980s, a reduction of oil prices by OPEC had the effect of killing off a variety of alternative fuel projects. It could happen again.

The realization that we have problems that need to be solved is dawning on the American consciousness. The 2008 presidential election campaign and cries of "Drill, baby, drill!" skirted energy, transportation, and environment issues, but managed to avoid tackling any of the real problems head-on. With all due respect to former vice presidents, few politicians understand the tough choices that we will need to make to enjoy a future that will allow us to retain the personal mobility represented by the automobile.

The opportunity to do nothing has passed. That was the option we chose to exercise over the last decade as we debated the existence of global warming and whether or not we would ever really run out of oil. All we can hope to do now is make decisions that will make the impacts of the challenges that we face less severe. To avoid calamitous climate change over the next forty years, accounting for the need for the third world to grow its economy and for the estimated increase in world population by three billion people, we in the U.S. and Western Europe will need to find a way to reduce our fossil fuel usage by 70 percent, and the emerging economies of China and India will have to curtail their emissions as they continue to grow. If you think that we can do that through the profligate use of coal, oil, and natural gas, continuing blithely with a business as usual attitude, you won't be allowed to play in this high stakes game in the future.

Two things are clear: the problems and possible solutions presented by little available oil and runaway global warming from greenhouse gases are being poorly communicated to the public, and most people have little idea of the vast amount of work that is already taking place in America and around the world to ensure a sustainable future. Significant television airtime and advertising paid for by energy companies and special interests are leading the public down a crooked path to make energy alternatives even more confusing, or to promise solutions without any mention of consequences.

The good news is that there *is* a range of solutions to our problem that are being explored. The bad news so far is that none of those solutions will fix all of our problems, and most of them introduce entirely new challenges that will need to be addressed. We must keep our options open, adapt as we learn, and avoid a wait-for-tomorrow complacency. Given the conflicting opinions offered by scientists, oil companies, politicians, environmentalists, and a host of other special interests, how do we move forward on the most viable course?

## Chapter 2
## Old Carbon

*Bang, chuff, chuff, chuff, chuff.* Every twenty seconds
the silence surrounding the Drake Well Museum near Titusville,
Pennsylvania is broken by the sound of the 10-horsepower single-
cylinder 1904 Klein engine in the Silver Run Pump Station. In the
early days of oil exploration, the man in charge of the pump engine
would tune the tip of the exhaust pipe so that the *bang* it made was
distinctive. That way the men who ran the wells would know from the
bang whether their particular rig was up and running.

*Bang, chuff, chuff, chuff, chuff.* This is hallowed and
consecrated ground. On August 27, 1859, precisely at this place, the
oil industry began. I've driven to Northwestern Pennsylvania on a cold
and rainy Saturday in October to see what Edwin Drake saw when he
sank his first well. It's a narrow valley, cut by Oil Creek, named such
in the eighteenth century because petroleum flowed out of the ground
from seeps and floated on the surface of its flowing waters. The Drake
Museum has done a good job of collecting artifacts from the early days
of oil. The Klein engine in the pump house is the real thing, running
on a supply of natural gas, just as it might have done at the turn of the
century. Just idling, it fires once and then makes four or five chuffing
revolutions of its huge flywheel before firing again. Nearby is a board-

for-board replica of Drake's 1859 well, created in 1945 on the exact spot of that first-ever oil well. How often is history so clearly defined?

*Replica of the Drake Well on the orinal spot where Drake found oil*

*Bang, chuff, chuff, chuff, chuff.* On my way into Titusville, the gas gauge on my beat-up, flex-fuel, Ford Ranger pickup truck was heading toward empty. I stopped at a convenience store masquerading as a gas station and asked if there were any stations with E85 ethanol nearby. The blank stare from the clerk said it all. I filled up with unleaded regular. Old carbon. Old carbon is coal, oil, and natural gas. It comes primarily from holes in the ground. Sometimes, those holes are on land, but more often lately, in the case of oil and gas, sometimes those holes are located on the sea bottom under thousands of feet of water.

*Bang, chuff, chuff, chuff, chuff.* Drake's well changed everything. For the remainder of the nineteenth century and all of the twentieth century, oil dominated our economy, our politics, our society and our position in the world. I stand among the bare dripping hardwoods in Drake Museum Park, next to the gently flowing Oil Creek, listening to the sounds of the past. This is why I have come: to find a small part of an answer to a much bigger question. How much of the twenty-first century will continue to be controlled by old carbon and how much of a role will new carbon play?

Prior to the 1840's in the U.S., the standard of energy

excellence for lighting was whale oil. It burned cleanly with a bright
flame and, if you were sufficiently wealthy, you had whale oil lamps,
just as your forbears had for the previous 500 years. By 1850, with
more than 700 ships in the American whaling fleet, the number of
whales rapidly decreased as they were hunted to near-extinction and
whalers had to travel further distances to find their prey. The higher
costs for these longer journeys and the decreasing supply drove
the price higher until prices reached more than $2.50 a gallon and
promised to go as high as $5.00 a gallon in 1850 dollars. (Without
accounting for inflation, those prices have an eerie resonance with
today's gasoline prices...) The promise of higher costs for the energy
represented by whale oil (an admittedly new carbon material, but
one that was a neither sustainable nor renewable resource at the rate
at which it was being consumed) prompted the search for alternative
sources of energy. There were plenty of options to choose from,
including turpentine made from sap from the abundant pine forests,
camphene (a purified oil from turpentine), and other rosin oils from
plants. None of the solutions produced satisfactory results. Enter old
carbon.

In 1846, Dr. Abraham Gesner demonstrated a lamp that
burned a type of oil that he had distilled from asphalt from the Great
Pitch Lake in Trinidad. Gesner, a Canadian who was fifty at the time,
had already made a name for himself with a career as a physician,
geologist, author, and full-time inventor. In 1853 he moved to New
York, applied for patents for the creation of illuminating oil from coal,
and set about creating a company to manufacture the new material that
he called kerosene. The acceptance of kerosene spread rapidly, and
by 1859 more than 5,000 gallons per day were made from Scottish
coal, imported across the Atlantic Ocean at a rate of 30,000 tons per

year. England's export of coal to the European Continent dated from the 1200s, so diverting some to the New World was apparently easier than finding a North American source. Gesner's plant made a variety of lubricating oils and solid paraffin for candles in addition to the kerosene that sold for $1.15 per gallon. Gesner was doing his part to save the whales.

Petroleum was well-known centuries before the first oil well, of course. Oil was in limited production in the U.S., usually by skimming it from seeps or tar pits where it had made its way to the surface. In Canada, a "well" was dug by hand in the summer of 1859 to augment the surface production, but "drilling" for oil was still unknown.

The Pennsylvania Rock Oil Company of New York was incorporated on January 13, 1855, with the objective to "raise, procure, manufacture and sell Rock Oil." This was the world's first oil company. In 1858, the company was reorganized and renamed the Seneca Oil Company. Colonel Edwin L. Drake, who at various times has been described by historians as the "father" of the oil industry and as an out-of-work railroad conductor, was not actually a Colonel. The rank was added to his name after he was hired by the Pennsylvania Rock Oil Company of New York to go looking for oil. He'd had the good fortune of staying at the same Hartford, Connecticut hotel where the directors of the Pennsylvania Rock Oil Company were meeting. They needed a man to send to assess some property along Oil Creek Valley in northwestern Pennsylvania, and Drake needed a job. The fact that he, as a former railroad employee, had a pass to travel by rail for free sealed the deal, making him the ideal choice.

Drake left his Connecticut home in December 1857 to begin his investigations. Over the course of the next year, the story goes that by noting that wells were drilled to obtain salty brines, he evolved a theory that more oil could be produced much quicker by drilling through the rock near places where oil was found above ground. Drake supposed that a layer of rock covered a reservoir of oil that lay beneath the ground. He convinced his backers and began drilling alongside the aptly named Oil Creek near Titusville, Pennsylvania in the summer of 1859, but had trouble when water kept filling the hole. His solution was to drive an iron pipe down to bedrock and to drill inside this pipe. On August 27th his well, drilled to a depth of only sixty-nine and a half feet, filled with oil. His well pumped twenty barrels of oil per day—double the production rate of any other source of oil at the time. A barrel of oil, which was standardized in 1866, was set at forty-two gallons, and it remains the method by which quantities of oil are measured today. A few weeks after it started producing, a lantern started a fire that burned Drake's oil derrick and the building above the well to the ground, but the word had already spread.

Kerosene could also be made from oil rather than coal, and soon the entire Oil Creek Valley was filled with oil derricks. By chance, Drake had actually hit a tiny pocket of oil at a shallow depth. Subsequent wells in the area needed to go between 600 and 1100 feet deep to find oil. His discovery had important political ramifications: he had helped begin a new industry on the eve of the Civil War, an industry that provided the Union with a huge export trade. When President Grant visited Titusville in 1871, he said to the inhabitants of the Pennsylvania's oil region, "…your efforts in the discovery and production of petroleum, aided materially in supplying the sinews of war, as a medium of foreign exchange, taking the place of cotton."

All of this is the "official" history of petroleum and of Colonel Drake, the one endorsed by the petroleum industry. No doubt the Horatio Alger-like image of the courageous Drake going it alone

to found the oil industry is appealing, but several researchers have
suggested that Edwin Drake was little more than an employee of the
Pennsylvania Rock Oil Company, and that the real hero of the story
should have been James M. Townsend, the leader of the New Haven,
Connecticut businessmen and capital-providers who had hired Drake.
Townsend later claimed it was he who first had the idea of drilling for
oil and that Drake was really only operating under his instructions.
Edwin Drake had never held any military positions and the "Colonel"
had gained his distinguished rank when his employers in New Haven
began to address his mail sent to Titusville to "Col. Edwin Drake"
in an effort to boost his standings within the small rural community.
Drake was a quiet and reserved man who was fond of stove-pipe
hats and whose life seemed to be filled with failure. He never moved
beyond the first well, even when others were buying up drilling sites
all over Titusville. In all, he made $10,000 from his oil venture in
Pennsylvania and later, shortly after leaving the oil business, he lost it
all stock speculating on Wall Street in 1863. His health failed and he
died penniless in 1881 in Bethlehem, Pennsylvania.

The oil industry needed its heroes and in 1902, Drake's body
was exhumed from its pauper's grave and placed in an elaborate
memorial in the Forest Lawn Cemetery in Titusville, Pennsylvania.
The memorial inscription describes him as the "…founder of the
petroleum industry, the friend of man."

In 1859, at the time when Drake sank the first oil well, nobody
was entirely sure exactly what petroleum was. Today, 150 years later,
the same is true. One thing it is not is crushed-up dinosaur bodies,
despite what all of those old 1960s Sinclair gas station signs with the
big green dinosaurs might have wanted us to believe. The prevailing
theory among geologists is that oil and natural gas result from fallout

of organic materials from tiny plants and algae and microorganisms onto the seafloor. These tiny plants and animals once captured and stored solar energy when they were living organisms. The fallout formed layers of sediments rich in organic materials. Later, thanks largely to movement of the tectonic plates forming rift zones where the plates separated, these organic sediments were buried deep within the earth. Those buried deep enough (7,500 feet would be deep enough) were raised to a temperature of around 175° F, providing the energy to, in the absence of oxygen, break down the long chains and rings of organic carbon from the plants and animals into smaller pieces. Those smaller chains with five to twenty carbon atoms became liquid crude oil. Those with fewer than five atoms formed natural gas. This is a simplification of course; actual crude oil contains thousands of different hydrocarbon chains and rings. Exactly how this takes place remains a mystery, but typically millions of years of heat and pressure are involved. This process didn't suddenly end millions of years ago; it is still taking place today, but the time required to complete the process is so long that waiting for recently buried organic matter to become oil isn't practical.

If the sediments are buried too deep (say below 15,000 feet) where temperatures are much higher, they tend to form pure methane gas, also called natural gas, a compound consisting of a single carbon atom and four hydrogen atoms. So, if oil forms from sediments that contain organic materials that were once on the surface and then are buried to a depth of 7,500 to 15,000 feet, then why did Colonel Drake find his oil sixty-nine and a half feet below the surface of the Pennsylvania countryside?

Oil is less dense than rock and floats on water. This means that it travels upward once it has been liberated from the shale rocks made up from sediments that were rich in organic materials. For oil to rise, cracks and pores in the rocks are required. Contrary to the image of immense subsurface caverns filled with liquid petroleum, oil is actually trapped in the pores of rocks like sandstone and limestone as if absorbed by a sponge. The oil and gas floats on water and will travel all the way to the surface, forming seeps and tar pits, unless it is stopped by an impermeable layer of rock that holds and collects the rising oil, preventing it from reaching the surface. Drill through the impermeable rock (which is often also a shale) and you'll reach the oil waiting beneath it. Sometimes, thanks to pressure exerted by natural gas, the oil will flow freely from the porous rock once it is tapped by a well. More often, it must be pumped to bring it to the surface. Gushers in the old days were powered by significant natural gas pressure behind the oil.

In the early days of oil production, explosives were sent to the bottom of the oil well to form cracks that let the oil flow more easily to the pump. Today, these cracks are often created with high pressure blasts of steam or carbon dioxide. In Drake's case, a small amount of oil that had been destined to make its way to the surface got trapped beneath an area of impermeable rock and Drake was just lucky enough to drill in that spot.

Less than 1 percent of sedimentary rocks contain the over 5 percent of organic carbon needed to form oil. Areas without an impermeable cap have already lost their gas and oil. When the $2 billion, 8,000 foot deep Mukluk well in the Beaufort Sea, fourteen miles off the north coast of Alaska ended up being a dry hole in 1983, Richard Bray, the president of Sohio's production company is reported to have said, "We drilled in the right place, we were simply thirty million years too late."

Some sediment gets buried so deeply that the temperature converts the organic materials entirely to methane. All of these conditions make it pretty difficult to find oil. When it all works perfectly, you get an oil region like the Middle East, West Texas, or the North Sea. It rarely all works perfectly.

At first, oil was easy to find and the demand for kerosene fuel was easily met. Early refineries processed the oil into paraffin wax and kerosene, which could be sold, and gasoline, although much more dangerous and volatile than kerosene, found use in stoves and lighting. It was dangerous stuff and newspapers from the 1870s and 1880s were filled with accounts of house fires caused by gasoline that claimed hundreds of lives.

Meanwhile, in the 1860s the German engineer Nikolas August Otto was developing a stationary engine that ran on a gaseous fuel derived from coal. An engineer named Gottlieb Daimler went to work for Herr Otto and together they perfected the concept four-stroke Otto-cycle engine that is still used today. Daimler and Otto had a falling out and Daimler left in 1882 to develop a more portable engine that used liquid gasoline as a fuel. After initial trials in a boat, in 1885 the engine was placed in a three-wheel contraption that could move under its own power. Ironically, another German, Karl Benz, was working on the same concept at the same time and his gasoline-powered motorized tricycle also appeared in 1885. Benz got his machine into production by 1888 and Daimler followed in 1889. Others, like the Duryea brothers (in the U.S.) in 1893 came up with their own designs and the automobile age began. While at first, automobiles served as expensive play-toys for the rich, machines like the Curved Dash Oldsmobile (1902) and the Model T Ford (1908) resulted in a growth in popularity and by the early teens, demand for petroleum refined into gasoline skyrocketed, and has never declined since.

By the late teens, researchers, convinced that crude oil supplies were limited, were looking for additives that would improve fuel economy and stretch the remaining petroleum reserves. General Motors, under Charles Kettering was in the forefront of this work and his top researcher, Thomas Midgley worked assiduously from 1919 until 1921 to find a material to reduce engine knocking and allow higher compression ratios for better fuel economy. Although a variety of additives, including ethyl alcohol, or ethanol, were found to have the desired effect, Midgley and Kettering finally settled upon a material that, while effective at reducing engine knock, would prove to be harmful to the health and well-being of every living creature on the planet for the next sixty years.

The stuff was called tetraethyl lead (TEL), a laboratory oddity that when added in small quantities to gasoline, would reduce engine knock. The fact that lead was a powerful neurotoxin seemed unimportant to the researchers at General Motors. Midgley himself suffered the debilitating effects of lead poisoning and had to take time off to recuperate, yet he would often pour the substance onto his bare hands to demonstrate its supposed safety. In 1924, General Motors formed a joint venture called the Ethyl Gasoline Corporation with Standard Oil and DuPont to produce leaded gasoline. DuPont owned a significant part of General Motors (43 percent) and was looking for ways to enhance its investment and producing vast quantities of the highly poisonous tetraethyl lead seemed just the ticket. Things got off to a rocky start. In October of 1924, a miscalculation at a Standard Oil refinery in New Jersey led to the deaths of seventeen refinery workers and many agonizing and disabling injuries. DuPont also managed to kill several of its workers in its TEL plant in Delaware. The workers called the stuff "looney gas."

The public outcry against leaded gasoline was led by Yandell Henderson from Yale University and Dr. Alice Hamilton, a physician who trained at the University of Michigan, the first female professor at Harvard University, and the founder of the field of occupational medicine. Hamilton had written as early as 1910 on the dangers of lead exposure in children. Henderson and Hamilton provided what amounted to the first attempt at environmental activism by objecting to the use of lead in gasoline. Although the toxic effects of chemicals on human neurology was an emerging science, they convinced the government to hold a hearing and gave scientific testimony on the harmful effects of lead, especially on small children. The government's own Bureau of Mines did research into the safety of lead (subsidized by the lead industry) and found leaded gasoline to be perfectly safe.

The public face of the lead industry was a toxicologist named Robert Kehoe. Initially, he was hired by Kettering in 1924 to study the hazards of tetraethyl lead in manufacturing plants, and in 1925 rose to the position of chief medical consultant to the Ethyl Corporation. He was also the first director of the Kettering laboratory—founded with a $130,000 gift from GM, DuPont, and Ethyl Corporation at the University of Cincinnati. Kehoe believed that lead was a naturally occurring substance in the body and fought any attempt to characterize the substance as a poison. With substantial funding from the lead industry, his laboratory published reports and findings clearing lead of any health hazards. He even sat on the Surgeon General's Board that exonerated lead against the charges by Henderson and Hamilton. Kehoe would continue working for the lead industry, promoting leaded gasoline as perfectly safe, until shortly before his death in 1992 at the age of 99.

Eventually DuPont and Standard Oil devised ways to handle the deadly TEL more safely in the plants and the risk of lead in the atmosphere was largely forgotten until the 1960s. The Ethyl Corporation grew in power during the 1930s and would tolerate no criticism of its products from its competitors. In a restraining order, the Federal Trade Commission told competitors to stop criticizing Ethyl gasoline as it "…is entirely safe to the health of [motorists] and to the public in general when used as a motor fuel, and is not a narcotic in its effect, a poisonous dope, or dangerous to the life or health of a customer, purchaser, user or the general public."

The oil companies made sure that gasoline (containing tetraethyl lead) was the fuel of choice, defending it vigorously against all comers, including ethanol, which was proving popular in other less oil-rich parts of the world.

Gasoline and its procurement played a major role in World War II. In the 1920s, German scientists had developed ways of synthesizing gasoline from coal. During the Second World War, Germany's Luftwaffe was kept aloft with synthetic leaded aviation gasoline. At first, this synthetic fuel was inferior to the petroleum-based aviation gas used by the Allies and the performance of German aircraft suffered as a result. In fact, in tests during the early part of the war, captured enemy aircraft were found to have superior performance to many Allied fighter planes when fueled with the high-performance fuel that the Allied powers used. Before the war started, General Motors (under direction from DuPont) and Standard Oil of New Jersey had formed a joint venture, Ethyl G.m.b.H. with the giant chemical company, I.G. Farben, to produce tetraethyl lead to use in the gasoline for German military aircraft. By the end of the war, Germany's synthetic gasoline, bolstered by tetraethyl lead provided the same performance levels as the gasoline used by the Allies.

Over time, oil did become increasingly difficult to find, but large deposits like the huge East Texas oil field, discovered in 1930, and the super-giant Ghawar field in Saudi Arabia, the largest in the world, discovered in 1948, made many people in the oil industry believe the quantity of oil in the Earth was unlimited. Except for one man named M. King Hubbert.

Marion King Hubbert was born in 1903, grew up in central Texas, and went to the University of Chicago. He studied not only geology, but also math and physics and earned his doctorate degree in 1937. He began working as a geophysicist at Shell Oil in 1943. He made numerous contributions to the field of geology but his most lasting contribution came in 1956 when he presented a paper titled *Nuclear Energy and the Fossil Fuels* at the meeting of the American Petroleum Institute. In his controversial paper, using mathematical models that supposed that oil production would follow a bell-shaped curve, Hubbert predicted that U.S. oil production from the lower forty-eight states would peak in 1971. Predictions of a limit to oil production had been made before, and despite his high standing among geologists and geophysicists, his conclusions were generally rejected. That is, until the early 1970s, when it became clear that U.S. oil production had reached its peak and had begun a decline. Hubbert had been right.

On person who believed Hubbert had been Ken Deffeyes. At an age when many retired college professors might be playing with their grandchildren, Kenneth S. Deffeyes is writing books and giving lectures about "Hubbert's Peak" and worldwide peak oil. Having grown up in the "oil patch," the son of a petroleum engineer, Deffeyes worked with M. King Hubbert at Shell Research in the late 1950s. He accepted Hubbert's argument that the oil industry would eventually decline and left that industry, eventually ending up in 1967 as a professor of geology at Princeton. He retired a few years ago as Professor Emeritus. After retiring, Deffeyes's somewhat simplified the mathematical approach used by Hubbert to calculate the peak in worldwide oil production. His calculations, reported in his 2001 book *Hubbert's Peak,* gave a peak of worldwide oil output of sometime in 2003. He has since revised that estimate, now saying that peak production occurred sometime at the end of 2005. Others, reputable geologists, and oil industry observers among them, have placed estimates in the 2010 to 2020 time frame. The opposing camp, including some oil companies and the Organization of Petroleum Exporting Countries (OPEC) claim that oil production will never peak or that the peak is at least a century away. Web sites and books have been dedicated to "Peak Oil," often predicting the exact instant that Hubbert's Peak will be reached and describing in great detail the mayhem in terms of starvation, pestilence, and warfare that will befall all of civilization shortly after that point has been reached.

Even if he hadn't achieved notoriety from his "peak oil" predictions, Deffeyes (rhymes with "the maze") was already famously depicted in John McPhee's 1999 Pulitzer Prize-winning book *Annals of The Former World.* Deffeyes and McPhee had traveled across the United States together with the geologist acting as an Earth sciences tour guide to the writer. I met Ken Deffeyes at the 43rd Annual Nobel Conference at Gustavus Adolphus College in 2007, in St. Peter, Minnesota. Deffeyes had just given a talk titled *Peak Oil: Here and Now* to the 6,500 assembled conference attendees. McPhee had described the geologist as "… a big man with a tenured waistline," and that "His hair lies behind him like Ludwig van Beethoven's." Standing in front of me was a big guy with longish white hair who fit the description.

I asked Deffeyes how soon he thought the peak oil situation would make itself known.

"I'm afraid the crunch is going to happen in the term of the next president," Deffeyes said. "Who we elect right now is going to be our president through a time of major crisis." I then asked him how he saw the transition from our dependence on oil to some other form of energy.

"Painful!" he said. "I don't see any of them [referring to the current crop of politicians] as another Kennedy, Churchill, or Roosevelt."

According to the U.S. Government, the idea that the oil resources in the Earth are finite is a sound one. In February, 2007 the United States Government Accountability Office (GAO) provided a report to Congress with the catchy title "Crude Oil: Uncertainty about Future Oil Supply Makes it Important to Develop a Strategy for Addressing a Peak and Decline in Oil Production." Using estimates of the total amount of oil left in the ground from a 2000 study by the United States Geological Survey (USGS), the GAO report quoted an Energy Information Administration (EIA) estimate that worldwide oil production would peak in the year 2037.

The amount of oil used each day in the world is almost inconceivable in its scale. Ever since the 1860s, oil has been measured in an archaic system called the barrel. A barrel of oil used to be made of wood and was about nineteen and a half inches in diameter and slightly more than thirty-three inches high with a volume of forty-two gallons. Oil isn't shipped in barrels anymore, but if all of the 83,607,000 barrels of oil used every day worldwide was actually contained in standard wooden barrels they would cover an area about

5,067 acres or, in that most American of measurements, the barrels would fill up 3,839 football fields. Placed side by side the barrels would extend 25,731 miles, which conveniently is just a bit more than the circumference of the earth at the equator.

Only slightly more manageable to get your head around, are the 9,253,000 barrels (or 388,600,000 gallons) of gasoline used in the U.S. each day. That's enough to fill 588 Olympic-sized swimming pools (at 660,253 gallons each). If each of these barrels were placed side by side, they would form a line 2,848 miles long, easily covering the distance from Times Square in New York, to the Hollywood Bowl in Los Angeles, with some extra for sightseeing on the way. Remember, this is the amount of gasoline used each day, every day, by Americans driving to school and work and just about everywhere they want to go. The United States is well past its "peak oil" in terms of production, and we now import 60 percent of our oil from a world that is rapidly reaching its own peak in production.

Today, tomorrow, or thirty years from now? What is the significance of "peak oil?" The one thing it doesn't mean is that the world will run out of oil the moment the peak has been reached. What it does mean is that we will have used half of all of the oil that we will ever produce. If we are able to economize or find alternative forms of energy, we can stretch the time over which the remaining 50 percent will be used up. There are lots of arguments that new "unknown" oil supplies could be found, but the estimates for the peak of oil production already take into account that new supplies will come on-line as other known oil fields begin or continue their decline. Practically speaking, after that point in time that represents peak oil, the amount of oil available worldwide each year will be less than the year before, and we will have to learn to live with that reality.

The idea that worldwide oil production will peak suddenly and drop off precipitously, causing an oil-starved doomsday may not be the correct model. Oil production may remain at high levels over a decade or more as the remaining conventional oil is used up to maintain our current energy intensive lifestyle. This was the case in the early 1970s, when U.S. production peaked as predicted by M. King Hubbert, we simply and dramatically increased our imports of foreign oil to ensure that our economy and way of life wouldn't falter. Today, we could be using the remaining oil to find suitable energy alternatives if we would have the discipline to do so. Perhaps more likely, given our past history, we will use the remaining resources to fuel "business-as-usual" until we suddenly find ourselves without the energy resources needed to get to the next stage in the energy game.

Critics of the peak oil position point to "unconventional" oil supplies as providing all the energy that we will need through at least another century. "It's not a matter that the stuff is running out," said Shell Oil's Neil Golightly at a 2008 Mobility Conference in Michigan, "but it is getting a whole lot harder to get to it— and a lot more expensive." Unconventional oil refers to petroleum that comes from sources that are harder to process than the traditional hole-in-the-ground oil well. These include deep sea oil platforms, drilling at depths of more than 10,000 feet below the water surface or in the harsh regions of the Arctic Ocean. "The stuff that's left tends to be under either very cold ice, very deep water or very, very complicated governments," said Golightly.

A fourth of the nation's oil production comes from the Gulf of Mexico and BP's Thunder Horse platform is a good example of the lengths that oil companies will go to produce that oil. Thunder Horse sits 150 miles southeast of New Orleans in the Mississippi Canyon area of the Gulf. The water is more than a mile deep here (6,200 feet) and the oil is pumped from twenty-five wells on the Gulf floor that drill down another three miles below the seabed. Thunder Horse, which is the world's largest floating platform, produces 250,000 barrels of crude oil a day and 200 million cubic feet of natural gas. The production and drilling facility is operated by BP, which owns 75 percent of the enterprise, while the remaining 25 percent is owned by ExxonMobil.

Shell Oil is also in the deep sea exploration game and its latest project is the Perdido Development, 200 miles from shore in the Gulf of Mexico in water that is 7,500 feet deep. The technology for Perdido (which means "lost" in Spanish) is all-new, consisting of a 555-foot long, 118-foot diameter cylindrical spar that's tied down to the sea-floor. The spar is capable of processing oil and gas from seafloor wells drilled as far as nine miles away, along with the twenty-two wells drilled directly beneath it. Oil and gas are separated at the spar's base and then pumped to the surface with pumps powered by 1,500-horsepower gas turbines. Shell owns 35 percent of Perdido, while Chevron owns 37.5 percent and BP 27.5 percent.

Unconventional also refers to oil from oil sands like those in the vast Athabasca oil sand region in Northern Canada or the oil shale deposits in the American West. Depending upon who you talk to, oil shale is either America's greatest chance at energy independence, or an environmental disaster of epic proportions just waiting to happen.

Oil shale isn't really oil at all, it's sedimentary source rock that hasn't yet undergone the necessary heat and pressure to become oil. There is a lot of it under Colorado's Western Slope; some estimates put the amounts at the equivalent of more than 800 billion barrels of oil which is three times more than Saudi Arabia's proven oil reserves.

The problem is that nobody knows how to create oil from the fine-grained shale rock and researchers from major oil companies have been trying since the mid-1970s. Shell Oil is the latest to try and has devised a scheme that is promising. The old method was to remove the rock, pulverize it and then raise it to a temperature above 900 degrees Fahrenheit to convert it to oil.

Yields in this process were low and the costs were prohibitive. In Shell's new process, a series of wells are drilled, into which are lowered 2,000 foot long heating elements that, over the course of a year or more, raise the rock to 650 degrees Fahrenheit. What emerges from the wells is a high-quality (technically synthetic) oil that can be further refined into gasoline and diesel fuel. The problem is that the underground oil can contaminate the ground water if no barrier is put in place. Shell's proposed solution is to circulate aqueous ammonia in deep wells beneath the mine area to produce a wall of ice that contains the shale oil. How well this hot and cold system will work is problematic as Shell has yet to test the concept. What is known is that any technique for oil shale processing so far suggested requires huge amounts of energy and large quantities of water, a resource that is already scarce in the region and one that will soon become critical.

Western water will have a huge effect on every future energy project, including oil shale, in the region. With as much as 90 percent of Colorado's available water dedicated to agriculture, some of the state's cities and towns that depend on groundwater wells for their water source are expected to exhaust their accessible supplies by 2050. The source of underground water in the west from northern Texas through the Dakotas is the vast underground Ogallala Aquifer, fossil water whose level is rapidly dropping and that is not being replenished. Nonetheless, at the end of 2008, the Bush Administration gave energy and oil companies steep discounts in royalties and opened 1.9 million acres of federal property in Wyoming, Colorado, and Utah to potential oil shale development. With the technology in its infancy, even the most optimistic energy experts say that oil shale commercialization is at least a decade or more away.

If oil shale is off in the future, Canada's Athabasca oil sands in Alberta are producing enough oil to help Canada become the United State's top oil supplier; we import more oil from Canada than we do from Saudi Arabia. The oil sands (also called tar sands) are in an area of northern Canada that is the size of Florida. The thick tar is literally mixed with sand, which is dug from huge open pit mines and then treated with vast quantities of hot water to remove the oil from the sand. Another method of mining involves injecting steam deep into the ground and then pumping out the oil. Extracting the oil from the sand produces three times the amount of carbon dioxide compared with producing conventional crude oil and the process leaves behind vast wastewater ponds that are highly toxic to birds, animals, and humans.

The crude oil from Canada's tar sands is pumped through a pipeline whose terminus is Superior, Wisconsin, located on the shores of Lake Superior. Some of the oil is refined there, while much of it is shipped to other oil refineries throughout the upper Midwest.

Canada's oil sand reserves are estimated to be more than 173 billion barrels, but the environmental costs are clearly high in terms of water used, energy to heat the water and process the oil, water pollution, air pollution, greenhouse gas emissions, and harmful effects to the population living near and downstream from the pit mines and processing. The land that has been disturbed for the mining process was once a part of Canada's pristine and ancient boreal forest.

For America, peak oil is real. Regardless of whether the

worldwide peak oil has already happened, is happening now, or is
still decades in the future, America's ability to obtain and exploit
cheap energy has already reached its peak and is headed for a decline.
Perhaps the most oft-quoted statistic in any energy discussion is that
Americans use 24 percent of the world's oil, while we account for only
2 percent of the world's population.

The world is changing. We are no longer the only large-scale
energy users in the game, and the stakes have increased dramatically.
Countries that were once energy exporters will, as their energy
resources begin to decline, look to fill their own needs with any
reserves that they have left. The GAO estimates that 85 percent of the
world's oil reserves are in countries with medium to high investment
risks or where foreign investment is prohibited. We won't be able
to buy our way into this oil. Others, most particularly China, are
emerging as massive energy users and are forming alliances with
countries that produce oil to ensure their own continuing supply.
The GAO also reports that 60 percent of the world's oil reserves are
in regions where political instability could hamper exploration and
production. America's ability to access cheap energy has peaked
because much of the world's oil has already been removed from our
grasp.

It can also be argued that "cheap oil" has never really existed,
particularly for Americans. Although our gasoline prices have
traditionally been less than half of what Europeans or Asians pay for a
gallon of gasoline, the price we pay at the pump is a small percentage
of what that gasoline really costs us. During the past decade there have
been more than a dozen studies that have tried to quantify exactly
what a gallon of gasoline costs an American consumer. It isn't an
easy project. Researchers have to consider the subsidies paid by the

American government to U.S. based oil companies so that they can compete with international companies to ensure comparatively low prices at our pumps. Even at a time when they are making record profits on their oil sales, U.S. oil companies receive tens of billions of dollars in tax breaks and subsidies to make sure that they will be able to continue to search for more oil and develop new oil fields, if and when they are found.

To make accurate fuel cost estimates, the social costs of gasoline usage need to be considered. For example, each tank of gasoline you burn through adds an incremental amount of air pollution to your city or town. This increase in air pollution results in a small increase in health problems that include asthma, emphysema and pneumonia, which add to the costs of health care. These unseen costs are ultimately paid by society, through higher health insurance rates, higher medical costs to offset the uninsured, and through the premature loss of individuals who would have been able to continue to contribute to society. In Europe, significantly higher taxes are levied against transportation fuels, helping to subsidize nationalized health care and other social costs that result from gasoline and diesel fuel usage.

Each tank of gasoline burned also makes a contribution to global warming through carbon dioxide release, which will eventually lead to sea-level rise, desertification, species extinction, global food shortages, and a host of additional unpleasant and extremely expensive consequences. Because carbon dioxide lasts for decades and freely diffuses into the entire stratosphere, the enormous greenhouse gas emissions from China, the U.S. and Europe add to the societal costs in every part of the world. The costs of limiting those emissions or mitigating the damages on a global scale caused by climate change are enormous, but are as yet unaccounted for in the price of a gallon of gasoline.

Perhaps the most visible of the "external" costs are the military expenditures needed to protect oil supplies and shipping lanes from the Persian Gulf to customers around the world. The best way to ensure your own energy security is to ensure the energy security of your enemies (and friends). The Persian Gulf supplies a quarter of the world's oil and about 14 percent of the U.S. oil needs. The U.S. has committed to ensuring that shipping lanes remain open and that oil flows from the highly volatile region of the mid-east to places like Europe, South America and Japan. It can be argued that protection of our national interests is the reason for which the U.S. military exists in the first place, but yearly costs of $50-$80 billion can be directly attributed to this role of oil shipping-lane traffic cop.

Then there is Iraq. We are told that the U.S. yearly expenditures of $200 billion are being used for security and to rebuild that country. According to the U.S. Energy Information Agency (EIA), "Iraq holds more than 115 billion barrels of oil— the world's second largest proven reserve." The question as to how much of the money going into Iraq should be reflected in our "true" cost of a gallon of gas can be endlessly debated. Accounting for the lives of several thousand U.S. servicemen and the deaths of hundreds of thousands of Iraqis is also an impossible task.

Estimates of the contributions of some or all of these factors to the cost of a gallon of gasoline have been made and range from $5 per gallon to over $15 per gallon. The amount we pay at the pump, even at prices well over $3 and higher per gallon, doesn't come close to reflecting the real cost of a gallon of gasoline. The least we can do is try to burn it efficiently.

# Chapter 3
## Aiming For Efficiency

Even after more than 100 years of continuous development, our automobiles are remarkably inefficient machines. A modern gasoline-powered internal combustion engine, the kind you use to drive your car to work everyday, has a peak efficiency of 25-30 percent and an average efficiency of 15-20 percent. In theory, an internal combustion engine is limited to a maximum efficiency of about 50 percent by the temperature tolerance of the materials used to make an engine. The Carnot cycle is the basic thermodynamic model of the internal combustion engines that we use today and is named after Nicolas Leonard Sadi Carnot, who proposed a hypothetical heat engine in 1824. No amount of tinkering can improve on this "Carnot" efficiency of about 50 percent. Actual engine efficiency is lower because of internal friction and combustion characteristics—both of which are amenable to tinkering. Still, what's important to us is that an efficiency of 20-30 percent means of the energy available in each gallon of gasoline, more than 70-80 percent of it is wasted as an unavoidable cost of using and engine in the real world.

Where does this energy go? Much of it (about a third) is lost as heat in the exhaust system and cooling system. The temperature in the combustion chamber at the instant of ignition can be higher than 1,500° C and the exhaust system conducts much of this heat energy away from the engine, releasing it to the atmosphere. Likewise, the engine cooling system pulls heat away from the cylinder heads and combustion chambers and using the engine's radiator, releases it to the surrounding environment. Some of the energy from the gasoline (about another third) is also consumed by the engine itself through the internal friction generated as the pistons slide up and down inside the cylinders and the crankshaft and camshafts rotate in their bearings. Equipment such as the electrical alternator, power steering pump, water pump, and air conditioning compressor exact their toll from the gasoline's energy. Further, the transmission, final drive gears, and tire rolling resistance consume energy that reduces efficiency. Lastly, the vehicle must move over the ground and through the air and as its speed increases the effects of tire rolling resistance and aerodynamic drag significantly impact the amount of energy consumed (the final third of the energy available from the fuel).

The past twenty years has seen remarkable innovation and improvement in the reduction of internal engine losses through the use of low-tension piston rings, reducing the surface areas of engine bearings, the application of super-slippery synthetic lubricating oils, and improved and more efficient design of accessory belts and drive systems. Gasoline engines have also seen a revolution through microprocessors that monitor and control ignition timing and fuel delivery that improves combustion and emissions. Unfortunately, at least in the United States, automakers have largely applied these innovations and technologies in an effort to increase horsepower and vehicle performance instead of dramatically reducing fuel consumption. Our vehicles have gotten bigger and heavier (caused in part by their larger size and in part by the addition of safety systems such as airbags) and significantly faster during the past two decades, but fuel economy has stayed relatively constant over the past twenty years.

There are ways to make both internal combustion engines and vehicles that are more fuel-efficient. Car companies and research laboratories are working to design smaller engines that consume less fuel, but provide the same levels of performance. The Europeans have placed a great deal of emphasis on diesel engines for both passenger cars and sport utility vehicles. Diesel engines are more efficient than gasoline engines (a theoretical Carnot maximum of about 55 percent), largely because they squeeze their air and fuel mixtures to much higher pressures in the combustion chamber through significantly higher compression ratios (20:1 or more) compared with those found in a modern gasoline engine (about 10:1). Diesel engines do not use spark plugs; instead, the heat caused by the enormous compression in the cylinder causes spontaneous combustion of the diesel fuel and air mixture.

Most modern diesels use a turbocharger to force even more air and fuel into the cylinder before combustion to increase power output, allowing for a smaller engine displacement. Modern turbo-charged diesel engines are reaching efficiencies of around 40 percent.

In the U.S., we have had a tendency to associate diesels with large trucks belching vast amounts of soot into the air, but unlike earlier models, modern diesel engines inject fuel at extremely high pressures directly into the combustion chamber, resulting in low emissions, impressive performance and high fuel economy results. Mercedes-Benz and Volkswagen have led the charge for diesel engines in the U.S., developing vehicles that can be sold in all fifty states

(California and a few other states have had restrictions on previous diesel designs due to the emission of particulates). Although they are expensive (especially when fitted with the high pressure injectors and turbochargers needed for low emissions and high economy), diesels promise to be an increasing part of the reduction in carbon dioxide emissions and reduced fuel consumption. But that Carnot efficiency of around 50 percent still vexes us in a diesel or a gasoline powered vehicle.

The problem with most advanced and highly efficient gasoline and diesel engine designs is that they are typically being placed back into the same heavy and inefficient vehicles that for more than a decade we have loved so much. In the U.S. we often drive 6,000 pound vehicles (SUV, pickup trucks and full-size sedans) with engines that produce 300, 400, and even 500-horsepower and deliver less than twenty miles per gallon. Each gallon of gasoline or diesel fuel from fossilized carbon that is consumed is one gallon less that remains for the future. The vehicle manufacturers have defended themselves saying that they deliver what the public wants and, although I am embarrassed to say so, car magazines like the ones I have written for the past fifteen years have been pouring gasoline on the flames of automotive passion by embracing and celebrating such examples of rolling excess.

The idea that Americans would always want big SUVs and pickup trucks fell apart in the middle of 2008 when oil prices surged to more than $140 per barrel and gasoline price nationwide topped $4.00 a gallon. Although undoubtedly also influenced by a soft economy, SUV sales dropped 55 percent compared to a year earlier and pickup truck sales dropped by 40 percent. Companies like GM and Ford, American icons that had existed for more than 100 years, and whose bread and butter was selling light trucks and SUVs, were caught without a strategy to ensure survival. GM's stock closed well below $10 a share, the lowest it had been in more than fifty years. Even Toyota, whose Prius hybrid set an example of the kind of vehicles Americans suddenly wanted, was stuck with stocks of its now unwanted full-sized Tacoma pickup truck on dealer's lots.

A few months of $4.00 a gallon gasoline had done what environmentalists, urban planners, and economists had been unable to do for decades: move Americans away from their love affair with rolling excess. When gasoline prices rose, Americans responded by driving less. In the fourth quarter of 2008, the financial crisis dramatically affected the price of oil, dropping it below fifty dollars a barrel and cutting gasoline prices to less than $2.00 a gallon at the pump. Faced with lower prices, there is evidence that American consumers responded by driving more and reconsidering the purchase of those big SUV's that they thought would be gone forever.

The key to improved fuel economy is light weight. It is also, ironically, the key to greater performance. Racing car designers know this and it's the reason that exotic materials like carbon fiber and titanium are used in modern racing car designs. The common wisdom in the U.S. is that lighter weight cars are unsafe in an accident. This view has been promoted by a variety of sources, usually quoting information from studies done more than a decade ago. Modern cars have come a long way with safety systems such as crush zones, front and side airbags, and energy management systems, and if a vehicle like the 1,800-pound Smart Car can meet the impact and safety standards of a full-size car, the argument doesn't seem to hold any longer. Instead of using technology to build in faster 0-60 mph times, the technology must be used to make lighter cars that are as safe as or even safer than the current full-size models.

Unfortunately, lighter weight and more efficient conventional gasoline engines are not going to bring us to the next level of efficiency and low fuel consumption that will be needed in the near-term future. This will require a rethink of how automobile power plants work.

I remember driving a variety of electric and hybrid cars during the 1990s. At the time, I was the Technical Editor at *Automobile Magazine* in Ann Arbor, Michigan and it seemed like every week I was driving some new and sometimes hare-brained automotive concept car. The California Air Resources Board (CARB) had mandated in 1990 that by 1997, at least 2 percent of vehicles for sale in the state of California by a manufacturer had to be Zero Emission Vehicles (ZEVs). CARB also required that number to increase to 10 percent by 2003. The domestic U.S. carmakers screamed that it couldn't be done and that the technology didn't exist to meet the mandates. Except, back in 1988, Roger Smith, the CEO of General Motors (GM), had agreed to fund a research and development project with an advanced technology firm in California called AeroVironments. This small company had worked with GM on its successful solar car project, and it was just the kind of place where new ideas would flourish. Mr. Smith had bragged about the possibilities of electric cars from GM and now CARB was going to hold him to it.

General Motors showed off its Impact electric vehicle concept at the Los Angles Auto Show in the beginning of 1990. By 1996, when the EV-1 was introduced in California and Arizona, it had a new name, but retained the same basic shape, lightweight aluminum skin and a whole range of technologically advanced features. Unfortunately, its lead-acid storage batteries were probably the least high-tech part of the

*GM's Impact show car became the all-electric EV-1 (General Motors)*

car. Weighing almost 1,200 pounds alone, the batteries allowed the EV-1 to travel between fifty-five and seventy-five miles on a full eight hour charge. Except, if you drove the EV-1 like a normal car, you'd be lucky to get more than forty miles from a full charge. The EV-1 was quick, with a zero to sixty miles per hour time of just over six seconds, but all that battery weight made its handling sluggish and you were always aware that you were driving an urban commuter and not a sports car. Around the same time, Honda offered its EV Plus, while Toyota had an all-electric RAV4-EV and Ford did an electrically powered Ranger pickup truck. As if to prove that CARB couldn't regulate the laws of physics, each of these was massively heavy and suffered from disappointing range. None of these cars were actually for sale but were only available through lease schemes in California and sometimes in Arizona.

If electric cars didn't provide adequate range, why not carry along a generator so that you could recharge the batteries on the fly? The concept is nothing new. In fact, more than a hundred years ago a twenty-four-year-old engineer named Ferdinand Porsche developed and raced just such a machine during the earliest days of the development of the automobile.

Porsche worked for Jacob Lohner & Company in Vienna,

Austria in 1899 and had created and patented a wheel-hub electric motor that eliminated the need for a transmission and drive system. The Lohner-Porsche electric car created a sensation on April 14, 1900 when it was introduced Paris World Exhibition. Standard output was two and a half horsepower at 120 rpm, but the hubmotors (one in each front wheel) were capable of seven horsepower each for up to twenty minutes. Using a forty-four cell battery with 300 ampere hours and eighty volts, Porsche's vehicle could provide speeds of just over ten miles per hour and a top speed of about thirty-one miles per hour and had a range of about thirty miles. Lohner went on to sell more than 300 of the Lohner-Porsche electric vehicles.

Porsche continued development in throughout 1900, adding electric hubmotors to the rear wheels to create a four-wheel drive electric vehicle. He also added additional batteries to boost range, but by now his machine weighed more than 4,000 pounds and suffered from reduced performance. To combat this problem, Porsche

*Lohner-Porsche gasoline-electric hybrid (Dr. Ing. h.c. F. Porsche AG)*

added a pair of De Dion Bouton gasoline engines that powered a generator to charge the batteries, thus creating a series gasoline-electric hybrid vehicle. This new concept debuted at the 1901 Parisian Auto

Salon and used the three and a half horsepower combustion engines to
drive dual generators to supply current to the two wheel hub motors
on the front wheels. The gasoline engines could be run after start up to
keep the battery charged. Porsche created variations delivering five to
twelve horsepower. In 1902 he piloted his hybrid during trial runs at
the Exelberg race, finishing first in the large-car class and third overall.
Porsche went on to bigger and better things, working on racing cars for
Mercedes-Benz and Auto Union, designing the ubiquitous Volkswagen
Beetle, and sowing the seeds for the sports car company that bears his
name.

Electric cars held a strong position in the U.S. in the earliest
part of the 1900s. Companies like Baker and Detroit produced quiet
comfortable fully electric cars, primarily for in-town usage. Electric
cars were particularly attractive to women; they didn't need to be
cranked by hand to get them started, as gasoline-powered cars did.
The advent of the electric self-starter in 1913 changed the world and
electric cars soon lost their favor.

Several other manufacturers played with hybrid designs and in
1938, General Motors Electromotive Division introduced its diesel-
electric railroad locomotive that revolutionized rail power and made
steam obsolete. During the 1970s, General Motors and others, like
Volkswagen and Fiat, tested various concepts, but they were definitely
back burner projects.

In 1993, the Partnership for a New Generation of Vehicles
(PNGV) was formed by the Clinton Administration with membership
of seven federal agencies, universities, national research labs, parts
suppliers, and DaimlerChrysler, Ford, and General Motors. Its goal
was to help automakers develop technologies (including hybrids)
that would bring highly fuel efficient (eighty miles per gallon), five

passenger vehicles to market by 2003. By 2000, all three automakers had developed lightweight diesel-electric hybrid concept cars that achieved seventy to eighty miles per gallon fuel economy. The PNGV spent more than $1 billion of taxpayer money before the Bush administration cancelled the program in 2001, at the request of the automakers.

In 1995, Chrysler put its significant public relations clout behind a new hybrid concept. The company claimed that it would compete with its new Patriot racing car at long distance races, like the twenty-four hour race at Le Mans in France. The Patriot was monstrously complex, using a gas turbine and powerful flywheel to generate electricity that would power an advanced technology electric motor. It was doomed to failure before it ever got off the ground, but it did bring the idea of a hybrid drivetrain to the attention of automotive journalists and a small segment of enthusiasts. Chrysler followed the Patriot with concept cars like the Dodge Intrepid ESX in 1996, which I remember driving at the company's proving ground. The Intrepid had a three cylinder turbocharged diesel engine that drove a generator sending power to a 300 volt battery and to a pair of oil-cooled electric wheel motors. It wasn't refined, but it was a small step along the right direction.

Hybrids come in several flavors. A series hybrid typically uses a gasoline engine to power an alternator that generates electricity, which then either gets stored in a battery or is used directly to power an electric motor that moves the vehicle. There is no direct mechanical connection between the gasoline engine and the drive wheels; the electric motor or motors produce all of the force that propels the car. Because the gasoline engine is only used to charge the batteries, it can be designed at a single optimum speed (rpm), providing better efficiency than an engine that must run over a range of revolutions per minute to accelerate and then sustain the speed of the vehicle. The batteries in a series hybrid generally need to be bigger than those in other hybrid designs as they must provide electric energy for maximum performance without any assist from the gasoline engine. In addition, when coasting or slowing down, the motor acts as a generator to help recharge the onboard batteries, a process called regenerative braking. The biggest problem facing series hybrid designs is the need for low-cost high energy-density batteries.

A parallel hybrid uses both the gasoline engine and electric motors to drive the vehicle's wheels. Honda introduced its Integrated Motor Assist (IMA) hybrid system in 1999 for its lightweight two-seat Insight model. IMA uses a small and light electric motor that replaces the vehicle flywheel. When additional torque is needed to enhance performance, the motor is energized and adds its torque to that produced by the vehicle's gasoline engine. I was so impressed with Honda's IMA that I chose it to receive *Automobile Magazine's* Technology of the Year award in 2000, noting that, "The Insight is just the beginning of a future that will be easy for automotive enthusiasts to live with." Parallel hybrids like the Honda IMA system also provide recharging of the batteries through regenerative braking, putting energy back into the batteries. Parallel hybrids can use smaller battery packs and electric motors because the gasoline engine does the majority of the propulsion work. In stop and go driving, because the gasoline engine must operate at various speeds, efficiency is compromised.

When Toyota introduced its first generation of the Prius at the Tokyo Motor Show in 1997, it chose to combine the attributes of both kinds of hybrid systems into what is now called a series/parallel hybrid

*First Generation Toyota Prius (Toyota)*

driveline. In the Prius the engine can drive the wheels directly (as in a parallel hybrid system) or can be disconnected from the drive system so that only the electric motor provides power to the wheels (as in a series hybrid). Both the engine and electric motor can come into play under full acceleration. During deceleration and braking, the motor acts as a generator to help recharge the batteries through regenerative braking. Such systems that can use the engine, the electric motor or both together, are also sometimes called Full Hybrid systems. In contrast, a Mild Hybrid system uses the electric motor just to restart the gasoline engine when it is shut down at a stop (saving the fuel used for idling) and to generate electricity through regenerative braking.

In the early 2000s, with hybrid vehicles on the market from Toyota and Honda, and no anticipated breakthroughs in battery technology, the California Air Resources Board backed off on its mandate for Zero Emissions Vehicles. In 2001 CARB modified the ZEV mandate to allow partial credits for hybrid vehicles and in 2003 removed the ZEV mandate altogether. 2003 was also the year when General Motors cancelled its EV-1 program. Despite switching away from traditional lead/acid batteries to more advanced Nickel Metal Hydride (NMH) batteries in 1999, which gave a theoretical range of seventy-five to 150 miles, the EV-1 couldn't or wouldn't perform up to GM's expectations. Other car makers with ZEV models, who were never excited about building electric cars for the California market, quickly cancelled their programs. The fully electric car appeared to have died once again, but the battery, electric motor, and electronic control innovations that were spawned by the doomed electrics would soon find a place in a new lineup of hybrid gasoline electric vehicles, like the Toyota Prius.

"The first Prius wasn't special, but this one [the second generation] is. I'm going to take credit for it because I was in charge of product planning for this car," said Bill Reinert, the National Manager of Toyota's Advanced Technology Group in the U.S. when I caught up with him at Toyota's display stand at the North American International Auto Show in Detroit. Reinert is justifiably proud of his

*Second Generation Toyota Prius (Toyota)*

career that started with the Japanese carmaker in 1990. "We fiddled with hybrids for about thirty years, in 1992 we started to get serious about building a car for the twenty-first century," said Reinert. "We looked at small engines, we looked at cylinder deactivation, we looked at light weight, and we looked at hybrid designs: series-parallel and parallel-series. Through our investigations our goal was to double the fuel economy of the average car. We settled into a series parallel hybrid design that eventually became the Prius."

I can remember driving a test-mule with the Toyota hybrid

drive system in Phoenix in 1997. It was easy: turn the key on, shift into drive, and press the throttle pedal. The car started off with a whir of the electric motor and after a second or two the gasoline engine started up and added its power to the wheels. I found the transition between electric and gasoline power difficult to detect and my story described the whole system as "seamless."

That first generation of Prius, when it was launched at the Tokyo Show and on the Japanese market in December 1997, was a bit ungainly. Some said it was ugly. Reinert gave me some of the background. "We didn't have an existing chassis that would allow us to do it. The car was all purpose-built. With the Prius we never expected to sell 2,000 cars a month. The execs were hands-off—let those crazy guys do what they are going to do. They want to make a five-door hatchback? We think that's a stupid idea, but go ahead and make a five-door hatchback." The first generation Prius came to the U.S. in 2001, but was a slow seller.

Reinert's chance came when the Prius was redesigned for its second generation that arrived in 2004. "Prius meant 'to come before' [in Latin], to do wacky things." said Reinert. "Not just the hybrid drive but the engine start-stop and the styling and other stuff." The wacky things paid off and the Prius quickly became more than just a niche market automobile for Toyota. "I think there are two things that the Prius has become. One, it has become an icon, and two, and more importantly, its made the environment an aspirational part of the market, just like performance motorsports or luxury is an aspirational part of the market. Now hybrids are."

Toyota has gone on to offer hybrid drive systems on its Camry line and on a range of Lexus luxury cars and sport utility vehicles. The Prius remains the torch-bearer of the company's environmental credibility. This is quite a responsibility, especially as a new redesign of the Prius is due out in 2010. Reinert, in his early 60s, isn't all that far from retirement and worries about what the next generation of Prius will bring.

"Honestly, if we knew how to capture that Prius magic and put it in a bottle, we would," he said, also noting that the Prius outsells all other hybrid vehicles combined and has become a brand for Toyota. "The people who are doing the product planning on the next Prius don't know what makes this one special," said Reinert. "But they are trying to make it special and here is my concern: They are trying to keep it special but at Camry volumes. When you have a bread and butter car like the Camry, you don't take chances. So my challenge to the kids is: *Will you take a chance on this car and how will you take a chance?* Prius is an aspirational car and that tells me that as long as that condition exists we'll need a unique car."

Perhaps feeling burned by its EV-1 experience, General Motors came later to the party, but has embraced hybrid vehicles in a big way. In 2006 it opened a brand new engineering facility at its Milford, Michigan proving grounds, dedicated to designing and building hybrids. Milford, which opened in 1924, was the industry's first automotive proving ground and so it seems appropriate that some of GM's most important research and development work is taking place on its 4,000 acre campus. I went to Milford to see Micky Bly, Director of Engineering for Hybrid Integration and Controls of General Motors. Bly is a fortyish engineer with a slight southern accent, no doubt a result of time spent achieving his engineering degree from Georgia Tech. To him, the questions faced by the auto industry and General Motors in particular are simple: "How do we increase fuel efficiency significantly and also reduce emissions, hopefully down to zero?"

Bly explains that GM has three answers to these questions. "Our short term strategy was to go after efficiency improvements in our internal combustion engine and our transmissions. We've been doing that for about fifteen years now and they have been very incremental improvements," said Bly. He notes that those incremental improvements have added up to over 85 percent efficiency improvement in truck fuel economy and over 110 percent improvement in car fuel economy. "We've gone from four-speed to five-speed to six-speed transmissions. We've been working on higher compression ratio and higher efficiency engines; we've been doing turbocharging and supercharging. Another [area of development] is active fuel management, we used to call it DOD, for Displacement on Demand, where we can actually take out some of those cylinders that you don't need when you are cruising down the road, so an eight cylinder engine becomes a four-cylinder engine," Bly explains.

Vehicles benefiting from GM's strategy of engine efficiency improvements are hitting the market now. But what of the long term? "Our long term strategy was really fuel cells, and that's kind of the buzz for all the scientists and researchers around the world," said Bly. It won't be an easy transition to hydrogen power. "There is the dilemma of the hydrogen fuel economy and the infrastructure supporting that versus the cost of the fuel cell technology." Bly predicts hydrogen to be at least ten or more years away, expecting to see small hydrogen fuel-cell cars on the market in the 2030 time frame.

GM's mid-term strategy of producing gasoline hybrids is perhaps the most important to the survival of the company, and the one getting the most attention. "We started this project in January 2006, co-locating of everyone working on hybrids. One hundred people at first, now more than 550 people, all working on hybrids. If you are working on hybrids, you are working here," said Bly. His enthusiasm for the mission is clear. "There is not a better place to be working in General Motors. I'll speak for my team. I've got a huge population of younger engineers who have a passion and desire to break out of what they were doing and get into this stuff. They are absolutely passionate about this. It is grassroots to them. This is where they want to bring up the technology and make a difference. I also have a population of very senior engineers that have seen what we've done in the past. They really want to turn GM's image back to that high-tech, innovative, setting the benchmark kind of company, so they have gravitated to this position," said Bly.

The challenges facing Bly and his team are formidable. "We committed to rolling out three different hybrid technologies and twelve different hybrid models over the next five years. Since that time we've delivered on our commitment," said Bly.

The first project was a full-hybrid diesel transit bus that appeared in 2004. "If you really are going introduce technology and you are going to make a big impact, you need to do it where you are going to save the most," said Bly. Transit buses operate primarily in urban settings with lots of stop and go driving—the perfect environment for fuel savings from a hybrid system. GM's big hybrid buses offer a 50-70 percent fuel economy improvement over conventional diesel buses and over a thousand vehicles have been delivered to the marketplace.

"The next technology we introduced was our BAS—Belt Alternator Starter, what we called our mild-hybrid or entry hybrid, value hybrid system," said Bly. His engineers mounted an electric device that consists of a five-kilowatt electric motor and alternator and on the front of the engine and driven by the accessory belt. Nickel

Metal Hydride (NMH) batteries store up energy produced by the
alternator and provide that electric energy back to the system. "It has
all of the capability of a hybrid; its got regenerative braking, electric
engine start-stop and has some amount of electric propulsion, fairly
small two to three miles per hour off the start, and then it has assist
where we can take that battery energy and propel the vehicle to get
even better zero to sixty miles per hour times," said Bly. "It allows
you to have a 15-25 percent fuel economy improvement for a very
reasonable price of around $2,000. We introduced it in 2007 on the
Saturn Vue. It's on the next generation Vue, the Buick in China, and
has many more applications," he added. Bly notes that sometime
in 2010 or 2011, the NMH batteries will be replaced with Lithium-
ion batteries produced by Hitachi. The greater energy density of the
Lithium batteries will allow a boost in motor power to fifteen kilowatts
and improve fuel efficiency by a further 5-8 percent.

In some ways this "mild" hybrid has been an uphill battle.
"The media was very skeptical of it being successful, because it didn't
generate big numbers, but what's really turned around is that they
realized that it's 20 percent improvement [in fuel economy] for $2,000:
that's a great bargain for the customer who wants to get into a hybrid,
but can't afford the high-end $50, $60, or $70,000 hybrid, let's give
them something for $2,000," said Bly.

The cost and complexity of the development of hybrid
technologies is daunting. If it could be shared with other vehicle
manufacturers the risks and development costs could be spread around.
"About three years ago we started discussing and negotiating with
other manufacturers if they would like to partake in the two-mode
technology; we had the patents from the buses," said Bly. "Everybody
is trying to break into the hybrid game, it's very expensive technology

and everybody can't go off and do their own thing. So we went out to ask the best of the best of the OEMs if they wanted to join with us. It was Daimler-Chrysler [now it's Chrysler and Mercedes], and BMW. They use the same technology and same power flows and they are extremely pleased with the fuel economy numbers." The two-mode system is similar to the parallel-series hybrid system used in the Toyota Prius, providing power to the wheels either from the engine or the electric motor, depending upon performance requirements. GM's two-mode hybrid system was launched on the Tahoe, Yukon, and Escalade full-sized SUVs and on GM's line of full-sized pickup trucks. Fuel savings of 50 percent in city driving have been realized, using a 300-volt NMH battery produced by Panasonic. The system costs $4,500-$5,000 extra and adds about 150 pounds of batteries to the full-sized trucks.

GM's third hybrid technology is perhaps the most interesting. "Our final version is going to be the e-flex, which is an extended range electric vehicle," explains Bly. As shown at the 2007 North American International Auto Show in Detroit, the first application of the new technology is the Chevrolet Volt, due out in late 2010. The Volt will be

*Chevrolet Volt Concept Car (General Motors)*

a series hybrid—only the electric motor will provide propulsion to the wheels, the gasoline engine works as a range extender to provide electric power when the charge in the Lithium-ion batteries has been depleted. "That will be using a Lithium-ion battery; the only way you can make that vehicle work at a forty mile ev [electric vehicle] range capability is with a lithium-ion battery because of the energy density requirement. We are taking up every conceivable space underneath that vehicle to put battery cells in there," notes Bly. The lithium-ion battery pack must be specifically designed for its use in the vehicle.

GM worked with two possible battery suppliers for the Volt. A123, located in Massachusetts, used a lithium-iron nano-phosphate chemistry that was developed by scientists at the Massachusetts Institute of Technology (MIT). A123 had partnered with German auto parts firm Continental to package the cells into a battery that would fit into the vehicle. The other potential supplier was Korean battery giant LG Chem, one of the world's largest lithium-ion battery producers and a company that has hitched its wagon to a lithium manganese-oxide chemistry. In January, 2009, GM, citing better heat dissipation and more energy storage, announced a winner and LG Chem will build the lithium-ion cells for the Chevrolet Volt.

The e-flex system in the Volt receives its charge from a plug-in charger and only uses its three-cylinder turbocharged gasoline to charge the batteries when the electric vehicle range of forty miles is exceeded. With alternator and electric motor efficiencies over 90 percent, and electricity coming from the wall socket in the garage, fuel economy figures of 150 miles per gallon have been suggested for the Volt. But how do you measure the fuel consumption on the twenty mile EPA fuel economy test when the all-electric range of the vehicle promises to be forty miles? "We are working with the regulators to see how they will rate it. Maybe run the test five times in a row, or ten times, or fifteen times and then average it. Maybe [there will be] two ratings on a label," said Bly.

One way to quantify fuel economy that has been suggested is

to combine the electric range with a gasoline range. For example, the Volt has a projected forty mile all electric range. If the gasoline engine kicks in and is capable of achieving forty miles per gallon, then a sixty mile trip would require a half a gallon of gasoline (40 miles on electric plus twenty miles on gasoline), resulting in a fuel mileage of 120 miles per gallon. On the other hand, a 100 mile trip would require one point five gallons of gasoline (forty miles electric plus sixty miles on gasoline) so the fuel economy is now 66-miles per gallon. See why the EPA is having trouble deciding how to rate a plug-in hybrid?

Bly expects hybrids to beat the odds by rolling out quickly. "Hybrids will, once established, continue to grow faster and faster. An engine program technology gets refreshed every twenty years. We tool them for twenty years, and that's about when we turn over an engine. On the hybrid at GM we are already working on the generation two stuff in five years. I think it will turn over faster, faster, and faster," said Bly.

President Obama's energy plan calls for 1 million plug-in hybrids, using technology like e-flex, to be on the road by 2015, which seems an aggressive target. "I think it will increase at a rate based upon acceptance in the region. In North America, hybrids will continue to go up because my neighbor has them, because of fuel efficiency, because there are techno guys who want to be cool and have them. I think there will be a huge push for hybrids in the Asian markets. I go there [to China] three times a year now, and we are working on a strong hybrid rollout. They are very anti-diesel because of the particulates emissions. It's impressive the number of batteries. There are millions of electric bikes being produced with two to three cell lithium-ion batteries," said Bly.

The strategy for hybrid vehicles might be different in China.

"We're trying to make our hybrids low-cost, great fuel efficiency, last forever. I think the play in China for their marketplace is going to be very low cost, don't worry about how long they last, we'll dispose of them or recycle them and give me another battery in two years and we're fine with that, with very good fuel efficiency," said Bly. "Right now our batteries are warranted eight years, 100,000 miles. They may do a two-year battery. Get fuel efficiency, put them in a recycling heap and keep going."

With so much riding on hybrid vehicles for General Motors, rolling out a new hybrid every three months for the next five years, I asked Micky Bly if the company has bet the farm on them. His answer: "I don't think we are betting the farm on hybrids. This isn't where the money will come from for a very long time. We have to get our core business healthy: small cars, mid-sized cars. I would not say we are betting the farm. But there is a big wager on the table." GM's President Rick Wagoner, testifying before a senate committee at the end of 2008, said that the plug-in hybrid technology in the Volt won't begin to become profitable until at least 2016. As much attention as the Chevrolet Volt has received from the press and the politicians on Capital Hill, with an estimated price-tag of over $40,000 and a sales volume predicted to be just 10,000 cars in the first year, it's clear that, initially at least, the Volt is going to be little more than an image maker for General Motors.

In China, BYD Company is looking at hybrids as more than just good for its image. The company, better known for its cell phone battery prowess, has introduced the F3DM—China's first mass-produced hybrid electric vehicle. The plug-in hybrid is reported to have a sixty-mile range on battery power, at which point the small gasoline engine kicks in to extend the vehicle's range. The F3DM is a modified version of the gasoline-powered F3 sedan that brought BYD into the automobile market in 2003. The battery chemistry for the hybrid is the same lithium-iron-phosphate combination that the company uses in its cell phone and computer batteries. The first plug-in cars from BYD went on sale in China at the end of 2008, and the company announced that it would begin sending cars to the U.S. in 2011. If the Chevrolet Volt is delayed by even a small amount, it is quite possible that the first plug-in hybrid vehicle for sale in the U.S. will come from China. BYD also sells an all-electric version of the F3, called the F3E, primarily for use as Chinese government vehicles.

Hybrids are hot and every carmaker wants to have one in its lineup. Even Mercedes-Benz, where an executive engineer told me just a few years ago that it was too expensive to have two complete drive trains in a vehicle and that he had no interest in the concept, developed a hybrid version of its ML sport utility vehicle for 2009. There are more than twenty-five hybrid vehicles of one sort or another presently on the market and more are coming.

If hybrids are hot, they are also expensive. Although some hybrids qualify for a tax credit, many of the more popular models no longer do. Hybrids exact a price premium that ranges between $2,000 and $7,000 over the equivalent non-hybrid vehicle from the same company.

## TABLE 1: YEARS TO BREAK EVEN WHEN OWNING A HYBRID

| Vehicle 2008 | | Hybrid | EPA mpg | Years to break even |
|---|---|---|---|---|
| Ford Escape XLS | $20,005 | — | 20/26 | |
| Ford Escape Hybrid | $26,505 | $6,500 | 26/30 | 24.2 |

| | | | | |
|---|---|---|---|---|
| Honda Civic DX | $15,810 | — | 25/36 | |
| Honda Civic Hybrid | $22,600 | $6,790 | 40/45 | 20.8 |
| Lexus GS460 | $52,620 | — | 17/24 | |
| Lexus GS450h Hybrid | $54,900 | $2,280 | 22/25 | 10.6 |
| Saturn Vue | $21,250 | — | 19/26 | |
| Saturn Vue Hybrid | $24,170 | $2,920 | 25/32 | 8.9 |
| Toyota Camry | $19,620 | — | 21/31 | |
| Toyota Camry Hybrid | $25,200 | $5,580 | 33/34 | 18.5 |
| Toyota Corolla CE | $15,205 | — | 26/35 | |
| Toyota Prius Hybrid | $21,100 | $5,895 | 48/45 | 14.9 |
| Toyota Highlander | $28,750 | — | 17/23 | |
| Toyota Highlander Hybrid | $33,700 | $4,950 | 27/25 | 12.2 |

In general a hybrid will deliver a fuel-savings of 12-50 percent, depending upon which vehicle, and where and how you drive. Unfortunately, even with gasoline costs over $3.50 a gallon, for a driver covering 10,000 miles a year it can take between ten and twenty years, or more, to make back the investment that a hybrid's premium price demands (without the tax savings.) Of course as gas prices go higher, the payback time grows shorter. Then again, saving fuel and reducing carbon dioxide emissions should be its own reward, and the improved fuel mileage offered by hybrid technology does both.

David E, Davis, Jr. is one of the legends in the automotive industry. The founder of *Automobile Magazine* and my boss during the years I worked there, he has been an automotive journalist, publisher, and keen industry observer for more than five decades. He has a long view on hybrids. "I drove a hybrid at Fiat in 1980, it was diesel and I thought then that this is the answer—this solves what's wrong with electric cars," said Davis. "That's basically the way I feel. I think that we have only scratched the surface with hybrids so far, their lifespan has been very short and there is a whole lot of stuff we don't know about how this technology is going to develop." As long as I have known him, Davis has always been a fan of new technologies in automobiles. He is enthusiastic about driving hybrids. "I love the quiet of them. I love the performance of them. There is something kind of fun about your relationship with that technology, and your relationship with the special instrumentation that constantly is telling you whether you are burning gas or electricity. I just love all the sensations of driving it."

Davis feels like Honda missed an opportunity with its hybrid strategy. "I liked the Honda attitude, where they designed the interface of the electrical motor as a kind of supercharger that really gave the car some rorty acceleration. It was fun to pull out at fifty-five or sixty miles per hour and pass someone. It really did get up and go. I always felt that Honda misunderstood that market. When they came with the Insight, it was just too much of a 1939 World's Fair rocket ship

*First Generation Honda Insight (Honda)*

for a whole lot of people who might have been interested to get interested. It wasn't until the Prius came along, and then some of the sort of regular production sedans and coupes with the technology, that the thing found its legs and got going. I always thought that Honda shot themselves in the foot by expecting people to first accept the really peculiar-looking little car— it looked like a Woody Allen science fiction movie or something— and then to accept the technology. It was a hell of a lot easier to accept the technology in a Prius, or a Camry, or an Accord."

Davis also is optimistic that General Motors will get its

technology act together. "I think it testifies to the enormous strength of General Motors when properly applied that, after all the time that was wasted in trying to prove that hybrids didn't work, when they decided they had to do something, they did really good ones. The hybrid Tahoe is just a peach of a car to drive."

It isn't just the big guys like Toyota and GM who are working on hybrid vehicles. Fisker Automotive, located in Irvine, California has plans to build a futuristic four-door sedan that has been designed by Henrik Fisker, one of the company's founders. The Danish designer worked at BMW and was responsible for the Z8 Roadster. He subsequently went to work for Ford and was in charge of design for Aston Martin, designing the DB9 and Vantage. These are impressive credentials for a designer, so when he left the big-time to join a start-up, people noticed. "We want to be a new American green car

*Fisker Karma Concept Car (Fisker)*

company. All of our cars will be plug-in hybrids," said Fisker, when I met with him in Detroit at the Auto Show.

Fisker has designed a low-slung sedan called the Karma that promises a zero to sixty miles per hour acceleration time under 6 seconds and a top speed of more than 125 mph. "The interesting thing about this vehicle and the whole idea behind it is that so far green cars and environmental cars have always been small and somewhat awkward and we want to change that image. A green car can be good-looking, sexy and it can be fast as well." The series-hybrid technology used in the Fisker is similar to that of the Chevrolet Volt; an electric motor is used to drive the vehicle while a small gasoline engine extends the range beyond the fifty-mile range that is expected using just the battery pack. The Karma has two control modes; a stealth mode that uses just the battery system for commuting, and a sport mode that brings in the power from the gasoline generator for maximum performance. Although it was initially announced that the Fisker Karma would go into production in 2009 at a North American plant, the projected build date for the $87,000 sedan has slipped to late 2010. Really though, it doesn't matter if the Fisker ever reaches production—simply the idea that designers and visionaries are breaking out of the traditional concepts has its own merit.

The Karma's series-hybrid system uses a lithium-ion battery, specifically built for Fisker. "We have a very large lithium-ion battery pack," said Fisker. To accommodate the large battery Fisker has designed the car with a long wheelbase that allows the battery to be located in a tunnel in the center of the vehicle. "It's a very low sexy vehicle, but it's quite a large footprint. You can fit four grownups in the car with luggage," said Fisker. "We have a life expectancy of ten years for the battery—in the end it depends on how you drive. The battery doesn't end, like an engine that blows up. It just starts to go down in the ability to produce electricity."

The power performance required from a battery used in a hybrid depends largely upon what kind of hybrid vehicle you are driving. If you build a system like Honda's Integrated Motor Assist (IMA), or GM's mild hybrid BAS system, each with limited pure-electric propulsion capability, you need little battery storage capacity. On the other end of the spectrum, if you choose to build a series-hybrid with a forty-mile range, like the Chevrolet Volt, you need lots of batteries with high energy density and a rapid recharge rate.

Batteries are not all created equally and, depending upon

their electrochemistry, can have different charge and discharge characteristics. Some, like lithium-ion batteries, work best in a state of charge range of 40-80%. Discharge them to a state less than 40 percent and they can be damaged. Charge them over 80 percent of capacity and they can overheat and create a safety hazard.

Some industry leaders believe that an optimal hybrid in the future will have a bigger engine and a smaller battery, and that in fact the size of the battery depends more upon the usage cycle and longevity requirements than strictly the hybrid operation. Most companies target ten years and 150,000 miles as the projected life of the battery system in a hybrid. Mike Tamor, Executive Technical Leader for Hybrid Electric and Fuel Cell Technology at Ford said, "Contrary to popular expectation, the battery energy required to achieve the hybrid efficiency benefit is very small." Tamor says that the key to an affordable hybrid is to size the batteries by regenerative braking, accessory loads and durability requirements, and not by a significant electric driving range. Even when electrification of transportation is the goal, as in a plug-in hybrid, the battery can be kept surprisingly small. His numbers show that a thirty-mile electric range, for example, would "electrify" 60 percent of all travel. Tamor argues that providing greater range from the battery requires greater expense and more weight and that the extra range would be rarely used.

So, the ultimate key to any successful hybrid vehicle is its battery pack. One major reason why electric vehicles didn't attain more acceptance by the public was their short range. Vehicles like GM's EV-1 were launched using traditional lead-acid batteries that provided a practical range of less than fifty miles. A switch to advanced Nickel Metal Hydride (NMH) batteries doubled that range, but it still wasn't enough to overcome the fear of being stranded on the side of the road with dead batteries. NMH batteries have gone on to find a home in hybrid vehicles from Toyota, Ford, and GM, and have proven to be safe and reliable, even if the price of nickel has made them somewhat expensive.

Battery research has continued forward, resulting in today's most promising candidate, the lithium-ion battery.

What is lithium? It's the third element in the Periodic Table, slotted between helium and beryllium. Elemental lithium is an alkali metal and the lightest solid and would float on water, if not for the fact that it is highly reactive and would explode and burn if exposed to water or air. For that reason, batteries made from elemental lithium, although explored in the early 1970s, were too dangerous for practical use. Instead, lithium-ion batteries were developed, where the anode and cathode contain materials made with ions of lithium rather than the element itself. Ions are simply charged versions of atoms of a material, produced by adding or removing electrons. While not delving too deeply into electrochemistry, like all batteries, lithium-ion cells are made up of three principle components—the anode, the cathode and the electrolyte. For lithium-ion batteries, the anode and cathode are made of materials into which lithium can migrate, while the electrolyte is lithium salt in an organic solvent, such as ether. The transfer of lithium ions produces an excess of electrons, which flow through a wire running from the cathode to the anode, powering an electrical device along the way. The average voltage produced by a single lithium-ion cell is three-point-five to four volts, depending upon the chemistry used.

The first commercial lithium-ion battery was produced by Sony in 1991 and began a revolution in consumer electronics. The battery pack in your laptop, cell-phone, and PDA are all lithium-ion cells. The initial lithium-ion cells used lithium cobalt oxide, while subsequent work has explored nickel, titanium, iron, phosphate, and other cathode materials that reduce cost and improve safety. In 2004, nano-sized particles of iron (less than 100 nanometers across) were used in lithium iron-phosphate batteries, showing an improvement in heat resistance and a reduction in cracking. These batteries are now found in consumer-level cordless drills.

Although there are three major components in a lithium-ion cell, the battery itself must also contain several mechanisms designed to keep the battery safe. Lithium-ion batteries can ignite or explode if exposed to high temperatures. Manufacturers have found that even slight contamination can cause the cells to short-circuit and ignite, a situation that resulted in the recall of ten million laptop batteries by Sony in 2006. If you've ever felt how warm your laptop computer gets when you are using it with batteries, you know that lithium-ion cells produce a lot of heat. Larger scale applications, like an electric car or hybrid vehicle require dedicated cooling systems to dissipate the heat that is produced during both charging and discharging of the battery packs.

If there is a catch to all of the hype surrounding hybrid vehicles, it is the problem of sourcing the uncommon materials that are required to build Lithium-ion batteries and super-powerful electric motors that use rare-earth element permanent magnets. The United States was once self-sufficient in these materials, but beginning in 1999, and in the years since, 90 percent of the rare earth elements required by U.S. industry have come from China. Presently, rare-earth elements are used in computer monitors, fiber-optic cables, lasers, medical imaging equipment, as alloying agents in metals, and as catalyst agents in oil industry processing and refining. In short, rare-earth elements are used in some way in just about every aspect of our modern high-technology society.

In 1984, Magnaquench and Sumitomo, using materials like neodymium, praseodymium, and samarium, developed the modern rare-earth magnet. These super-magnets form the basis for all of the electric propulsion motors used in electric cars and hybrid vehicles. At the time, Magnaquench was actually owned by General Motors as part of its Delco Electronic division, but apparently the company didn't see the strategic advantage that electric drive would someday present. The estimates are that a hybrid car will require twenty to eighty pounds of rare-earth elements for its motors.

The history of rare-earth element mining in the U.S. is an interesting one. In 1949, a vein of rock with extraordinary high concentrations of rare-earth elements was found at Mountain Pass in the upper Mojave Desert in California, about fifty miles south of Las Vegas. By 1966, this deposit, by far the world's richest single source, had become the source not only for the U.S., but also the world. Color picture tubes had pushed the demand for the materials and Molycorp Inc., the company that owned and operated Mountain Pass, became the source for rare-earth elements. Unfortunately, the solvent extraction method of mining used at Mountain Pass to obtain commercial quantities of the materials produced wastewater that was toxic to the environment, putting pressure on the operation. In 1985, the Chinese government began production of rare-earth elements in mines in Inner Mongolia and another in the tropical regions of southern China. The Chinese flooded the market and have been accused of driving the price of rare-earth elements down in order to dominate it. Indeed, by 1994 the Mountain Pass mining operation owned by Molycorp was shut down, as the cost of extracting rare-earth elements had exceeded their market value. This, despite having enough resources to supply significant levels of the global supply of rare-earth elements for at least the next thirty years. Molycorp was by that time owned by the oil company Unocal.

In 2005, when Unocal was up for sale and the Chinese national oil company, CNOOC, was the top bidder, there was outrage in the U.S. Congress that an American oil company might fall into the hands of the Chinese. What was ignored at the time was that Chinese government's real target was probably control of the Mountain Pass rare-earth element mine in the Mojave Desert. By taking over ownership of one of the world's few rare-earth element deposits, China would be in a position to control the future of technology. Congress turned to Chevron to rescue Unocal and in the process Chevron also acquired Molycorp. In 2008, Chevron sold Molycorp and its rare-earth element mining operation at Mountain Pass in California to a group of investors that includes Goldman-Sachs, Inc., the Wall Street investment firm.

Goldman-Sachs is well-connected with the Chinese industrial and banking sectors, and is already a major investor in Lynas Corporation, Ltd., an Australian rare-earth element mining company that began its field operations in 2009. With more than 90 percent of the production of rare-earth elements currently coming from China, and the critical importance such materials play in hybrid vehicle technology and future energy production, the idea that controlling our oil imports from the Mid-east and Venezuela will determine our future energy security is a myth.

If the availability of rare-earth elements is largely dependent upon Chinese sources, how about the lithium used in the lithium-ion batteries on which so much of plug-in hybrid technology is counting?

Lithium is produced two ways. either by processing the mineral ore spodumene dug out of open pit mines, or by extraction from brines, typically using solar evaporation. One of the world's largest spodumene ore reserves in the world is located in Kings Mountain, North Carolina, which started operations in 1955. Other smaller producers of lithium by hard rock mining are located in Canada, Australia, Russia, Zimbabwe, Portugal and China. Chemetall Foote Corporation, which in turn is owned by a German company, owns the Kings Mountain facility Chemetall GmbH. Mining of spodumene ore at Kings Mountain was stopped in 1997, as the hard-rock process was more expensive and more destructive to the environment than the brine process.

Foote Mineral Company had started processing lithium from brine at Silver Peak, Nevada in the early 1960s. The Silver Peak facility is now also owned by Chemetall GmbH. Brines are processed by pumping the salty liquids from between 180 feet and to up to 2,700 feet deep into a series of evaporation ponds. The sun evaporates the water from the solution, leaving behind salts that are further processed to separate out the lithium compounds. Depending upon the composition of the brine, it can take twelve to eighteen months to obtain a solution of lithium chloride that can then be further processed into the desired compounds. For a time Silver Peak in Nevada was the world's largest supplier of lithium, but in the 1990s, large scale production shifted to South America as other Chemetall-owned companies in Chile and Argentina began production of lithium, also from brines. The U.S., which is the largest user of lithium, currently imports almost all (>95%) of its lithium from South America.

In 1999 a new mineral, natural lithium carbonate, was discovered in the Chabyer salt lake in Tibet at an altitude of more than 14,000 feet. The Chinese, who were already producing lithium from brine at locations in Northwestern China, have begun production at Chabyer, and the facility is now regarded as the number one area of lithium reserves in the world. If there is any doubt about China's interests in Tibet, the vast amount of lithium in the salt lake at Chabyer should make clear their intent. Largely based upon the availability of lithium from Tibet, China has become the largest producer of lithium-ion batteries in the world, making more than nineteen billion batteries annually.

Engineers, politicians, environmentalists, and much of the general public have jumped on the plug-in hybrid concept as the way we will build better, less polluting, more climate change friendly cars that will ensure a future of energy security. Electrification of transportation is possible, but the electricity to charge all of those batteries has to be generated somewhere and then has to be sent to homes and businesses. How will this be accomplished?

# Chapter 4
## Power to the People

*Sheila Lawrence feeds her Trumpeter Swans*

Sheila Lawrence shuffles slowly, slightly stooped under the weight of the two white five gallon plastic buckets she holds in her gloved hands. Her motions are deliberate, her steps measured as she moves among more than 1,500 Trumpeter Swans that fill her Monticello, Minnesota back yard on the Mississippi River. She is careful not to startle the huge birds, which have a wingspan of seven to eight feet and weigh as much as thirty-five pounds when fully grown. The noise surrounding her as she transfers the corn feed from the buckets into bins on the ground is cacophonous. It's an assault of high-pitched squeaks, middle range screeches and squawks, and low rumbling honks, all combined into a constant din that can be heard from blocks away. The swans winter in Lawrence's back yard, just as they have since the first few showed up in the winter of 1986.

Trumpeter Swans were once common throughout the U.S. and

Canada, but by the late 1880s they were thought to be extinct, due to the trade in their long white feathers. In Minnesota, a swan restoration project began in 1966. Twenty years later. Lawrence began feeding her visitors and they stayed around and each year more of them arrived, drawn by the open waters of the Mississippi and the promise of a free lunch. Now, the birds in Monticello are the largest colony of the big birds east of the Rocky Mountains, and Shelia Lawrence is known as the "swan lady."

The birds are wary of humans, but tolerant only of Lawrence, as she moves slowly among them to feed them. They consume more than 1,500 pounds of corn each day. "It's all private donations," she says of the corn supply. "I have some supporters that have donated for ten or fifteen years." A specially designed gasoline-powered conveyer moves the corn from a hopper in Lawrence's driveway, through a series of pipes to a bin in her back yard, close to the river. From there, she hauls the corn by hand in the buckets each day feeding the swans, ducks, and geese that visit her safe haven. There are only about 2,700 Trumpeter Swans in the contiguous United States and the Monticello population plays an important role in rebuilding the population.

The reason that the Mississippi River is free from winter ice in front of Shelia Lawrence's home lies just a few miles upstream. The Monticello Nuclear Generating Plant is a single unit boiling water reactor located on the banks of the Mississippi, just about three miles northwest of the town of Monticello. The 600 megawatt plant went online in 1971, at which time it began warming the Mississippi River enough so that ice no longer formed on the river in front of Shelia Lawrence's riverfront home, even on days when the air temperature hovers around or below zero. "If the power plant wasn't there to heat up the water, there wouldn't be the swans—they would have to go somewhere else or go south," said Lawrence.

Visiting a nuclear powerplant in the post-911 security environment isn't easy. Arrangements must be made several weeks in advance to allow time for background and security checks to be made. Applications need to be filled out, e-mails and phone calls answered, and permission given. For me, it seemed like it would be worth the effort. After all, President Obama ran on a promise to get 1 million plug-in hybrids on American highways by 2015.

Recall that plug-in hybrids use electricity from the home to recharge batteries that then provide an all-electric range before resorting to a gasoline engine. That electricity has to come from somewhere, and in the U.S., about 20 percent of electric power comes from nuclear power plants. Besides, I wanted to see the Monticello plant that was the benefactor of all of those Trumpeter Swans living in the relatively warm waters of the Mississippi. The arrangements were finally made. I received a phone call the day before my visit, reminding me that I was going to a high security area and that I would see lots of guards carrying weapons, but that I shouldn't be concerned about this.

*The reactor building of the Monticello Nuclear Plant*

From County Road 75, running just south of the facility, the Monticello Nuclear Generating Plant looks like nothing more than a large metal cube-like building, surrounded by several smaller metal buildings. It could be a warehouse, or perhaps a light manufacturing plant—it certainly does not look like the embodiment of what Greenpeace calls "an unacceptable risk to the environment and humanity."

The big building holds the Boiling Water Reactor (BWR), containing 484 fourteen-foot long fuel bundles, each of which is about the diameter of a finger. Pellets of uranium fuel, each a half an inch long and a quarter inch in diameter are loaded into the fuel bundles. Each pellet of uranium oxide can produce the energy equivalent of 1,780 pounds of coal. When fuel rods are put into close proximity to one another, a nuclear chain-reaction occurs that creates heat. This heat is used to create steam that ultimately turns a turbine, which powers a generator. The turbine and generator are located in the smaller buildings surrounding the main reactor building. Boron carbide control rods, which absorb the neutrons that trigger the nuclear reaction, are used to shutdown the reactor and to maintain a uniform distribution of power generation across the reactor. The generators produce approximately 20,000 volts of alternating current (AC), which is then stepped up to either 230,000 or 345,000 volts by a transformer and sent out from the plant on the power distribution grid. After the steam has done its job, it is cooled by water from the Mississippi River and sent back to the reactor to start the cycle over again. The warmed Mississippi water, depending upon the season and river flow rates is sent directly back to the river, or diverted to a small pair of cooling towers before returning to the river. In the summer, the maximum daily average water temperature at the end of the discharge canal can't exceed 95° F, while in winter the maximum allowable temperature is 80° F. With a maximum river flow of 290,000 gallons per minute, it's easy to see why the Mississippi stays ice-free in winter for several miles downstream of the plant and benefits the Trumpeter Swans.

When I arrived at the Monticello plant, the security was all it was promised to be. Every guard I saw had not only a holstered pistol, but also an automatic assault rifle strapped across their backs. There are a lot of guards. Guests must be accompanied by an employee who must keep you in sight at all times. Everyone wears radiation detection badges. Going through security involves airport-type metal detecting and screening apparatus and several bomb-sniffing machines. Once inside, moving from area to area requires constant scrutiny and security checks. The plant takes on the guise of most industrial complexes, except the floors, walls and ceiling are incredibly clean, and the whole place has a military feel to it. There is nothing here that is not needed, no decorations and nothing to distract workers from the task at hand—keeping an extremely dangerous genie inside its bottle.

My guide at Monticello was Bill Guldemond, who has decades of experience working in nuclear power plants. The Monticello plant is owned by Excel Energy, but operated by a subsidiary called Nuclear Management Corporation (NMC), LLC. Guldemond's title on his business card is Nuclear Safety Assessment Manager—to me that means he must know something about just about everything that goes on inside the plant. He explains that the plant has 450 technical employees and about 150 who work in security. His view of nuclear power is predictable. "This is a very safe, reliable, economical, and environmentally friendly way of generating electricity," he tells me. Most of the workforce at the plant has been there a long time. "A lot of people have been here a lot of years and clearly they believe in the technology," adds Guldemond.

I am struck by the redundancy in the place. Every system seems to have a backup and the safety systems operate using thirty-plus year old technology. Guldemond explains that they understand the failure modes of the old-fashioned analog systems, while newer digital systems aren't yet as clearly proven. "Analogs are pretty easy to understand, but digital aren't," said Guldemond. "The progress of rolling over to digital safety systems has been slow." Although measurement systems use the latest digital controls, anything that impinges on the safety of the plant uses the tried and true, something the Nuclear Regulatory Agency (NRC) also seems to prefer. "What the NRC is concerned with when they license a plant is that you understand all of the failure modes of your support and control systems and safety systems."

After visiting pump rooms and control systems at the base of the reactor, we take an elevator to a large room located near the top of the building. I'm literally standing on top of the nuclear reactor and

somewhere beneath my feet billions of neutrons are bombarding uranium atoms, causing a controlled nuclear chain reaction. Directly in front of me there is a large pool; one section of which contains spent fuel rods. It is twenty-three feet deep, filled with deionized

*Standing on top of the reactor core*

highly pure water. The water keeps the fuel rods and the top of the reactor cool and also absorbs neutrons to keep any unwanted chain reactions from occurring. It also protects the workers from radiation. "By keeping everything underwater, we keep the doses [of radiation] very, very low," Guldemond tells me. "There is very little hazard to the workers from direct radiation."

In the spent fuel part of the pool, there are used fuel rods that are more than thirty years old, from the start-up of the reactor in Monticello. The Federal government is responsible for this spent fuel, and was supposed to remove it from nuclear power plants for reprocessing. That work halted during the Carter administration under fears that the reprocessed fuel could be diverted to become nuclear weapons material. "Like many other plants, we are reaching the end of capacity in our spent fuel pool," said Guldemond. The Monticello plant has received permission from the NRC to store the oldest fuel rods outdoors in dry casks until such time as the Federal government has created a program to reprocess or store the radioactive material.

More than the question of accidents, attacks, or sabotage, it is this question of spent nuclear fuel that continues to vex the growth of nuclear energy in the United States. France, a country that obtains almost 80 percent of its electricity from nuclear energy, has built fuel reprocessing plants that reclaim plutonium and unused uranium and refabricate these radioactive materials back into fuel. The remaining waste is small in volume (reportedly the volume of high-level waste for a family of four using electricity for twenty years is a glass cylinder about the size of a cigarette lighter...) and is currently kept in temporary storage areas. Soon, the French government will begin long-term storage of the highest level materials a third of a mile below the surface in a mine shaft in eastern France. The U.S. plan has included a waste facility in Yucca Mountain in Nevada, but that facility has been in the works for more than fifteen years and has yet to receive its first shipment of radioactive waste material. A plant like Monticello refuels every two years, replacing about a third of the reactor's uranium fuel rods. The spent fuel rods take up an amount of space that would almost fill a railroad box car, but for now they aren't going anywhere—they are moved into the spent fuel pool where they wait for the Federal government to come up with answers. Until a solution is found, it's hard to imagine, no matter how "green" its carbon-free megawatts might be, how nuclear power can grow beyond its current twenty percent level in this country.

Fully 50 percent of America's electricity is generated using coal, more than double nuclear power or any other single fuel source. The U.S. has more than 600 coal-fired plants in operation and hundreds more are planned to meet our ever-increasing demands for inexpensive electricity. That demand will further increase as plug-in hybrids are charged from the electricity grid. What is coal and where did it come from?

Biologists tell us that about 400 million years ago the first primitive life forms, single and multi-cell algae appeared in the oceans. After another 50 million years the algae moved onto land, becoming mosses, primitive plants and eventually trees. The seas rose during warm periods, flooding coastal areas for millions of years, then receding as the climate cooled and ice ages came and went. Geologists call this time the Carboniferous Period as it was during this time that the majority of fossil fuels that we have today were created. In the swamps of the costal areas along what is now the Atlantic coast, trees and plants built up layer upon layer of organic material—leaves, roots, branches and seeds. Near the surface, this material became peat. Geologic processes pushed this peat deep into the earth, driving off the oxygen, nitrogen and hydrogen gases and leaving behind carbon—coal. This is how the coal beds in Pennsylvania, the Appalachians and the central United States formed.

A large amount of coal is also found in West. It is a much

younger and softer coal, created about 55 million years ago during the late Paleocene Epoch when the Rocky Mountains pushed upward out of the plains, producing low-lying basins and swamps in northeastern Wyoming and southern Montana. Huge ferns, as large as trees, took hold and, with a hot and wet climate there was a rapid buildup of organic plant material in these lowlands. Runoff from the Rockies covered the swamps with mud, and in time the organic material was pushed deep below the surface, where it became thick beds of soft coal. The western coal doesn't have as high an energy content as eastern coal, but because it formed in freshwater swamps, it is extremely low in sulfur, making it particularly desirable for today's electric power generation. Coal coming from areas that were covered in oceans has higher sulfur levels because bacteria in theses swamps converted sulfates in the seawater into pyrites, which were incorporated into the coal.

Coal is found in seams, bands of black rock that can be anywhere from a few inches to tens or even hundreds of feet thick. Traditionally, coal was mined by tunneling deep into the earth to find a rich coal seam, and digging out the material from that seam. It was dirty, dangerous, and difficult and more than 100,000 miners have died in U.S. coal mines since 1900, and at least double that number died from black lung, a respiratory disease caused by inhaling coal dust. Mining is still done the old-fashioned way, and miners still die when roofs cave in, or methane pockets explode, but beginning about twenty years ago, the coal industry underwent some dramatic changes and most of today's coal-mining is nothing like the job it used to be.

Larry Gibson's people have lived on Kayford Mountain in West Virginia for more than 230 years. Gibson stands about five-foot-five, is in his sixties, cautiously friendly and a born talker. His picturesque fifty acres, a low hill of rugged cherry, oak, hickory, and other hardwoods is surrounded on all sides by land leased by coal companies. Once, his little hilltop sat nestled among bigger mountains. Now its treed summit stands hundreds of feet higher than the barren surrounding country. "You are looking at mountain top removal," Gibson tells me as we walk to the edge of an 800 foot high cliff. "You have a mountain here and a mountain here, with a valley in the middle," he says, gesturing with his hands. "You literally turn that

*Larry Gibson and "Dog" survey the damage MTR has done to his West Virginia mountaintop home*

mountain upside down into the valley. What goes in the valley first is what's on top of the land—trees, topsoil, everything that's valuable, everything that's needed for life. Nothing can grow without topsoil, and of course the topsoil is at the bottom of the valley fill."

About 70 percent of coal in the United States is mined using Mountain Top Removal (MTR). It is a form of strip mining that started in West Virginia in the 1980s. Gibson explains why it is popular with coal companies. "Deep mining requires anywhere from 400 to 600 men. Out here you're going to maybe see nineteen men and they take out maybe five to ten times as much coal as the 600 men do in the same time period. Instead of extracting the coal from the mountain, they are extracting the mountain from the coal. It's much simpler…"

Coal companies say MTR is much safer for miners, and the

numbers bear this out. Throughout the 1970's, an average of thirty-five miners died every year. By the beginning of the twenty-first century, when MTR was well established, the number of fatalities had dropped

to around thirty annually. The safest year on record was 2005, with a total of twenty-three coal mine fatalities. That's much better than China's annual toll of more than 4,000 coal miners who die in the country's deep mines. Instead of working with complex and specialized

*Mountain Top Removal (MTR) coal mining in West Virginia*

machinery deep underground, miners who work removing the tops from mountains sit in their bulldozers, dump trucks, and drag lines, working above ground.

"Over here is where they set up the last blast yesterday," said Gibson, pointing across the vast open pit to a pile of rubble about a half mile away. "They blast ten to twelve times a day, six times a week." MTR miners drill holes in the ground, plant explosives and blast out huge sections of the ground. Bulldozers and draglines then push the rubble into the valleys until they reach the seams of coal, which are dug out and transferred by dump trucks to a wash area. For every ton of coal that is removed, ninety-five gallons of water are used to clean it prior to shipment. The water must be kept in impoundments because it is too polluted to return to the environment. In 2000, an impoundment in Kentucky broke and spilled more than 300-million gallons of slurry. This was thirty times the size of the *Exxon Valdez* oil spill in

Alaska. The spill killed all of the aquatic life in streams, destroyed homes, and contaminated much of the drinking water in the eastern part of the state. In addition to the dangers, MTR coal mining leaves behind a landscape that looks like the surface of the moon.

Appalachia produced 377 million tons of coal in 2007, about a third of the nation's total coal production, with MTR accounting for about a third of that. Wyoming is by far the largest coal state, producing more than 453 million tons in 2007, more than 99 percent of it by Mountain Top Removal.

"Up there in the woods, there was 150 graves," said Gibson, indicating the edge of the cliff off to our right. "They took a dozer and wiped out 139 graves, pushed them over the high wall…That graveyard was almost 300 years old. It was my family graveyard."

These forests of the Appalachian Mountains are special. When the glaciers pushed south a million and a half years ago, they were stopped by the mountains. Plants and animals that were displaced by the sheets of ice found a home in the temperate region. The Appalachian region became the richest temperate forest in the world and today is home to more kinds of trees than exist in all of northern Europe. There are more than 1,500 species of flowering plants and incredible biodiversity that includes everything from salamanders to black bears.

The Surface Mining Control and Reclamation Act of 1977 requires coal companies to reclaim land to it approximately original contours. Most of the time the reclaimed land ends up as rolling grassy hills—not exactly the rugged mountains that once were the hallmark of the Appalachians. More than a half a million acres of Appalachia have already been rearranged by MTR and more than 1,200 miles of streams adversely affected by the mining process, with more than 700 miles of streams now buried forever. Gibson claims that more than 475 mountains have been destroyed by MTR. For a long time many coal companies got by with forfeiting their bonds, packing up shop, and leaving behind a disaster. In 2002, the Army Corps of Engineers changed their reclamation guidelines, requiring operators to do a better job after removing the mountains.

The big argument for coal mining at any environmental cost is national energy security. It has been claimed that the U.S. has at least 250 years worth of coal reserves within its borders. That number is probably too high, as MTR coal mining isn't efficient and much of the coal in the seams is left behind or pushed into the valleys. Still, with energy security at the top of our collective minds, and the justification for ripping apart the landscape, why is Appalachian coal being exported to other countries? "Most of the coal, believe it or not, goes out of the country," said Gibson. Total U.S. coal exports in 2007 were 59.2 million tons, 19.2 percent higher than in 2006 and the highest export level since 1998. Canada is the largest market for coal imports while Europe is the second largest market. In the past, the United Kingdom was Europe's largest importer of U.S. coal (we truly have been bringing coal to Newcastle…) but in 2007, the Netherlands was the biggest user of U.S. coal. Africa also is becoming a significant U.S. export market and South America is growing. U.S. exports to Asia are dropping off, as coal from Australia is closer and less expensive to ship.

Ironically, 2007 was also a record year for coal imports into the U.S., the fifth year in a row. A total of 36.3 million tons were imported, 73.9 percent came from Columbia. If you thought our interest in Columbia was just about the war on drugs, think again. Although South American coal has been the primary source for coal imports,

Indonesia surpassed Venezuela to become the second largest importer
of coal into the U.S. in 2007. And even though we export dramatic
amounts of coal to Canada, the Canadians also export coal back to us,
sending 2.0 million tons to the U.S. in 2007. Most coal exports come
out of coal mines in the eastern U.S. Which mean that West Virginia
and Kentucky mountains are being decimated, communities are being
disrupted, and people who live in Appalachia are being exposed to
a litany of health hazards, not to promote American energy security,
but to make more money for the coal industry by shipping it abroad.
Gibson just scratches his head. "If there was an energy crisis, would
they be shipping so much coal out of the country?"

More than 92 percent of coal production in the U.S. goes
toward electrical power generation. About sixty miles to the east by car
from Sheila Lawrence's Trumpeter Swan and the nuclear power plant
in Monticello, Minnesota stands the Allen S. King coal-fired electricity

*The Allen S. King coal-fired power plant*

generating plant. The King
plant is located on the St.
Croix River, designated as
one of America's National
Scenic Riverways, and
uses water from the river
for cooling. The King
plant produces almost 600
megawatts, about the same
as the Monticello Nuclear
Plant, and went online in
1968, making it slightly older than the Monticello facility.

From a security view, it is a lot easier to get into a conventional
coal-fired power plant than it is a nuclear plant. I needed no

background checks and when I arrived at the plant entrance, the guard shack was deserted and the parking barrier was broken, allowing me to park near the building. I used my cell phone to call Floyd Radinzel, the Scheduling Coordinator for the plant and the guide for my visit. Radinzel met me at the front entrance to the plant and we walked straight into the building and upstairs into his office without the hassle of metal detectors and bomb sniffers that Monticello had presented. If the Monticello nuclear plant felt like a military operation, the coal-fired power plant feels like an old ship—maybe an aging merchant vessel that is clean and orderly but also relaxed and friendly.

Radinzel knows a lot about producing electricity from coal. He started working at a power plant right out of high school in 1971. He transferred to the King plant in 1975. He's worked in the coal yards and on maintenance jobs for several decades. He also spent some time working at other plants in the system, including nuclear plants. "I've been there and done that," explains Radinzel. "I used to give my job description as anything from repairing a leaky sink to refueling a nuclear reactor—and anything in between." He's the perfect guy to walk me through how electricity is produced from burning coal.

Although the King plant is medium-sized in the world of power plants, the scale of the place is immense and is dominated by the 785 foot tall smokestack. A large rectangular building next to the stack, almost a third as high, contains the furnace, steam boiler, steam turbines and electric generators. A mile long, 600 ton-per-hour coal conveyer system is several stories high and moves coal into the coal yard to start the process. All of the low-sulfur coal that is burned at the King plant arrives by rail from the Jacob's Ranch Mine in Wyoming. The trains average 100 railcars per train and arrive around the clock. The conveyer dumps 100 tons from each railroad car, tipping the cars through 200 degrees without decoupling them. It takes about a two-and-a-half to three minutes for the coal to empty from a railroad car; about an hour for a whole train.

The coal is unloaded onto a live pile. "Because the plant burns so much coal in a twenty-four hour period, we can't store it in the plant, we have no room," said Radinzel. "We burn about 300 to 350 tons of coal per hour. A live pile is just a stack of coal on top of a conveyer." A lot of other coal plants pulverize coal until it is like talcum powder, but that method isn't used at the King plant. Instead, it is crushed into pea-sized chunks. The crushed coal is metered into burners attached to the outside of the cyclones, which are large twelve-foot diameter, ten-foot long drums. "It's actually suspended in mid-air by two electric 8,000-horsepower force draft fans as it enters the burners."

90 percent of the coal burns as it travels from the burners into the cyclones at between 3,500 and 4,000 degrees. The walls of the cyclone are covered with tubes filled with water. The heat from the coal fire transfers to the water and becomes 3,600 psi superheated steam. The steam is sent to a multi-stage turbine that powers the electric generators. Meanwhile, the flame from the cyclone next enters the furnace, that is lined with tubes, also filled with water, where more energy is recovered by changing the water into steam. The furnace is like a big room; it is 30 feet, by 50 feet, by 180 feet high. The entire system is designed to pull as much heat as possible out of the burning coal. "The temperature inside the cyclone is between 3,500 and 4,000 degrees, and when we discharge out the top of the stack the exhaust gases are about 350 degrees—so we've used about as much heat as we can," said Radinzel.

Floyd Radinzel tells me that about 20 percent of the coal

remains as ash and slag after burning. That means every two hours
the plant produces a railroad car full of waste, which is either sent to
a landfill or sold to a company that uses it to make grinding abrasives
and roofing material. That's a lot of waste, especially when you
compare the 100 ton railroad car of material produced every two hours
by the coal plant to the single railroad car of nuclear waste produced
by the Monticello plant over a two-year period. The Monticello stuff is
much more dangerous, but there is so much less of it.

The dangers of ash and slag were made clear at the end
of 2008, when an earthen dam next to a coal-fired power plant in
Tennessee failed, allowing 5.3 million cubic yards of waterlogged
ash to flow into the Emory River, a tributary of the Tennessee River.
The plant's pile of ash and slag had covered more than 100 acres to a
height of sixty-five feet and was the waste product of more than fifty
years of operation. The sludge breached its dam after heavy rains
made the pile unstable. More than a dozen homes were inundated and,
because of the high levels of heavy metals in the waste ash, there is
great concern about continuing problems with pollution of downstream
drinking water. Ash and slag at the King Plant that I visited is not
stored on-site, as was the case at Tennessee plant.

Despite sitting next to the St. Croix River, Radinzel told me
that the water from which the steam is produced comes from two 600
feet deep artesian wells located on the King plant property. The plant
uses between two and three million gallons of water per month. The
steam is condensed, using river water to cool the steam back into
water so it can return and become steam again. "Right now we are
using about 302,000 gallons per hour of river water going in and out
of the plant. We pull it in, it goes through the tubes and goes right back
out," said Radinzel. Like the Monticello plant, the discharge water

temperature is regulated to a maximum of eighty-five degrees. "The water going out picks up between fifteen to twenty degrees," adds Radinzel.

The plant uses a high-pressure steam turbine, an intermediate pressure turbine, and two low-pressure turbines. The high pressure and intermediate turbines are brand new and were just installed and the internal parts of the low pressure turbines are also new. Radinzel points out an interesting problem that is facing the power industry. "The turbine was ordered two and half years ago. It came from overseas. The United States does not have any places to build large turbines. We do not have that anymore. If we wanted to build a turbine in the United States, and do it all here, it would take a minimum of ten years to man up and tool up to do that job. We haven't got the facilities or the people who know how to do that anymore." I ask him who has the ability to make turbines for the power industry. "China, Japan and Europe." This problem also exists with nuclear power— not only steam turbines but the ability to manufacture a reactor vessel no longer resides on our shores.

"We've just gone through a major refurbishment of this plant, so as far as environmental concerns we are 'state-of-the-art' for burning fossil fuels," said Radinzel. "We have a Selective Catalyst Reduction—basically it acts the same way as your car's catalytic converter works, only ours has about 220 tons of catalyst. We inject ammonia into the flue gas stream—that ammonia reacts with the oxides of nitrogen with the catalysts to become water and nitrogen gas. That removes the nitrogen oxides," explains Radinzel. This explained the farm of ammonia tanks I had noticed earlier while driving into the plant. "We also have an SDA, a dry scrubber. We ship a special limestone from Superior, Wisconsin.

We process it into a lime slurry—a whitewash basically. We put
the whitewash through an atomizer, a high-pressure pump that sprays a
fine mist into the flue gas stream. When that mist goes into the flue gas
stream it removes the sulfur dioxide." Some of this gets recycled and
the remaining material is sent to a landfill. "We also have a bag-house
to remove particulates. We have 18-20,000 bags, each thirty feet long.
The air goes out the filters before going out the stack." It takes energy
to move the flue gas through all of the environmental controls. "We
had to add four 7,400 horsepower induced draft fans to suck the air out
of the furnace," said Radinzel. The electric energy it takes to run these
blowers, along with other pumps and atomizers take away from the
electric power that can go out onto the grid. The Allen S. King plant
may be state-of-the-art, but it still releases harmful pollutants into the
environment. Coal has small amounts of mercury, arsenic and other
heavy metals that are not currently removed from the flue gas, but
there are plans to add such filters to the King plant in the future. Coal-
fired power plants are the largest source of mercury in the environment
in the United States and mercury is known to cause birth defects and
cognitive problems in adults, even in small doses and low exposure
levels. Carbon dioxide emissions, another area of rapidly growing
concern, are uncontrolled at the King Plant.

Radinzel takes me on a tour of the plant. It is warm in the
building, not surprising given the heat provided by the 350 tons of
coal that are burned every hour. There is a slight, but almost constant
vibration, sensed through the feet, caused by the huge turbines turning
the generators to produce electricity. If you work at a power plant, it's
a reassuring vibration. We look at steam pipes and blowers and the
control room and again I am struck by how nautical it all feels. Finally,
Radinzel takes me up onto the roof of the building where a cold stiff

wind is blowing. Up the St. Croix River, I can see the picturesque
town of Stillwater. Looking south, past the Interstate 94 bridge where
it crosses into Wisconsin, I can see where the St. Croix widens out to
form a broad lake in front of the town of Afton. It is easy to understand
why this river has been recognized for its scenic beauty. Behind us, the
plant's single stack is puffing out a stream of white smoke.

The King plant is cleaner than it was—removing smog causing
oxides of nitrogen and acid-rain inducing sulfur dioxide has made
it one of the cleanest coal plants in the country. The coal industry
says that nationwide it has reduced harmful emissions by more than
70 percent since 1970. Like the King Plant the emissions that have
been reduced are oxides of nitrogen, sulfur dioxide, and particulate
materials. But I can't help thinking of how mercury and arsenic and
other heavy metals are affecting the fish who live in the river and
the people who live on the shore. And what is the effect of all of the
carbon dioxide coming from the burning of almost 17 million pounds
of coal that this one medium-sized power plant burns everyday? Is
there a better way to make electricity?

Two hundred and fifteen miles west of the Allen S. King Plant,
on the border of Minnesota and South Dakota is a low ridge near the
town of Lake Benton, Minnesota. Buffalo Ridge runs north and south
for sixty miles and, at 1,995 feet above sea level, is the second highest
point in Minnesota. Along the top of that long ridge sit more than 685
wind turbines, producing enough electric energy, when the wind is
blowing, to power more than a third of a million homes.

Windmills have been around for centuries, but today's modern
wind turbines are technological marvels. Most have huge three-bladed
fans whirling on towers that stand 240 feet tall. Internal computer
systems adjust the tilt of the blades, allowing the turbines to produce

electricity in as little as nine-mph winds.

Joe Mason and Tim Walker are iron workers who are employed by M.A. Mortenson, a construction company that, among a variety of other projects, builds wind farms all over the country. It's a Sunday afternoon and a stiff wind is blowing out of North Dakota, but the Mortenson crew is hard at work. Over the course of the summer of 2007, the two men and their crew erected more than 200 wind turbines on the Buffalo Ridge. The $2-million GE wind turbines each produce one-point-five megawatts, so over the course of the summer the equivalent of one half of a 600 MW coal-fired or nuclear power plant has been built along the ridge. "It's pretty simple," explains Mason. "You put one piece on top of another to build the tower, and then put the nacelle on top that contains the generator," said Mason. "It takes us about an hour and a half to do the footings and then the top off crew comes along. It takes about two hours to erect one," adds Walker. The

crew can build two footings a day, building a structure out of fifteen tons of steel rebar and pouring 176 yards of concrete. The turbine blades, which are fiberglass, and are 124 feet long, are painted black to help reduce ice formation during harsh Minnesota winters.

I'd heard lots of stories about wind turbines. I've heard that they are noisy, that they act as giant cuisinarts, chopping up birds as they fly into the blades, and that they are an ugly blight on the landscape. Standing

*A wind turbine on Minnesota's Buffalo Ridge*

next to one of the giants in a stiff wind on Buffalo ridge, I could just hear the swooshing of the turbine blades over the sound of the wind rustling through the stover in a nearby cornfield. I searched the base of the wind turbine, but couldn't find a single dead bird. In fact a 2002 study found wind turbines were the cause of less than 1 percent of bird fatalities. The biggest cause was buildings and windows at 58 percent, followed by cats at 11 percent. As for a wind turbine's aesthetics? I find the synchronicity of dozens of huge slender blades rotating as the wind blows to be a thing of beauty.

Apparently, I'm not the only person who finds wind turbines to be appealing. Oil billionaire T. Boone Pickens has made wind power the cornerstone of a push for a national energy policy. In May of 2008, I sat with Pickens and group of journalists at the Alternative Fuels and Vehicles National Conference in Las Vegas. Pickens, had just provided a keynote address to the conference where the eighty-year-old geologist made it clear that we are going to have to drill everywhere to try to find oil. At the same time, judging from the geologic structures involved, he doesn't believe that there is much oil to be found along the Atlantic seaboard or in the Arctic National Wildlife Refuge (ANWR) in Alaska. But he has another solution in mind and announced his plans for wind power to replace the 20 percent of the country's electric power generation, power that is currently produced by burning natural gas.

"Go to Texas where we are getting ready to build 4,000 megawatts," said Pickens. He has leased hundreds of thousands of acres on which he plans to erect 2,700 wind turbines. He hasn't had any problem convincing Texas ranchers to come on board. "The landowners stand in line to sign up with you," said Pickens. "They want the turbines on the property."

A recent Department of Energy (DOE) study found that wind generating facilities located along a corridor from the Texas Panhandle to North Dakota could produce up to 20 percent of the nation's electric power needs. "In the middle of the United States you can develop all of the power you want to [through wind], and that's fabulous when you can do that with a renewable," said Pickens. But generating power in the middle of the country is only part of the problem. "Then you've got to get it to the west coast or the east coast," said Pickens.

When electric power is transmitted over distances, an amount is lost (averaging about 7 percent) through the electrical resistance of the transmission lines. The longer those transmission lines, the more electric energy that is lost. The interconnection of the transmission lines makes up the electric power grid, which is a network of circuits that moves power around the country. But the grid isn't designed to move vast quantities of energy from the middle of the country to the coasts. "The west coast's not so hard; there's a way to do it with a grid," said Pickens. But the whole grid system needs an overhaul if the Pickens plan is going to work. "What you need to do is to do the same thing as in the Eisenhower administration where they said we have to have a network of highways because it's an emergency to do that. At that period, in the Cold War, they felt like they had to have it," said Pickens. "That's what they have to do on transmission— they've got to say it's an emergency and this is what we are going to do. You have got to have somebody steps up and takes the hill."

The power transmission grid in the United States dates back to the earliest days of electric power generation. The first central power generating plant was built by Thomas Edison and began producing electricity in lower Manhattan in 1882. It had one generator and produced enough electricity to light 800 of Edison's recently (1879) invented electric light bulbs. By 1893, the alternating current (A/C) generating system invented by Nikola Tesla and developed by George Westinghouse was chosen to transmit electric power from Niagara

Falls to Buffalo, spelling the end of Edison's direct current (D/C) industry. In 1898, Samuel Insull proposed that electric companies be regulated by state agencies that would set service standards and establish rates and by 1916, 33 states had created regulatory agencies.

The electric power industry grew quickly, with nearly 90 percent of urban dwellers electrified by the early 1930's. However, only about 10 percent of those who lived in rural areas were served by electricity—the electric power companies claimed it was too expensive to install rural lines for farmers. In 1935, the Roosevelt administration created the Rural Electric Administration (REA) to bring electricity to areas like the Tennessee Valley that were not being served by private utility companies. Many groups, including the utility companies, objected to government involvement in electricity distribution but by 1939, the REA had helped to establish 417 rural electric cooperatives serving 288,000 rural households. In addition to electric power, the Tennessee Valley Authority (TVA) helped farmers purchase electric ranges, refrigerators and water heaters at reasonable prices, moving forward the cause of rural electrification.

The patchwork of electrical distribution systems eventually were woven together into the electrical power grid that we have today. Electric utilities and several independent transmission companies own the distribution system.

Roughly speaking, there are three levels to the grid. Imagine the U.S. is covered by three wire mesh screens. The top level, with the coarsest wires is the 345-kilovolt (kv) grid—this is the highest voltage grid to which base load plants like coal-fire plants, nuclear power plants, and huge hydroelectric projects like Hoover Dam are connected. These plants are designed to operate continuously, providing a constant base level of electricity into the system without changing power output levels. A few major industrial facilities like steel mills that have huge electricity requirements are connected into this top grid. Power is transmitted along the 345-kv grid through the huge towers that are a part of the regional transmission grids, and there are more than 200,000 miles of high-voltage transmission lines in the U.S.

At certain spots, power is taken from the 345-kv grid, reduced down, and connected to the next level, the 115-kv grid. This is where most normal manufacturing plants are connected. This is the level where natural gas fired peaking generators, smaller hydroelectric dams, and wind and solar generation enter the electrical grid system. The 115-kv grid also feeds the lowest voltage grid, which at 13.8-kv, services local homes and small businesses after being stepped down at local substations to 230-volt and 115-volt household current.

Electric power companies like consistency and this is one problem with renewable sources like solar and wind power. Solar panels only produce electricity when the sun is shining, and wind turbines only produce electricity when the wind is blowing. Electric power industry groups claim that this variability can cause instability in the electric power grid that could lead to blackouts, reduce the system's overall reliability and necessitate costly backup generation capability.

Now, overlaid on top of the power grid is the prospective of plug-in hybrid electric vehicles (PHEV). "The OEM's [original equipment car manufacturers] want to make charging at home as simple and easy as possible. So the focus right now is charging at 110-volt," according to Efrain Ornelas who is the Electric Drive Supervisor for Pacific Gas and Electric's (PG&E) Clean Air Transportation Department and whom I also met with in Las Vegas. "They will be able to come home, plug into a standard 110-volt outlet for your typical PHEV, and in five to seven hours your car will be totally recharged." There is also discussion of using household 240-volt service to charge PHEVs. "The bigger the pipe, the quicker you can get the energy into the vehicle," said Ornelas.

Electric energy demand varies throughout the day— peaking around midday and into the afternoon (air conditioning and business usage), and significantly less demand during to so-called "off-peak" hours at night. It has been widely suggested that because PHEVs will recharge mostly at night, during off-peak hours, as many as 60 million cars nationwide (and for example 4 million in California) could obtain electric energy from the grid with no new electric generation capacity required. Remember, however that electric power companies like consistency and don't like to risk the possibility of electricity shortages. If PHEVs fill in the trough in electricity demand during off-peak hours, most electric utilities would interpret that as an increase in base demand and would add electric power generating capacity to meet this new perceived base-load demand. Because this is base load demand, it would likely be filled with a nuclear or coal-fired power plant.

In parts of the country like California, which already has significant wind power generation capacity and where the wind blows reliably between 10:00 p.m. and 5:00 a.m., during the off-peak hours, wind energy might actually be capable of supporting much of the requirement created by the charging of PHEVs. Electricity costs for off-peak charging are estimated by PG&E to be less than one dollar per the equivalent energy contained in a gallon of gasoline.

In the long term, there are some exciting possibilities that combine the electric power grid and a fleet of electrically powered hybrid plug-in vehicles. It starts with a replacement of the traditional home electric power meter with a "smart" meter.

"The meters that we are developing actually have the capability to send energy information one second to two seconds after it is actually used—almost real time energy usage from those meters," said PG&E's Ornelas. Utility customers who have the smart meters will be able to get electricity usage and rate information and will be able to track energy usage from month to month. In addition, appliance manufacturers are developing new smart household appliances that will communicate with the utility to allow optimization of energy usage throughout the day. The objective is to help the customer find the lowest cost for electricity and give the utility a chance to level peaks, avoiding the purchase of more expensive energy and maximizing the use of renewable energy sources during the charging process. The California utilities have all been approved for smart meter programs and are moving quickly in that direction. "Our goal is by 2012 to have all 5.4 million electric customers and 4.5 million gas customers totally converted to the smart meter," said Ornelas.

Once smart metering is in place, the next step is smart charging, where the utility company communicates with and controls the charger to optimize the type of energy and how it is used to charge a vehicle battery. "There is a certain hierarchy that starts with smart charging—we have to be able to get the energy into the vehicle first to get it rolling and make that practical and efficient, and give customer choices," said Ornelas. But electric utilities and car manufacturers see additional value to the charged batteries sitting in the car parked in the garage. "The next step is the vehicle-to-home component. The vision is that when we start getting maybe the second generation of plug-in hybrids and battery-electric vehicles— ones that will allow the export of energy out of the vehicle that customers will be able to utilize as an emergency power source— you can use it as a standby generator so that you can keep your lights on, your heater going, your refrigeration, and things like that in times of emergency."

It is the long-term possibilities that have electric utility companies excited. They call it vehicle-to-grid, or V2G in shorthand. "What we see even more long term, fifteen to twenty years from now, when we really get the penetration of vehicles out there—numbers like fifteen, twenty, forty, even 80,000 vehicles out there where we have significant numbers—at that point you start seeing a real resource for energy storage and that's when we start talking about real vehicle-to-grid." The objective is to use the hundreds of thousands or even millions of individual electric vehicle battery packs as extra electricity capacity, available to the power grid to meet sudden peaks in energy demand.

The industry calls this spinning reserve. It's the extra capacity that needs to be available at a moment's notice when the actual demand exceeds the actual capacity. Systems that are fast reacting, like hydroelectric plants and gas turbine generators, are good for spinning reserve. "If we have a resource out there, which is the batteries in the vehicles, that we can count on to meet that last few megawatts of energy that we need to get us over the hump—the peaking—that could be significant as that's typically the most expensive electricity. If we have that huge reservoir of stored energy that we can tap that may be a lot cheaper than traditional sources that we buy for peaking electricity," explains Ornelas. Working out the details, for example how does the utility company reimburse you for the energy it takes from your car, who pays for the degradation of the battery cells caused by the extra charge and discharge cycles, and how to ensure you aren't left with a dead battery, present significant challenges. Many in both the automotive and power industries see V2G as one of the important energy saving benefits of plug-in hybrid electric vehicles.

There are some visionaries that think that the sprawling electric power grid that we have had in place for decades is the wrong direction to go for the future. Instead of centralizing electric power generation at giant coal-fired and nuclear power plants and sending it through an extended high-voltage grid, they say that distributed power generators, small in scale but numerous, might be a better long-term bet, especially for developing countries. These small generators, running on natural gas, biogas, biodiesel, geothermal steam, hydrogen fuel cells, or other "clean" fuels, and supplemented by wind and solar energy, could supply small towns or even neighborhoods in larger towns and cities. Some have even suggested that small-scale and fully self-contained nuclear reactors could provide the base level power for such a system.

Virtually self-contained, these distributed power units would eliminate the need for a vast electric grid and provide power where and when it is needed. A distributed power system could also be a great deal more robust. Amory Lovins, the CEO of the Rocky Mountain Institute, a think-tank for energy and environment matters has written, "A more efficient, diverse, dispersed, renewable energy system can make major supply failures, whether caused by accident or malice, impossible by design rather than (as now) inevitable by design." These ideas would require a radical rethink of how we generate and use electric energy.

No matter how and where it's generated, if we have all of this electricity available, why not go fully electric and forget the complexity induced by the hybrid drive train? Renault Nissan is working on a series of all-electric vehicles that it hopes to have on the market by 2011 and a spokesperson for the company has said as much as 20 percent of the European market will be electric vehicles in ten years. Renault will work on the European market versions of the vehicle line while Nissan will concentrate on electric vehicles for Japan and the U.S. market. Helping the rollout, an entrepreneur has received endorsement from the Israeli government to create a network of Renault electric cars by 2011. In Israel, 90 percent of drivers travel is less than forty-five miles per day and none of the major cities are more than 100 miles apart, making fully electric cars practical. The company is called Better Place and their business model is interesting: make cars available cheaply (or free) and sell electricity through a network of automated battery exchange stations. The same system is under study for Hawaii and cities in the U.S.

Several smaller companies are looking at the high-torque characteristics of electric motors to build all-electric sports cars. Venturi, an all-electric vehicle producer in Monaco has produced a flagship model called the Fetish that can accelerate to sixty miles per hour in less than 4-seconds, and can go nearly 180 miles on a single charge. In the U.S., a company in California is building an all-electric sports car called the Tesla. The 2,750-pound composite sports car uses a platform built by Lotus in England and has 6,831

*Tesla's all-electric sports car (Tesla)*

individual lithium-ion cells, combined into a single battery pack. The

$109,000 Tesla is fast, with a 3.9-second zero-to-60 mph time and has a reported range of 221 miles on a charge. Charging the Tesla takes three-and-a-half hours on a 240 volt, seventy-amp service.

The charging issue is something that is becoming a clear stumbling-block for the work that is underway exploring the use of the electric power grid to power our vehicles. Not everyone has the kind of utility service that allows a seventy-amp charge in their garage. Heck, not everyone has a garage. How will cars be charged if they are parked at the curbside?

What if we could just pull into a charging station, receive a quick fill-up of electrons and be on our way? Although it sounds ideal, physics has some limitations for us. The average size battery for a full electric (non-hybrid) vehicle will require a capacity of something like 130 kilowatt hours. To recharge that battery in ten minutes will require a charging station that can produce 780 kilowatts. To move that much current that quickly requires a thousand amp circuit. Just cooling the eight kilowatts of heat produced during charging would require five gallons per minute of cold water, circulating through the vehicle to keep it from overheating. A station capable of filling four fully-electric cars at a time would require 4 megawatts of electrical capacity— roughly the size of an industrial electric substation. You can't beat physics. It just isn't workable.

Another possibility that fully-electric vehicle proponents suggest is to stock spare charged battery pack and have a quick-change system. Except that the battery is the most expensive part of the electric vehicle. Having at least one spare battery on the shelf for every electric vehicle on the road just doubled the cost of the most expensive part of the vehicle. Technically feasible, but not a financially viable option.

The basic problem, if you want to supplant the energy from gasoline with energy stored in a battery, is one of simple physics. The amount of energy stored in a kilogram (two-point-two pounds or slightly more than a third of a gallon) of gasoline is about 12,000 watt-hours. We've already said that gasoline engines are about 30 percent efficient, so about 3,600 watt-hours are used to move the vehicle. The amount of energy you can store per kilogram of lithium-ion battery is about 120 watt-hours. Electric motors are highly efficient, let's use 90 percent for the electric drive system, so 108 watt-hours available to power our vehicle. Therefore, you need about thirty kilograms (seventy-three pounds) of lithium-ion batteries to provide the energy you can get from burning one kilogram of gasoline, or about 210 pounds of batteries to give you the energy in one gallon of gasoline. It's hard to get around the fact that for a given weight of gasoline and lithium-ion batteries, the gasoline stores 100 times the energy. Even the latest nanotechnology lithium-ion batteries, which promise to double the energy density of first generation lithium-ion cells, are still limited in the amount of energy that they can provide in a vehicle.

The reality is that except for a few local inter-urban applications, if we want to use electricity to help power our transportation fleet, we are going to have to do it through plug-in hybrid electric vehicles. It will require an overhaul of our electric grid, new smart metering and smart charging technology, some breakthroughs in battery technology (primarily cost), and a clear understanding of where certain strategic materials will come from. But the sooner we do it, the sooner we will be able to deal with reduced oil supplies and another problem that is sitting on a rapidly approaching time horizon: Global Climate Change.

# Chapter 5
## What Have We Done?

*Will Steger in his element (Gordon Wiltsie photo)*

"What I've observed in the last twenty years on the Arctic Ocean is the disappearance of the sea ice. It is almost impossible now to reach the [north] pole by dogs from land. In another three or four years, it will be impossible." Will Steger knows something about polar travel. In 1986, his team of six was the first ever reach the North Pole by dogsled. He returned to the North Pole in 1995, crossing the Arctic Ocean from Russia to Ellesmere Island in Canada. Steger lives ten miles north of Ely, Minnesota, not far from the Boundary Waters Canoe Area, in an off-the-grid cabin powered by solar panel arrays. The day I met Steger at his homestead at the end of December in 2008 was cold, about 9° F, somehow it seemed fitting for a visit with a polar explorer. We sat in his cabin, warmed by a woodstove, and overlooking a picturesque frozen lake.

"We completed two expeditions in 2008—up in Northern Ellesmere [Island] by dog team, and then we crossed Greenland by kite skis in the summer," said Steger. "What we saw there was really quite shocking to me. It is alarming is what's happening in the Arctic. One example is the summer sea ice on the Arctic Ocean," he said.

The Arctic Ocean is larger in area than the United States. Normally, in the summertime about 95 percent of the ice stays, it only breaks up a little bit on the fringes. The energy from the sun hits that ice like a mirror and reflects back into space. That keeps the top of the earth cool and balances it with the warmer equator. But things are changing. "Last summer we lost 50 percent of that summer sea ice—in other words 50 percent of what used to be reflective melted, exposing a darker ocean, and now you have a large percentage of that energy absorbed," said Steger.

The absorption of extra solar energy works in ways that scientists aren't able to easily predict. "Last year, when that 50 percent broke up, it shocked even the conservative scientists," said Steger. "The new 25 percent area that broke up is called multi-year ice which is older thicker ice that is the breeding ice for the Arctic Ocean. The majority of that broke up. We actually experienced this breakup."

Steger says it won't take long before the Arctic Ocean has even less sea ice than today's levels. "The inside word from the Norwegian Navy working with American Navy is that within ten years you are looking at a sea route over the top," said Steger. "You hear all this talk about the Northwest Passage? Forget it. You don't need the Northwest Passage—just go over the top. They're planning in less than ten years to do a sea route for four months out of the year."

I asked Steger about how this will affect the native people who live in the Arctic. "The Inuit Eskimo people are very adaptable," he told me. "So they say, if the sea level rises, we'll just move our village, if the ice moves, we'll just fish instead of hunt seal on the ice. They often turn the question back on us: what will you do in your society when your climate changes? We are all interdependent on each other globally. They [the Inuit] can be self-sufficient and adapt and roll with the punches. We're not able, as we've seen with the economy. Everything is changing. Their traditional knowledge is based upon certain weather patterns and game migration over the millennia. You did have climate change in the past, but it happened over very long time periods and you could adapt to it. The rapid change is what is different now. It's remarkable what's happening in the last decade."

If the Inuit can adapt, can the animals who inhabit the arctic polar region? "It's moving too quickly," said Steger. "The [polar] bear is going to be extinct unfortunately. The bear relies on the ice. The bear is not going to move to land. It took 100,000 years for the bear adapt to ice and they just can't move to land that quickly. They are not adaptable."

Steger's experiences are not just limited to the North Pole. During 1989-90, he led the 3,471-mile International Trans-Antarctic Expedition, using dog sleds to travel from one side of Antarctica to the other, via the South Pole. "In Antarctica the ice shelves are going," said Steger. The ice shelves are important because they buttress against the continent and keep the huge glaciers and ice streams from flowing into the ocean. "The A and B Larsen ice shelves have both disintegrated [since 1990] so we no longer could take that route toady."

Apart from inconveniencing polar explorers, why should we care about melting oceans and glaciers? "Sea level rise is the crucial thing," said Steger. "To me, the challenge is going to be, as humanity, that we have to move quickly to stabilize the ice sheets. We have to keep this melting to a minor level so that we can adapt around it. But we have to move immediately. Time is out unless we move immediately."

We started using fossil fuels in a big way at the beginning of the industrial revolution, in about 1750, when coal was used to produce steam to power machinery. Our usage of fossilized carbon has been accelerating at a fantastic rate ever since. Unfortunately, so has our release of carbon dioxide into the atmosphere. Every gallon of gasoline or diesel fuel that is burned releases into the atmosphere a significant amount of carbon dioxide ($CO_2$). Actually, it's about 19.6 pounds of carbon dioxide for every gallon of gasoline that's consumed. Recall that hydrocarbon fossil fuels made from petroleum are actually the remains of living organisms that, millions of years ago, removed carbon dioxide from the atmosphere. By burning such fossil fuels we are returning this prehistoric carbon dioxide into the Earth's atmosphere.

For a long time, the effects of the buildup of $CO_2$ went largely unnoticed. As early as the late 1800s, scientists studying why the Earth is temperate wondered if a "greenhouse" effect might occur, but nobody paid much attention. The greenhouse effect is similar to what happens due to the heat-trapping properties of the glass panels that make up the roof of a greenhouse. Rays of light from the sun pass through the atmosphere just as they travel through a pane of glass. The light heats up the Earth, which radiates this heat back toward the atmosphere as longer wavelength heat radiation. These long wavelength rays would radiate back into space, but like the glass panes in a greenhouse, the presence of water vapor and greenhouse gases

such as carbon dioxide, methane, and nitrides of oxygen traps this
heat, causing the atmosphere to gradually heat up.

Some amount of this heating is beneficial, providing a
temperate climate that supports life. Too much of this heating
and the Earth becomes radically altered with the consequences of
melting ice packs in the polar regions, sea rise, desertification, and
wholesale extinction of animal species. This is no longer in the
realm of conjecture: it is the consensus of nearly every reputable
scientist and researcher in the fields of climate change, meteorology,
biology and environmental science, and the conclusion reached by
the Intergovernmental Panel on Climate Change (IPCC) in their 2007
report. Still, it is difficult to sort through the legitimate science that is
based on credible research work, and the conjecture that has often been
created by those with specific and sometimes hidden agendas.

The relationship between the atmosphere of our planet and its
temperature is enormously complicated. It is affected by dozens of
interrelated cycles of everything from the proximity of the earth to the
sun, the wobble of the earth on its axis, the frequency of sunspots, and
the presence of particles in the atmosphere discharged by volcanoes.
These cycles can span hundreds of thousands of years, short in
geologic time, but significantly longer than mankind has been around
to make measurements. To find out what happened in the distant past,
paleoclimatologists study ice cores from Antarctica and core samples
drilled into the mud of ancient sea beds to determine the temperatures
and makeup of the atmosphere at points in the earth's distant past.

Sixty-five million years ago, the earth was 10° C warmer than
it is presently and the carbon dioxide levels were between 1,000 and
2,000 parts per million (ppm). The greenhouse effect was going strong
and it was a different planet than the one we inhabit today. It was too

warm for ice to form and even Antarctica was ice-free. The continents
had more or less organized themselves into the pattern we see today,
except that India was still in the south Indian Ocean and, thanks to
motion between the earth's plates, was racing toward Asia at a rate
of about fifteen centimeters (about a half a foot) per year. About 50
million years ago, India crashed into the Asian continent and pushed
up the Himalaya Mountains and the Tibetan plateau. These mountains
ended up having an extraordinary effect on the history of the world's
climate.

Almost as soon as a mountain forms, it begins to wear down.
Rain, snow, ice, water, and wind erode the rock faces and the resulting
debris flows down streams and rivers on its way to the ocean. The
erosion debris is largely made up of minerals containing calcium,
which reacts with carbon dioxide to form calcium carbonate. The
carbonates eventually find their way to the ocean floor, where they are
subducted or folded deep into the earth. The sedimentary rocks that
are formed by these carbonates undergo a change, becoming basalts
and releasing their carbon dioxide in the process. Some of this $CO_2$
is eventually vented into the atmosphere through volcanoes; some
gets forced under pressure into water, forming naturally carbonated
sparking water. Much of the $CO_2$ simply remains trapped deep within
the earth. Although it is an extremely slow process, over geologic time,
this erosion and sequestration of the carbon dioxide under the sea floor
ended up removing 80 percent of $CO_2$ from the atmosphere. Plants and
animals took up the remaining 20 percent. Sediments, trapping their
carbon, sometimes in the form of petroleum and coal deposits, also
bury these organic materials.

With the huge upheaval that caused the Himalayas to form,
carbon dioxide turned into carbonates and slowly the atmosphere of

the planet began to change. As the $CO_2$ levels dropped, the average temperature also began to fall. About 35 million years ago, when the $CO_2$ level had reached 550 ppm, ice began to form on the Antarctic continent. Then, about 10-15 million years ago, the cooling effort got a big boost when the Andes Mountains formed, rising out of the South America plains at a rate of 1 kilometer per million years. The weathering of this huge new mountain range increased the pull down of $CO_2$ from the atmosphere, to a rate of perhaps 100 ppm per million years.

With the planet significantly cooler, normal fluctuations such as changes in the earth's orbit and the wobble of the axis of rotation were now enough to cause warming and cooling cycles, resulting in periodic ice ages, and large-scale changes in sea level. During the last ice age, some 20,000 years ago, sea level was 400 feet lower than it is today and a land bridge existed between Asia and North America. On global average, the temperature varies about 5° C between the ice ages and the warmer interglacial periods. The present interglacial period began about 10,000 years ago, and it is important to note that all of recorded human history has occurred during this short, somewhat unusual portion of the earth's geological and climatic history. Through most of that time the planet has remained warm enough to keep ice off of Canada, but cool enough to allow Greenland and Antarctica to retain their ice. During the past 7,000 years, sea level has also remained essentially constant, allowing the first human civilizations to grow and prosper along the coasts.

Natural processes release and recapture large amounts (735 billion metric tons) of $CO_2$ each year. The atmospheric concentration of $CO_2$ during the 10,000 years before the industrial revolution (beginning about 1750) stayed relatively constant in the mid-200 ppm level, with a nice balance of CO2 in versus CO2 out. Since 1750 however, by burning fossil fuels, humans have been gradually adding increasing amounts of $CO_2$ to the atmosphere. At first, the earth's systems (particularly the oceans) were able to absorb the excess carbon dioxide, but more recently (since say the 1950s) the extra $CO_2$ added by humans can't be absorbed and has started to slowly accumulate. Today the level in the atmosphere is about 384 ppm and increasing by about 2 ppm each year. This is why people are worried; the highly complex computer models say that getting to 450 ppm will be dangerous and 550 ppm catastrophic. We should reach 550 ppm by 2050 at the current rates of $CO_2$ emissions. To us humans, these parts per million numbers seem incredibly small, and they are, but they build up over time until they have a significant effect.

"There's a large gap between what is understood about global warming and what is known about global warming," said James Hansen when I interviewed him at a Nobel Conference on Energy in 2007. "I mean what is understood by the relevant scientific community and what is known by the people who need to know—that's the public and policy makers. The result of that is we really are at a crisis point. It is hard for the public to understand this because we don't really see much happening." Partly related to the inertia caused by the oceans that can be more than two and a half miles deep, it takes a long time for the atmosphere to respond to climate change effects: a few decades for half of the response and a few centuries for most of the response to occur. "The climate changes that have happened are small in comparison to the day-to-day weather fluctuations," said Hansen.

Hansen is an unlikely rock star in the world of global climate change. A mild physicist who spent his early career at NASA studying planetary atmospheres, he became interested in the earths atmosphere and has been working since the 1970s on trying to understand the human impact on the earth's climate. "I find that even more interesting and important than trying to understand the clouds of Venus..." As the director of the NASA Goddard Institute for Space Studies in New York, when he testified before Congress in the 1980s on the human impact of climate change, he raised awareness of global warming as an issue. His outspoken position that climate change was man-made was at odds with the official position of the Bush White House, and an attempt by bureaucrats to muzzle Hansen and other NASA scientists had an opposite effect.

"Even though the instigator of these [major] climate variations is changes in the earth's orbit, the mechanism by which the temperature changes [between the large-scale variations] is the change in atmospheric composition and the change in the surface albedo [the amount that the surface reflects sun back into space]," said Hansen. "Well, now those mechanisms are totally under the control of humans. The $CO_2$ and methane are now increasing far outside the range that they have existed in millions of years and the temperature is beginning to respond. Humans are now in control of the mechanisms of global climate change—without any question for better or for worse."

During the last century, the global average temperature has increased 0.8° C, or 1.5° F. It has gone up about 0.75° F in just the past thirty years. "There is another 0.5° to 0.75° C of warming in the pipeline due to the gases that are already in the atmosphere; even if we stopped increasing them, we would get this warming," said Hansen. It is important to note that these are average figures, but the earth isn't warming the same amount everywhere. Warming is greater at high latitudes nearer the poles than at lower latitudes near the equator. The Northern hemisphere is also warming faster because there is more land mass in there and more ocean surface in Southern hemisphere.

Hansen also notes that the carbon dioxide release by fossil fuels we burn today will be with us for a long time. "When we put a pulse of $CO_2$ into the atmosphere by burning fossil fuels, half of it appears to disappear within ten to twenty years. It's taken up, especially by the oceans," said Hansen. "But then, the uptake slows down—in effect the $CO_2$ in the ocean exerts a backpressure on the atmosphere. Even after 500 years, about one quarter of the $CO_2$ we put in the atmosphere is still there. That's the problem."

Hansen and other climate scientists warn of reaching a tipping point where only a small addition will cause a big change. "The big dangerous tipping point would be if one or both of the large ice sheets of Antarctica or Greenland would begin to disintegrate and get out of our control because it could cause sea level change of many meters in a short time period," said Hansen. "The formation of an ice sheet is a very slow process because it depends on the rate of snowfall. But the disintegration of an ice sheet, once it gets started is a wet process and you can get collapse. If you push it beyond a certain point, you can get very rapid change."

Because the burning of fossil fuels has been the problem, they also hold the key to the solution. Hansen looks at coal as the big culprit. "Oil by itself cannot take $CO_2$ to 450 ppm and it's practically impossible to capture $CO_2$ coming out the tailpipes of vehicles, and we are not going to be able to tell Saudi Arabia and Russia not to mine their oil and sell it," he said. "So the real issue comes down to coal and what's going to happen when oil runs out. Are we going to try to squeeze liquid fuels out of coal or tar sands or shale? That's what we really can't afford to do. We could keep $CO_2$ at less than 450 ppm if we would just agree that in the future we would begin to phase out the use of coal except at power plants where we capture the $CO_2$ and sequester it. That is the principle thing that we need to do to stabilize climate." If we continue on a business as usual path, we could see a 3° C increase in global temperature during this century. "The problem is that no one knows what dangerous is."

Carbon dioxide is not the only greenhouse gas that effects global climate change. Methane ($CH_4$) remains in the atmosphere between nine and fifteen years and is up to twenty times as effective as $CO_2$ in retaining the earth's heat. Methane is released during coal mining and oil production and also is formed by a variety of organic processes, including decomposition in swamps and bogs and during the digestion of grasses in animals like cows. Livestock such as cattle actually produce more greenhouse gases that have a greater effect on global climate change than does the entire transportation sector.

A major concern for the future is the vast amounts of methane gas that has been trapped in the frozen Arctic tundra that may be released as the planet warms. Other greenhouse climate effects occur from water vapor, whose presence can act to trap heat, or when in the form of clouds, reflect solar radiation to reduce planet heating.

Hansen sees the challenges of avoiding an increase in planetary temperature as difficult but possible. "It's not an impossible challenge to agree to only use coal in that way. It's important that we stretch the conventional oil and gas, because otherwise we are going to run out very soon and we are not going to be ready with the new technologies that don't require them."

The conference I attended and at which I interviewed James Hansen took place in the fall of 2007. At that time, he concluded with some optimism. "There is still time to in my opinion to avoid the disastrous climate effects and to keep global warming well under 1°

C additional warming, but in fact that path is not being pursued," said Hansen. "I think if we go even one more decade down the business as usual path with $CO_2$ emissions increasing 1 or 2 percent per year, then it becomes impractical to get onto a path which would keep additional global forcing less than the amount to keep global warming less than one degree."

In late 2008, a team of ten international researchers, including NASA's Hansen, published a paper in *The Open Atmospheric Science Journal* that suggested that a level of 450 ppm of carbon dioxide, previously thought to be a threshold for safety, would be a tipping point, beyond which the effects of global climate change would escalate and possibly could become irreversible. Much of the optimism Hansen has expressed in 2007 was gone. Hansen's team found that a level of 350 ppm would be a cutoff limit for causing damage to the planet. The authors also noted that we are already at a level above 385 ppm of carbon dioxide in the atmosphere. The paper indicated. "An initial 350 ppm $CO_2$ target may be achievable by phasing out coal use except where $CO_2$ is captured and adopting agricultural and forestry practices that sequester carbon." The researchers went on to warn, "If the present overshoot of this target $CO_2$ is not brief, there is a possibility of seeding irreversible catastrophic effects."

Hansen's views of global climate change have become much more widely accepted during the past decade. The Intergovernmental Panel on Climate Change (IPCC) was established in 1988 by the World Meteorological Organization (WMO) and the United Nations Environment Programme (UNEP). Its fourth assessment report of 2007 was reviewed by more than 2,500 scientific experts.

The conclusions of the IPCC report of 2007 were clear, but have often been misquoted and misinterpreted. The report's main conclusion was: *The observed widespread warming of the atmosphere and ocean, together with ice mass loss, support the conclusion that it is extremely unlikely that global climate change of the past fifty years can be explained without external forcing, and very likely that it is not due to known natural causes alone.* In another part of the report, the authors define *extremely unlikely* as a 5 percent chance and *very likely* as a 90 percent chance. The "external forcing" that is referred to in the report is something that causes the temperature to change. That could be solar variations, volcanic activity or even humans burning fossil fuels. So, what the scientists are really saying is that there is a 90 percent chance that humans are responsible for some of the global climate change that has been observed, and only a 5 percent chance that these observations result from ordinary climate variations. Or, stated a different way, the IPCC says that there is a 95 percent probability that global climate change is occurring and only a 10 percent chance that none of this warming is caused by the activity of human beings.

Having established a relationship between the burning of fossil fuels that releases carbon dioxide into the atmosphere and the observed rise in atmospheric and ocean temperatures and the loss of sea ice, the IPCC report has cautiously suggested a link between other global phenomenon and climate change. The IPCC was quite conservative in its predictions and connections. This is in contrast to others who have claimed that everything from the destruction of New Orleans by Hurricane Katrina, to the violence and number of Midwest tornados, to drought and desertification of China and Africa is directly caused by global warming. There is little or no hard scientific data to back up many of these claims, and because of the enormous complexities involved in predicting weather and climate change effects, scientific theory can only begin to suggest any cause and effect relationships.

Each of these events may have been related to climate change, but with our current level of understanding, it is extremely difficult to make the connections. With the manifestations of climate change taking place over decades, we may have problems determining causality. Thus far the confirmed effects of global climate change have been primarily seen in the Polar Regions. Observations over long periods of time, like those of the Arctic environment provided by Will Steger, can help fit the pieces together to build a picture of what we are doing to the planet. We are on a path that we have predetermined, and over the next decades we will see with ever-increasing magnitude the results of greenhouse gas emissions.

This does not imply that we shouldn't be concerned today with the effects of global climate change. On October 30, 2006, The Stern Review was released. Nicholas Stern, who was head of Britain's Government Economic Service, and a former Chief Economist of the World Bank, was in charge of this landmark document from the British Government that examined the economics of global climate change. His conclusion was that action now to prevent or at least slow down global climate change would provide a better return than waiting for calamity to occur and dealing with it then. Action— reducing greenhouse gas emissions to avoid the worst impacts of climate change— according to Stern, would cost us as much as 1 percent of the world's Gross Domestic Product (GDP) per year. The overall cost of inaction would result in impacts that might include hundreds of millions of people suffering hunger, water shortages and costal flooding. Stern estimated the financial effects of inaction would be the equivalent of losing 5 percent of the global GDP each year, and could rise as much as 20 percent of the world's annual GDP. This level of economic and social disruption would be on par or beyond the effects of World Wars I and II and the Great Depression.

The Stern Review noted, "If no action is taken to reduce emissions, the concentration of greenhouse gases in the atmosphere could reach double its pre-industrial level as early as 2035, virtually committing us to a global average temperature rise of over 2° C. In the longer term, there would be more than a 50 percent chance that the temperature rise would exceed 5° C." It went on to note that it is no longer possible to prevent the climate change that will take place over the next two to three decades. The best we can hope for over that time period is to provide better information and planning and work on infrastructure and drought resistant crops to help protect societies and economies during this period. Further, "The investment that takes place in the next ten to twenty years will have a profound effect on the climate in the second half of this century and in the next."

A year before President Obama chose Nobel Prize-winning physicist Steven Chu to be the head of the Department of Energy, I spoke with him at the same energy conference where I had met Dr. Hansen. "Five years ago the predictions were not pessimistic enough.," said Dr. Chu. "The northern polar region and Greenland are melting far faster than we thought. We didn't understand the soot in the air that lands on the snow was making it melt faster. We didn't understand that as it melted, there are these large moulins, these rivers that go down two kilometers deep and lubricate the ice packs with Greenland so that the ice runs off faster. We knew these things were happening; we didn't understand they would be happening to that degree."

Despite its enormous scale, Dr. Chu still sees the problem as solvable and in some ways comparable to other challenges that we have faced. "In World War II it was conceived as a national emergency and Americans were will to sacrifice and the whole machinery of the United States was asked to help solve the problem and we solved it. If we get one tenth the mobilization we got in World War II we can solve this problem." Still, the magnitude of the problems we face are daunting. "The changes are more or less worse than predicted ten years ago. That's the scary part. The American public and the world public doesn't know—this is serious," said Dr. Chu.

Perhaps one way to look at climate change is as a bet against the house. Based upon the philosophical argument of Pascal's Wager on the existence of God, we can come up with the following:

1. Global warming is false, and we do nothing

2. Global warming is false, and we do something

3. Global warming is real, and we do something

4. Global warming is real, and we do nothing

If we adopt strategies based on case one, we spend nothing extra, continue business as usual and there are no consequences. In case two, we spend large amounts for no real gain and it hurts our economy and reduces our GDP. In case three, we bet right, we took the right steps and we were able to mitigate societal collapse and disaster at some cost to GDP and the economy (although both survive). In case four, we end up with all of the Armageddon-like scenarios or famine, drought, plague, societal collapse and massive die out of species, possibly including our own. One can argue that it is worth betting some of our economy and GDP on case two, just on the chance that case three is correct, rather than take the risks inherent in case four, which will have really dire consequences. Except the evidence is clear; global climate change is real and we aren't doing enough to mitigate its detrimental effects on out future.

Investing in our future sounds fine, but where do we start? How about with the cheapest, most abundant, but dirtiest form of energy? The realities of the energy industry suggest that coal will be with us for a long time to come. Is there some way we can reduce or eliminate carbon dioxide emissions when coal is burned? We already do this in coal-fired power plants with sulfur dioxide and oxides of nitrogen. This idea that carbon dioxide might in some way be captured from a power plant smokestack and then stored or sequestered away for eons is an attractive one, especially if we are looking at a future filled with electric cars and plug-in hybrid vehicles.

The exhaust gas produced by a power plant is not pure carbon dioxide. Typically, flue gas from a coal-fired power plant is only 10-15 percent $CO_2$. This complicates the capture of the gas as it must first be separated from the gases it is mixed with before it can be secured. The large scale industrial process to absorb carbon dioxide uses amine-based solvents that absorb the $CO_2$. The process is common in oil refining and natural gas production, but has never been used on a large scale to remove $CO_2$ from a powerplant flue gas. Pulling $CO_2$ out of the flue gas is likely to be at least as expensive—experts estimate as much as 30 percent of the energy of the power plant will be needed to pull out $CO_2$ with the amine process, a significantly greater amount of energy than is required to remove other pollutants such as sulfur dioxide and oxides of nitrogen. New research in techniques such as chilled ammonia capture is under development to reduce this energy consumption, but the capture of carbon dioxide will remain energetically costly.

Our atmosphere is made up of 76 percent nitrogen. The majority of the gas in power plant exhausts is simply nitrogen that has come along for the ride. In the Oxycombustion process, an air separator strips nitrogen from the intake air, leaving oxygen to combust with coal, leaving behind almost pure injectable $CO_2$ after the sulfur dioxide and oxides of nitrogen are removed. There is hope that this could be done at a lower cost than treating the highly diluted stream of flue gas.

It has also been suggested that burning coal in a fundamentally different way might provide a more efficient method of removing $CO_2$. The system is called Integrated Gasification Combined Cycle (IGCC). The idea is to separate air into nitrogen and oxygen and then to react the coal, oxygen and water together to produce syngas, a mixture of hydrogen and carbon monoxide. The syngas can then be sent to a gas turbine where it is burned, running a generator to produce electricity. The gas coming out of the turbine is then used to create steam, that runs a second turbine and generator (which is why it is called a combined cycle). The $CO_2$ that comes out of the process is captured and stored for eventual geologic sequestration. Efficiencies of as high as 45 percent are expected from IGCC plants, compared to 35 percent for a standard coal-fired plant.

The U.S. Government had put its resources behind a 275-megawatt IGCC pilot plant called *FutureGen* to prove the concept. In early 2008, the government withdrew its support of the program before any real progress was made, the costs had gotten too great to justify continuing.

IGCC is one of the cornerstones of "clean coal," a catch phrase used by the coal industry and politicians, but that resonates as an oxymoron to environmentalists and much of the public. For the industry, the term includes the work that has been done to remove pollutants like sulfur dioxide and oxides of nitrogen from powerplant smokestacks. For critics, who point at emissions of tons of greenhouse gases like carbon dioxide and heavy metal pollution from mercury, "clean coal" does not exist. The Clean Coal Technology that President Obama publicly supported when he was a candidate does not yet exist, except on paper. Removing $CO_2$ from a coal-fired plant's smokestack has not been accomplished, and IGCC is still a dream. Then, once we've separated out the carbon dioxide, we have to find a place to put it.

Dave Barnes is a geology professor at Western Michigan University who left a job with an oil company to become an academic. "As early as the 70s, people have been using injected $CO_2$ to enhance oil recovery in depleted oil fields," Barnes told me when I visited the Michigan Geological Repository for Research and Education, in Kalamazoo, Michigan. "The pressure to drive the oil out of the formation in the subsurface has been depleted by the removal of those hydrocarbons. So the injection of $CO_2$ has been conducted and continues to be conducted at much greater rates these days since as early as the 1970s, unrelated to any concerns about emissions or anything else." Where does this $CO_2$ come from? "The $CO_2$ that's being used is naturally occurring in the subsurface. In other words, they are mining $CO_2$ and pumping it into reservoirs. In most cases, because carbon dioxide is an expensive material, it's fairly carefully contained. You do not just let it vent. When you produce the oil, part of what comes out is the $CO_2$ and that is captured. It's a commodity that costs $10, or $20, or $30 a ton."

Barnes points out that the game is now changing. "The development of carbon capture technologies makes that whole business different. There could now be these human sources of $CO_2$ that could become available."

Finding the right place to inject carbon dioxide into the substructure of the earth is not trivial. Carbon dioxide takes up a lot of space as a gas, but it can be changed into a supercritical fluid at a pressure of 1,100 psi and a temperature of 31° C. The volume of the fluid is 300 times less than that of gaseous $CO_2$: a ton of supercritical $CO_2$ occupies fifty cubic feet, while at atmospheric pressure, that same ton takes up 18,000 cubic feet. It's important to inject the carbon dioxide to a depth where the pressure of the rocks above will keep it above 1,100 psi. That depth ends up being about 2,600 feet below the surface. Drilling a hole below 9,000 feet becomes cost prohibitive and other technical problems arise, so the range of 2,600 to 9,000 feet is considered optimal for sequestration.

It is also important that the rocks into which the carbon dioxide is injected are porous enough to accept a high rate of injection. It costs a million dollars to drill a bore hole to a depth of 2,600 feet, and therefore it is useful to have a porous rock structure that can accept the injection of CO2 quickly. "What you'd like is formation that is sufficiently thick and has sufficient injectivity and capacity to store with is commensurate with the amount you want to inject," said Barnes. He told me that a 500 megawatt coal-fired power plant generates about four megatons of $CO_2$ per year; that's about a million gallons of the supercritical fluid per month that needs to be injected from a single plant.

Then, there is the potential for leakage. The density of supercritical carbon dioxide is 0.7, making it float on water. This buoyancy allows it to migrate upward and, unless it meets an impermeable cap rock, it can eventually reach the surface." We know that there are common rock formations that are sufficiently impermeable to prevent the vertical migration of a buoyant fluid," said Barnes. "How do we know that?" he asks rhetorically. "Oil and gas accumulations. We know that there are rocks that are sufficiently impermeable to retain in the subsurface a buoyant fluid over geologically significant time frames." Rocks such as shale, and other very fine grained dense materials like halite or anhydride rocks, and gypsum work well to cap the escape of $CO_2$. What geologists are looking for are a succession of sedimentary rock layers which contain both porous rocks with lots of void space, interlayered with impermeable rocks that are capable of retaining the leakage of the CO2. "Virtually anywhere where there has been oil production is going to be a place where injection of a fluid into the subsurface is going to be feasible," said Barnes.

Curved, bent, or folded sedimentary layers allow the buoyant fluid to migrate along the layer where they are eventually trapped against an impermeable layer. In fact, these are the kind of structures oil companies look for when they go looking for oil. They migrate slowly, depends on permeability. What is important in choosing a site is the indication that there are no fluid migration pathways to which results in the $CO_2$ entering ground water, soils, or the atmosphere.

Not all parts of the country will work for carbon sequestration. Barnes says that virtually all of Lower Michigan has some potential, because it was once the basin of a large inland sea. He tells me that perhaps half of the surface area of the continents are ancient sedimentary basins and therefore have some potential for sequestration of $CO_2$. Other regions, like the areas surrounding Atlanta and Minneapolis are poor choices because their substructure won't keep the carbon dioxide in place for the required time frame of millions of years. Again, areas with a history of oil production, like Texas, Pennsylvania, Oklahoma, and Louisiana will work just fine. If you can't inject the $CO_2$ locally, it might make more sense to locate a power plant in a place where sequestration is possible and send the electricity through wires, rather than building pipelines to move huge quantities of carbon dioxide.

Knowing what is underground comes mostly through boreholes that have been drilled in search of oil, natural gas or brines. "The information that we derive from tools we send down a four or five inch diameter bore hole, and the cylindrical core samples of rock material provide fundamental information of what lies below the subsurface." A state like Michigan, with an early history of oil and gas production, has more than 55,000 bore holes, drilled to depths of up to 16,000 feet.

Can we really inject that much $CO_2$ into the earth's substructure? "The technologies for injecting fluids in the subsurface have been known for decades," said Barnes. "The scale of injection of fluids into the subsurface is well established. The equivalent of about two billion tons of wastewater is injected annually into rock formations in the U.S. The scale of the injection of fluids (mostly brines produced with oils) into the subsurface matches the scale of potential $CO_2$ injection, given the deployment of carbon capture and geological storage. In other words there is an equivalent order of magnitude in scale of fluids that are currently injected using known given available technologies to the scale of $CO_2$ that can be captured from other sources."

That much carbon dioxide, even as a supercritical fluid, takes up a great deal of space underground. "I'm doing calculations right now that suggest that a 500 MW power plant, in a reasonably optimal geological circumstance that exist in Michigan, will produce a plume of $CO_2$ that is on the order of six or eight miles in radius over the lifetime of the powerplant," said Barnes. With luck, it should stay there. "It's a reasonable geological assessment. It's only reasonable— it's by no means proven or guaranteed—there is absolutely no way we can guarantee this. We can be reasonably confident that it is not going to move sufficiently far that it's going to escape."

Carbon sequestration won't be cheap. Industry watchers have said that the process could double the cost of electric power. Barnes points out the significant energy required to compress carbon dioxide into a supercritical fluid and to drill the bore holes. "The steepest hill to climb is public acceptance. Not only acceptance of environmental hazards, but also public acceptance of the fundamental expense entailed in changing the way we do business."

The issue of sequestering away huge volumes of carbon dioxides for millennia led me to Battelle Laboratories in Columbus, Ohio. There I met with David Ball, a program manager and Neeraj Gupta, a research leader in geologic sequestration. Gupta has worked on a DOE program studying sequestration of $CO_2$ since the mid-90s. "The question is when you have a power plant with 20 million tons of emissions per year. That's a huge amount of $CO_2$," said Gupta. "It's a scale-up challenge. How big an area would you need? How many wells will you need and how will you do it safely? And how does it tie in with the power plant operations?" Gupta tells me that a single 500 MW coal-fired power plant produces 3.5 million tons of carbon dioxide a year—that's about 10,000 tons a day. "In terms of volume," said Gupta, "you are roughly looking at a similar scale to oil and gas production." In other words, the amount of carbon dioxide that needs to be injected into the geologic substructure and sequestered there each year is approximately equivalent to the amount of oil that we pump out of the ground every year. "Nobody is talking about injecting all of it," said Gupta. "Even if you do a fraction of it, it's still a major dent in the climate problem."

Many of the power experts with whom I had spoken had

suggested that carbon capture and sequestration would end up doubling the cost of electric power generation. I asked Battelle's David Ball how that compared with his estimates. "We've seen numbers all over the map," said Ball. "If you look at the cost of capture, add the capital costs, the costs of compression and everything that goes with it—I think it is fair to say that you are looking at a significant cost increase to undertake this goal of stabilizing $CO_2$ concentration. But geologic sequestration may, in the long run, be less expensive that any other way of getting to a stable $CO_2$ concentration in the atmosphere."

One reason why a fuel such as coal is so cheap is that there is no accounting of the real costs associated with the release of carbon dioxide into the atmosphere that occurs when it is burned. There are several ideas how this might be handled. One proposal is to levy a "carbon tax" on the amount of carbon dioxide that is produced when fuels are burned to produce electric power or in our vehicles. As anything with the word "tax" in it is a death sentence to any politician's reelection hopes, carbon tax proposals are rarely discussed among those who have the power to enact them.

A more often discussed way of accounting for the carbon content of an energy source is called "cap and trade." In this system, credits are given to energy producers and manufacturers, based upon and capping the amount of carbon dioxide that they are allowed to emit. If they add technologies that reduce the $CO_2$ output from their process, they can sell the difference between the amount they emit and the amount they are allowed to emit. If they emit more than their allotted amount of $CO_2$, the manufacturer can purchase "offsets" from a company with credits to sell. Over time, the amount of allowable $CO_2$ emissions decreases, causing an overall reduction in the level of greenhouse gases in the atmosphere. It should be noted that cap and trade has already worked to help reduce sulfur dioxide emissions from power plants and industry.

The tough details to be worked out in a carbon cap and trade system is how to give away or sell the initial credits, how to establish a value for the credits (some say the market should decide this) and how to set the limits and the reduction in those limits. Critics say that the system still allows the dirtiest polluters to keep polluting, that it won't work fast enough to reduce greenhouse gases in a way that will prevent catastrophe and that it will result in a system that will be corrupt on many levels. Nonetheless, it is the system that seems the most likely to pass into law as both liberal and conservative politicians have embraced the idea. Carbon credits are already for sale in other parts of the world and can be purchased in the U.S.

If a cap and trade system were adopted, how would it effect transportation? Depending upon the credits for carbon, fuels like ethanol made from cellulosic materials would become much more financially attractive than gasoline or diesel fuels made from petroleum. Electricity generated by hydro, wind, or solar and used to charge a plug-in hybrid would be much cheaper than that from a coal-fired plant. Coal would necessarily change to IGCC technologies with carbon sequestration to remain cost competitive. Canadian oil sands and oil produced from shale in Western states as well as coal-to-liquid fuels would be much less attractive if the cost of carbon dioxide released during their production was factored into their price. In short, and in an ideal world, the major changes necessary to reduce carbon dioxide emissions would gradually fall into place, and as the Stern Review suggests, at a cost lower than that projected if we do nothing. If it worked the way it's supposed to, it would change all of the paradigms of cheap energy and transportation. If it proved a failure, either through greed or political maneuvering, it could doom vast portions of the human population to catastrophe.

Public acceptance of global climate change is significant right now, but will it stay that way? The World Meteorological Organization (WMO) reported that 2008 was the coolest year since the beginning of the twenty-first century, fractionally warmer than the year 2000. Critics of climate change point to data like this and claim that global warming is a myth. The WMO points out that 2008 still ranked among the ten warmest years on record and NASA's Goddard Institute for Space Studies ranks it as the ninth warmest year since 1880.

Cooling La Niña conditions in the Pacific Ocean are credited with bringing the year's temperature down and may result in several years of slightly reduced temperatures. The warmest year on record was 1998, when a strong El Niño event in the South Pacific sent thermometers higher. A 2008 NASA report indicated that, based on satellite data, two trillion tons of land ice in Greenland, Antarctica and Alaska have melted since 2003, and that is evidence that global climate change is not abating.

There is a danger that a few years of slightly cooler temperatures will change the public's focus away from the issue and lessen the desire to do what is necessary to fix the problem. Others will try to lead us away from doing the right thing. "The planet we can see in the future if we do take the actions that we need to take is actually a very attractive planet and has advantages over the present situation with a much cleaner environment and a stable climate," said NASA's Hansen. "The problem is that special interests who are more interested in short term profits are making it difficult to make this story clear."

We need to stay focused and work to solve the problem before it becomes unmanageable. As Hansen said, "We are less than ten years away of passing a tipping point where it is going to be impossible passing the level of dangerous $CO_2$ in the atmosphere. We are making the problem harder and harder for ourselves by waiting longer and longer to get started."

## Chapter 6
## New Carbon

It takes energy to make energy. The roaring diesel engine in Brian Kreps' 11-year-old Case International Model 2188 Farm Combine consumes just under a gallon of diesel fuel for every acre of corn that he harvests. Diesel is old carbon. It comes from plant and animal organic matter folded deep into the earth. Over millions of years, heat and pressure have turned that mulch into petroleum that an oil company subsequently refined into the diesel fuel in the combine's tank. Kreps' combine burns old carbon to harvest new carbon: sunlight that has been absorbed by the chlorophyll in corn and combined with carbon dioxide and stored as complex carbohydrates (cellulose) and other parts of the plant. Corn will be consumed as food or feed by humans or livestock, or more recently, turned into ethyl alcohol (ethanol) as a replacement for

*The view of the corn fiield from inside the combine*

gasoline in our cars.

I'd never been in a combine before. It's a huge red beast with a small glassed-in cubical sitting ten feet above the rake-like corn harvesting tool at the front of the machine. The combine's four drive wheels are each powered by a hydraulic motor. The diesel engine runs a hydraulic pump that builds pressure in a reservoir. The hydraulic pressure travels through a hose to each wheel to move the machine forward and back. In this way, the Model 2188 Farm Combine is in fact a hybrid vehicle, although different in detail from other hybrids— say, for example, the Toyota Prius. Kreps climbs the short ladder that leads to the cabin where he settles into the independently sprung bucket seat behind the small steering wheel.

It's a bright Sunday morning in mid-October and I've come to Kreps' Southeast Michigan farm to find out how his new carbon crop is harvested. The farm is about fifty miles south of Detroit and just north of the Ohio border; it is flat land cut into a grid of corn, wheat, and soybean fields by intersecting dirt roads.

"We don't like to work on Sundays," says Kreps, "but this time of year we usually have to."

I follow him up the ladder; the first step is a stretch and I balance on each rung before getting to the top and climbing into the cab. I find a spot on an upholstered bench seat next to the door. The cab is surprisingly roomy. As I slam the steel-framed glass door shut behind me, the pitch of the engine rises although it never gets really loud in the cabin, and Kreps eases the combine into the field.

Kreps' left hand rests lightly on the black steering wheel of his harvesting machine while his right sits atop a yellow and black joystick. As he guides the machine along the parallel rows of corn stalks, he operates buttons on the joystick, constantly adjusting the

height and gap between the steel finger-like spears that project ahead
of the corn harvesting tool that is attached to the front of the rig. His
machine can harvest eight rows of corn at a time.

"I'm running eight rows," he frowns. "If I had a newer machine
a little bit bigger, I could be taking twelve rows at a time." Still, the
results are impressive. Every other pass of the thirty acre field he is
harvesting fills the 250 bushel hopper on the back of his combine
with kernels stripped from the ears of corn by a thirty-inch rotating

*"It's making me smile" 200 bushels of corn per acre*

drum and rasp inside the
combine. Let's see, 250
bushels of corn at fifty-
six pounds per bushel;
that's 14,000 pounds
of corn in two passes
through the field. The
kernels are the only part
of corn that Kreps keeps;
the remaining cobs and
plant stalks, called stover,
are chopped into small pieces and left in the wake of the combine.
This organic material helps hold the soil in place over winter and, in a
practice called "no-till" farming, will act as a sort of mulch when new
corn seeds are planted in the spring.

Kreps has planted 1,100 acres of corn this year, some of it on
land that he owns, most of it on land that he leases from others whose
fields might otherwise lie fallow. In a day, Kreps can bring in about
100 acres of corn, at close to 200 bushels of corn an acre. This is a
pretty good yield for Southeastern Michigan, and even a corn farmer
in Iowa, Minnesota, or Nebraska wouldn't be disappointed in those

results.

"It's making me smile," says Kreps of the corn building up in the hopper just behind his head. "They are increasing the genetic ability of the corn plant so fast—the drought tolerance and the stress tolerance of the plant is way higher than it ever used to be, and we've just had four or five years of good growing in a row right here in this area. So this will be the fifth or sixth year in a row that I can go 200 an acre."

Corn may be one of the most extensively bioengineered crops in the world. There are currently sixteen varieties of GMO (genetically modified) corn on the market. Fourteen of them contain the DNA from bacteria or a virus to provide resistance to insects and pests; one has a boost in lysine for animal feed, and the other is designed to allow easy hybridization. GMO corn for human consumption has met with resistance from the European Community and others, but so little corn in the U.S. is grown for direct human consumption that this hasn't affected exports. Meanwhile, DuPont Agriculture Enterprise and Monsanto are designing hybridized corn with boosted starch content to improve ethanol yields by 2 to 4 percent compared with regular corn.

Corn is an energy intensive crop to cultivate. It must be planted new every year, and it requires added fertilizer and pesticides, both of which are made from oil or natural gas. Kreps points out an ironic twist on the idea that ethanol might someday help to break our dependence on foreign oil. Much of the nitrogen fertilizer used on his corn is imported from the countries like Kuwait in the Persian Gulf. Just a few years ago, the U.S. was the largest exporter of nitrogen fertilizer; now, we are the largest importer. There isn't a large market for natural gas in the Arab oil producing regions, so much of it gets converted into a solid, urea, which is rich in nitrogen. Our own natural gas is being used to generate electricity, a move on the part of American utility companies a few years ago when natural gas was cheap. The urea from the Persian Gulf is shipped to North America and up the Mississippi River to the Corn Belt, where it is mixed with water and applied to crops.

Corn also requires lots of water, upwards of 6,000 gallons or more for one acre throughout the year. In the Midwest, this water comes from rain; roughly twelve to twenty inches are required during the growth season. In the West, corn cannot be grown without irrigation, resulting in an increased depletion of deep subsurface aquifers like the Ogallala aquifer that also supply drinking water to the population of many western cities. Growing corn in places like China and central Africa also requires irrigation, and an increase in corn crops puts further stress on already endangered fresh water supplies.

The water that runs off cornfields is often charged with high levels of nitrogen from the fertilizers. Corn production is responsible for more than 40 percent of fertilizer use in the U.S., and many growers use far more fertilizer than necessary. As these nitrogen compounds run off and are carried downstream, they can eventually result in huge dead zones, like the one in the Gulf of Mexico at the mouth of the Mississippi River.

"We don't need to map it anymore. What you see instead is a ring of shrimp boats around the edge of the dead zone. They all stop when they get to it." Don Scavia is talking about the dead zone in the Gulf of Mexico off the Louisiana coast. Scavia is a Professor of Natural Resources and Environment at the University of Michigan. Before donning his academic hat, he was the chief scientist at the National Oceanic and Atmospheric Administration's (NOAA) National Ocean Service. He's been studying hypoxic dead zones for much of his career. Sitting in his basement office in the University of Michigan's Department of Natural Resources on a cold autumn afternoon seems pretty far removed from the warm waters of the Gulf of Mexico.

"Two things are required for a dead zone to form. First, the water volume involved has to stratify. Warm fresh water from the Mississippi River floats out on top of the cooler salty water of the Gulf. It doesn't have to be much warmer—a few degrees. What that does is form two layers—if you've ever dived down in a lake you've felt the cold layer under the surface. This is stratification and what it does is prevent oxygen from the surface from reaching the lower layer. This is a natural condition and it's very common. The second thing needed is a lot of organic matter has to get into that bottom layer. The decay of the organic matter uses up the oxygen and since it isn't resupplied, you get a dead zone."

The term for a lack of oxygen is hypoxia—and regions characterized by this lack, where fish and sea animals can't survive are called hypoxic areas or dead zones.

"Algae growing on the surface of the Gulf of Mexico provide a source of the organic matter. As they grow they get eaten by zooplankton in the food chain which produce fecal matter that settles to the bottom along with some of the algae that aren't eaten. Excessive algae blooms because excessive nutrients, primarily nitrogen, are carried down the Mississippi in the spring. This flush of nutrients stimulates over-production of algae. In the past that production led to tremendous fisheries in the Gulf. But if there is too much algal production, it settles to the bottom and uses up the oxygen."

Where do the nutrients come from? In 2000, Scavia led an integrated assessment of the dead zone for the White House Office of Science and Technology Policy. Data from the USGS demonstrated

that three quarters of the nitrogen that gets into the Gulf gets into
the Mississippi north of the Ohio River—it's coming from intensive
corn production in the Corn Belt. The discharge of the Mississippi
River has only changed about 10-15 percent since the early 1900s,
but the amount of nitrogen being discharged tripled since the 1950s.
The amount of nitrogen applied onto corn fields during that time has
continually increased. The action plan based on the 2000 assessment,
recommended reducing the nitrogen load from the river by 30 percent
to reduce the 20,000 square kilometer (7,700 square mile) dead zone
to 5,000 square kilometers (1,900 square miles) by 2015. The plan was
largely ignored however, and the 2007 Gulf dead zone was the third
largest on record.

"While we need to be reducing the amount of nitrogen getting
to the Gulf, interest in corn ethanol is pushing us in the opposite
direction," said Scavia. The drive to ethanol and higher corn prices
means that farmers are planting more corn. "In the last three or
four years, people are starting to see impacts in the fisheries. They
are fished so hard that when they go, they go fast. There could be a
collapse. There is also evidence of a regime shift in the ecosystem in
the Gulf after creating this dead zone year after year. The very food
webs are fundamentally changed so it could be setting up a condition
where the fisheries at risk could go fast if we don't turn things around.
We are starting to see declines in shrimp catch."

Global climate change is adding to the problem. Warmer water
means faster algae growth and stronger stratification between the
top and bottom layer. But the effect of global warming on the land
is even greater. "It's already happening, and the models confirm that
precipitation in the mid-continent is going to become more intense
with stronger storms. If you get rain in strong and intense storms,

you flush more of the land and more nutrients are going to wash into the Gulf. The models say that even if you do everything necessary to reduce nitrogen by 30 percent, the climate change effect will overwhelm it," said Scavia.

There are solutions. If farmers would only apply the recommended amounts of nitrogen fertilizer to their fields instead of using 50-60 percent more than is recommended, the nitrogen load to the Gulf would be reduced by 20 percent. Wetlands also help. By allowing field runoff to flow through a wetland before entering the rivers nitrogen loads can be reduced by 30 percent.

In the late fall, as the surface water temperature cools and the winds begin to blow, the stratification breaks down and the dead zone disappears over the winter. The next spring it will return again: the causes are well known and it won't get smaller unless the amount of nitrogen traveling down the Mississippi is reduced. "It's just logical: If you have more acres of corn, you have more nitrogen washing down the river resulting in larger dead zones," said Scavia.

Back on the farm, Kreps is surprisingly precise in the way in which he harvests his corn. He carefully counts over the number of corn rows before he enters a section of the field to make sure his eight-row harvester will harvest all of the corn with the minimum number of passes. He maneuvers the big machine deftly as he works into the corners of the field to get every ear of corn. At one point, backing into a tight corner, his combine flattens a few stalks of corn and he grimaces and says, "That just cost me forty cents."

Most of Kreps' corn will feed chickens, cows, and pigs. The USDA estimates that a bit more than half, some 54 percent, of the U.S. corn crop goes to animal feed. That's expected to drop to around 50 percent as more corn is diverted to ethanol production. Only

18 percent of corn is consumed by humans, while between 4 and
5 percent is turned into High-Fructose Corn Sweeteners (HFCS),
primarily by agricultural-industrial giants like Archer Daniels Midland
(ADM) or Cargill. Corn sweetener is found in many of the processed
foods that Americans eat and critics have blamed its overuse (per-
capita consumption in the U.S. is about sixty pounds a year, or about
200 calories a day) as one cause for widespread obesity and the onset
of diabetes, especially among American children. The remaining
corn, some 20 percent of the total harvest, goes to making ethanol.
Incidentally, this is about the same percentage of corn that is currently
exported to foreign buyers. A new ethanol plant in nearby Blissfield,
Michigan takes about 20 percent of Kreps' yearly production. A bushel
of corn will produce 3 gallons of ethanol, so if he sold the entire thirty
acres of corn that we are harvesting this day to the ethanol plant, it
would produce as much as 18,000 gallons of alcohol: E10 with 10
percent ethanol and E85 with 85 percent ethanol mixed with gasoline.

Brian Kreps, at age thirty-four, is lean and fit with close
cropped hair. He looks more like a soldier than the stereotype of a
farmer. He has worked his own Michigan farm for more than seven
years. Kreps grew up on the farm that was bought by his grandfather
in the mid-1940s and is the third generation of his family to farm the
same land. During that time he has grown a variety of crops. In most
years, that's been a mix of corn, soybeans, and wheat. He still grows
the other crops, but in the last several years, corn has been king. This
results partly from a subsidy legislated in the Farm Bill. The U.S.
Government provides a direct subsidy of twenty-eight cents per bushel
of corn that a farmer grows. Additional payments are made based upon
the season-average market price and an additional payment that comes
into play when the market prices drop below a specified loan rate.

In times when there is a surplus of corn, this subsidy acts as a price support, easing what would have been the financial losses stemming from too much low-priced corn. In 2002 U.S. corn subsidies amounted to more than $3.2 billion. Over the past three years, however, thanks to the demand for corn created by ethanol to mix with gasoline, corn prices have risen to more than $8 a bushel, higher than at any time in the previous decade, and farmers are riding the wave.

Eight rows at a time, the combine works through the cornfield . Kreps points to a beautiful ring-neck pheasant that has stepped out of the rows just ahead of the combine.

"You should have brought your shotgun," says Kreps. The bird, which would have been flushed by an encounter with a human or dog seems unafraid of the machine the size of a small house that is working through the corn field.

As he works, Kreps tells me of his latest efforts growing apples and an interest in trying to grow grapes to make wine. He also confesses a desire to open a restaurant: a place with really fresh vegetables directly from his farm.

It's a late fall day, and as the sun streams through the huge windows of his combine, for a moment the Michigan farmer becomes philosophical. "That's all this is—solar energy," he says pointing out the windshield at the field of corn. "That's what we do; sun, carbon, and water."

It goes by a lot of names. White lightning. Moonshine. Corn liquor. Grain alcohol. Ethyl alcohol. Ethanol. Chemists say that ethanol is made up of two carbon atoms, six hydrogen atoms, and an oxygen atom ($C_2H_5OH$). Structurally, the two carbon atoms are bonded to each other and to five hydrogen atoms with a hydroxyl group (OH) bonded to one of the carbon atoms. It is this oxygen-hydrogen (OH) hydroxyl group that makes ethanol a liquid alcohol instead of simply ethane gas $(C_2H_6)$.

Mankind has long consumed ethanol for the inelegant purpose of getting drunk. There is residue of ethanol on 9,000 year old pottery from China and every civilization has had its own preferred variation of the cocktail. By itself, ethanol is a colorless flammable liquid that mixes completely with water and exceptionally well with cranberry juice. In fact, ethanol has such a strong affinity for water it's called hygroscopic—it scours water from wherever it can find it.

Any moonshiner can tell you the recipe for ethanol. Mix sugar, water, and yeast and let it ferment for a day or two. The yeast uses the glucose sugar molecules $(C_6H_{12}O_6)$ as an energy and carbon source to support growth and form ethanol and carbon dioxide as byproducts. Don't have any sugar? Don't worry. You can use almost any starchy food like potatoes, wheat, or corn, use heat to break down the starches into sugars with the help of naturally occurring enzymes, and then use yeast to make alcohol. Ethanol is actually toxic to yeast, so about the strongest a batch of "mash" can get is 15 percent alcohol. That's where a still comes in.

Separating the alcohol from the water using a still is a simple process called distillation. Ethanol boils at 75.4° C, significantly lower than water's 100° C boiling point. If you heat the mash that contains 15 percent alcohol above ethanol's boiling point, but below water's boiling point the ethanol will vaporize. All you have to do is collect the vapor with a tube and condense it back into a liquid by cooling it and you have 190 proof (about 95 percent pure mixed with 5 percent water) alcohol. Moonshine. Serve it in a Mason jar if you are a traditionalist.

Aside from its virtues as an intoxicant, the energy contained in ethanol has real value as a fuel. The V-2 rocket used by the Germans during World War II was powered by burning liquid ethanol mixed with liquid oxygen. This same fuel was used in the Redstone rocket that launched America's first satellite into space. Long before that, ethanol was recognized as a potential fuel to power the automobile.

"The run was made in the last week of January, occupying three days. The conditions were very severe. Snow was encountered throughout the entire journey, and the temperature was close to zero. With the exception of a few miles near three or four of the larger cities, the roads had been little traversed, the ruts were deep and irregular, causing a heavy strain upon the motors. In some instances second speed had to be used in descending grades." That's how the February 12, 1907 edition of *The New York Times* described a 249-mile test drive between New York and Boston to evaluate the effectiveness of alcohol as a motor fuel. Three automobiles built by the Maxwell Company were used; one using gasoline, driven by Thomas Toner, one powered by kerosene, driven by Charles H. Fleming, and one burning denatured alcohol, driven by H.A. Grant of Tarrytown, NY. All three cars reached the headquarters of the Bay State Automobile Association in Boston at 1:15 in the afternoon on January 30, 1907. The total distance traveled was sufficient "to allow of accurate comparisons between the three fuels" according to the comparison committee who sanctioned the test. The results, certified by official observers who accompanied the three Maxwell cars gave an average of 10.1 miles per gallon for gasoline, 7.4 miles per gallon for kerosene, and 8.1 miles per gallon for the alcohol fuel.

The price of the alcohol fuel was its primary drawback, costing four times as much per gallon as gasoline. But *The New York Times* was optimistic. "... it is believed that within a short time the price will be materially reduced so that it may be a successful financial competitor with gasoline. At present the price is the only drawback. In all other respects alcohol more than verified the expectations as a fuel possessing excellent motive power."

World War I resulted in a shortage of oil and U.S. ethanol production jumped to fifty to sixty million gallons per year. After the war, ethyl alcohol as a fuel continued to fascinate motorists and researchers. The University of Michigan's Professor of Chemistry Eugene H. Leslie wrote a book in 1923 titled *Motor Fuels: Their Production and Technology*. He noted, "The value of ethyl alcohol as a motor fuel when used in a mixture with gasoline... has been amply demonstrated." Leslie surveyed a variety of sources including molasses, beets, potatoes, sweet potatoes, and artichokes, but found that, "If any other grains are to be used for alcohol manufacture in this country corn will be the one." This was 1923, and in a premonition of an argument used against corn ethanol today he noted, "The better grades of corn cannot be used for alcohol manufacture because of their greater value for feed and food."

By the early 1930's, the use of alcohol blended with gasoline as a motor fuel was common in many parts of the world. Argentina, Austria, Brazil, France, and Italy all decreed that alcohol be mixed into gasoline supplies to reduce imports of foreign oil or refined gasoline. In Germany, alcohol, produced chiefly from potatoes and also from grains and molasses, was mixed extensively to extend that country's limited petroleum supplies. In the U.S. however, a dark cloud formed on alcohol's horizon. The oil companies decided to flex their muscle and oppose the dilution of their profits that they perceived would come from a gasoline and alcohol motor fuel. A 1933 article in *The New York Times*, titled "Motor-Fuel Blend Decried By Oil Men" reported,

"The proposal that Congress enact a law requiring that all gasoline sold in the United States as motor fuel be blended with 10 percent by volume of alcohol made from agricultural products grown within the Continental United States is opposed by oil companies on the grounds that it would give motorists a fuel inferior to that which is obtained solely from crude oil and that the prices would be higher." Big agriculture wanted into the fuel business and the oil companies wanted to keep them out.

The warfare between big agriculture and big oil came to a head on April 14, 1936 at the meeting of the American Chemical Society in Kansas City. As reported in *The New York Times*, the oil men were represented by Dr. Gustav Egloff, director of research of the Universal Oil Products Company of Chicago and Dr. J.C. Morrell, the company's associate director. Dr. Egloff and Dr. Morrell summarized their arguments: "Alcohol-gasoline is a distinctly inferior motor fuel in performance, consumption and upkeep of the motor. Difficult starting, slow acceleration, overheating of engines, and rougher driving can be expected. Economically, blending can result only in economic loss to society, and additional unestimated losses will result to the country at large from the political, moral and health hazards." Faced with this argument, Dr. Leo Christensen from the Farm Chemurgic Council could only point to a new market for farm products, extra farm income, and the potential for 2 million new jobs as reasons to blend gasoline with alcohol. The oil men, seemingly without irony, came back with an argument on "moral and political grounds" *The New York Times* wrote, "Tests show, they assert, that the grain alcohol could easily be extracted from the gasoline mixture and would provide good drinking liquor at 'automobile bars' at a cost of only five cents per quart. This, they say, would add considerably to drunken driving and motor accidents."

Dr. Egloff also addressed the supply of oil. "… the supply, at the present rate of discovery of new fields, is practically inexhaustible, and that the hydrogenation of coal would provide a supply of oil for 10,000 years." He smugly concluded with the remark that, "If it were desirable, from a purely technical point of view, to produce alcohol for motor fuel use, the oil industry can make it in enormous volumes, from cracked gases from petroleum refining, at a price highly competitive with any produced from farm products." When Dr. Oscar C. Bridgeman from the National Bureau of Standards supported the position of big oil, old carbon and the oil companies ended up the big winners. The idea of using new carbon, ethanol, as America's motor fuel was put back onto the shelf where it would more or less stay for the next sixty years.

Davie Spitznagle works at The Andersons ethanol plant in Clymers, Indiana. It's a new plant, built over an eighteen-month period. The plant started ethanol production in April of 2007. Despite an array of overhead stainless steel pipes and a maze of huge buildings, tanks and grain silos, in essence, the Clymers ethanol plant is no more complicated than a moonshiner's still. Its scale is larger. Much larger. The plant processes 115,000-120,000 bushels of corn a day. Recall that each bushel weighs fifty-six pounds; that's roughly 6.5 million pounds of corn. Each day. Trucks carrying 60,000 pounds of corn enter the plant in a nearly constant stream, dump their loads, and head back to the fields and corn silos for more.

Corn ethanol plants are most profitable when they can get corn from within a fifty mile radius. Farther than that and the fuel costs of transporting corn by truck becomes prohibitive. On site, the plant has two corn silos that can each hold a million bushels and one that can hold two million bushels. Spitznagle, friendly and open, offers: "You do the math; a million bushels of corn doesn't last us very long."

Spitznagle takes me to the hammer mill. This is the first step of

the process of turning corn into fuel. The corn kernels are pounded into a coarse dust by the electrically powered mill. As you might imagine, the noise in the mill building is nearly deafening. From there the corn flour is transferred to the processing building into a slurry blender where

*The Andersons Clymer Corn Ethanol Plant*

it is mixed with water and enzymes and heated to over 200° F to begin breaking the corn starch down into sugar. It's where I met Jeremy Frerichs, the production manager for the Clymers Ethanol plant. Frerichs is young and his recent college diploma is posted proudly on the wall behind his desk. On his desk is a computer whose monitor displays diagrams of various parts of the process and the current status of operations. "90 percent of the plant is automated," Frerichs tells me. He uses his desktop computer to switch to different diagrams as he explains how it all works.

"If you looked in a microscope the starch molecule would look like it was all wound up in a ball. The enzymes chemically attack the starch and break it down into long chains of sugar molecules. One enzyme takes it to long chains and then another enzyme breaks it down further into glucose molecules," he explains. "Basically, that's what we are doing in the cooking process, taking the starch, adding enzymes and heat and getting those glucose sugar molecules."

Switching the computer screen I now see seven cylinders represented. "Then we run it [the glucose mix] into the fermenters," he says. "We have seven of those. That's what the yeast will eat—it will take this sugar molecule and make alcohol, $CO_2$ and heat." For the fermentation process to work most efficiently, the yeast must be kept at less than 93° F. The heat generated by the process must be removed from the system and this is done with a water cooling system. Outside are a row of huge cooling towers with water vapor flowing skyward from each one. "We use a million gallons of fresh water a day—our biggest loss of water is through cooling tower evaporation. No process water is discharged from the plant, it's all recycled," says Frerichs. Spitznagle tells me that the plant has eight wells on its 150 acre site that supply the daily water needs.

Fermentation takes fifty-five hours and there is always one tank draining and one tank filling. Filling a tank takes eight and a half hours. With seven fermenters the system is finely balanced to keep the plant running continuously. After fermentation, the mash is about 13 percent alcoholic and is called "beer." Maybe this is because it smells much like that beverage, a fertile smell that permeates the processing building. The beer is transferred into the beer well, a big surge tank that feeds the distiller. The fermenters work in a batch process— everything else in the plant works continuously. The beer well feeds the distillation towers where the alcohol boils away from the mash, is captured and then condensed into 95 percent alcohol. "We return the 190 proof to molecular sieves—like a water softener with ceramic beads. The molecules of alcohol flow around the beads and the molecules of water are trapped inside the bead," says Frerichs. "That's how we make 200 proof alcohol. It's a big distillery on a big scale," he adds. The Clymers ethanol plant makes 315,000 to 320,000 gallons of ethanol a day: about 110 million gallons of ethanol a year.

The process results in an interesting outcome. One third of a bushel of corn entering the process ends up as alcohol, one third ends up as a solid waste that is dried into an animal feed called Dried Distiller's Grain (DDG) and the final third is carbon dioxide gas. If 6.5 million pounds of corn are processed each day, that means that something like 2 million pounds of carbon dioxide are being produced. "We're not capturing the $CO_2$," says Spitznagle. "We thought that somebody would invest in a plant here—dry ice or a beverage plant." With no use for the carbon dioxide, 2 million pounds of this greenhouse gas, $CO_2$ captured from the atmosphere while the corn plant was growing, is vented directly into the atmosphere each day.

There is a strong market for Dried Distiller's Grain (DDG), a byproduct of the ethanol from corn process. One thousand tons of DDG are produced each day and it is shuttled into a natural gas heated drier. This is another place where some of the water coming into the plant goes as it evaporates during the drying process. From there it moves into a huge building where it dries for another two days before being shipped out as chicken, beef and dairy feed. The DDG looks like corn meal and the building has a pleasant odor, like slightly burnt oatmeal. It carries on the breeze and downwind of the plant you can smell the DDG.

The alcohol produced by the Clymers plant is mixed with a small amount (2-4 percent) of gasoline to denature it. This is necessary so that it isn't taxed as a food product. It is shipped out by rail car, eight to ten cars carrying 30,000 gallons each, and by truck, twenty to-twenty-five trucks a day, each one carrying 8,000 gallons of ethanol. It travels by truck to an oil refinery or blend facility where it becomes

E10 (a mixture of 10 percent ethanol and 90 percent gasoline) or E85
(85 percent ethanol and 15 percent gasoline).

I have a personal interest in E85. I drive a 2000 Ford Ranger
pickup truck. It's an XLT model with a 3.0-liter V-6 engine and

four-wheel drive and is
equipped from Ford to
use E85 Flex-Fuel. My
beat-up old truck has more
than 160,000 miles on
it and some rust around
the edges, which makes
it perfect for blending in
while traveling through

*Getting a fill-up with E85*

Midwest farmlands and
small towns. It is estimated
that there are around 5 million Flex-Fuel capable vehicles in the
U.S. Production of a few vehicles able to use E85 began in the late
1990s and has continued slowly since then. General Motors, perhaps
the biggest E85 proponent, has stated that half of its new vehicles
available in 2012 will be Flex-Fuel.

When alcohol first was blended into gasoline at a 10 percent
level in the 1980s, some vehicles had problems with corrosion of
metal fuel lines and degradation of rubber parts in the fuel system.
Car makers quickly changed the materials specifications to make fuel
systems impervious to the effects of alcohol. Therefore, when E85
came along, it wasn't a big issue to build Flex-Fuel vehicles. The
biggest concern is the difference in the ratio of air to fuel that ethanol
requires compared with gasoline. When you run gasoline in an engine
that ratio is about fifteen parts of air for each part of fuel. Meanwhile

ethanol needs about nine parts of air for every part of fuel.

The problem is that if you fill up your tank one week with E85, run it down halfway and then fill it with regular gasoline the next, the mixture is no longer E85 with 85 percent alcohol, but somewhere in between that and pure gasoline. To combat this, car companies first put a sensor in the fuel line to detect the amount of ethanol present and then adjusted the engine's fuel injection system to provide more or less fuel to reach the proper air to fuel mixture. Eventually, car makers figured out how to do away with the fuel-line sensor and use the existing oxygen sensor between the exhaust manifold and the catalytic converter to control the amount of fuel delivered by the fuel injection system. Although some people do it, the car companies say it's not a good idea to run non-Flex-Fuel vehicles on E85; they claim that standard fuel injection systems aren't able to adapt to the changing air-fuel mixture requirements.

My Ranger has a nineteen-point-five gallon fuel tank. If I fill it with unleaded regular gasoline I can go about 380 miles on the highway on a nineteen gallon tankful, getting around twenty miles-per-gallon if I stay below seventy miles per hour. There are two gasoline stations near my home that carry E85 ethanol fuel. Each has a special tank in the ground and a special pump on a separate island from the other fuel pumps, a reflection of oil company rules to franchise stations about selling products not directly endorsed by the parent oil company. There are only about 1,400 E85 ethanol pumps in the country, mostly located in the Midwest, near where the most corn is produced. I've driven my old truck through a harsh Michigan winter without any of the cold-weather starting problems that have been reported as one problem with using E85. If I fill up my truck entirely with E85, I can get about 285 miles on the highway on a tank, about 15 miles-per-gallon and accurately reflecting the roughly 25 percent less energy contained in a gallon of ethanol compared to a gallon of gasoline. From a miles-per-gallon or vehicle range perspective, E85 ethanol looks pretty grim, but that's not looking at the whole story.

Gasoline prices have been wildly fluctuating recently, but $3.10 a gallon seems an average. E85 prices are even wilder: in Michigan I have paid anywhere from $2.40 to $2.80 a gallon. In Minnesota, a huge producer of ethanol, I've seen pump prices as low as $2.20 during the same timeframe. A nineteen gallon fill up of $3.10 unleaded gas costs me $58.90 and will allow me to travel 380 miles, resulting in a cost of 6.45 miles per dollar spent on fuel. If I buy my E85 in Minnesota at $2.20 a gallon, the nineteen gallon fill will cost me $41.80 and my 285 mile trip costs me 6.82 miles per dollar spent on fuel, nearly a half mile further for every dollar I spend on fuel when I am running just gasoline. Unfortunately, if I buy my E85 in Michigan for $2.40 a gallon, I can only go 6.25 miles per dollar, and it quickly is apparent that the price paid for E85 makes a huge difference in whether using E85 allows me to break even economically when using E85.

But here is another way to look at it. Even at $2.40 per gallon for E85, when I fill my nineteen gallon tank, I am only filling 15 percent of it or 2.85 gallons with gasoline made from nonrenewable petroleum energy. So if I drive 285 miles on 2.85 gallons of gasoline, my tired old Ford Ranger pickup is actually getting 100 miles-per-gallon of gasoline! If the objective is to save oil, that black gooey stuff that we pump from the ground and refine into gasoline, my Ford Ranger is doing an admirable job.

The example of my pickup truck, extending the work a small amount of gasoline can do when mixed with a high-percentage of alcohol was exactly Brazil's justification in the 1970s to switch away from gasoline and toward ethanol. In the 1930s, Brazil was one of a dozen or so countries that experimented and to a limited extent blended ethanol in to extend its supply of gasoline. In 1975, faced with a huge bill for importing oil, and blessed with a perfect growing climate located in a tropical zone near the equator, Brazil decided to divert some of its excess sugarcane capacity to make ethanol. Sugarcane is a particularly good crop from which to make ethanol as, unlike corn, it is mostly sugar instead of starch and doesn't need to have an extra step in the production process. The program was successful and Brazil offered Gasohol with around 24 percent ethanol content, as well as pure ethanol.

When oil prices were high and alcohol prices low, almost 70 percent of Brazil's cars ran on ethanol. Unfortunately, in the late 1980s and early 1990s, an alcohol shortage caused by soaring sugar prices and cheap oil hurt the program. Recent high oil prices and the development of Flex-Fuel vehicles in 2003 have reinvigorated Brazil's alcohol fuel program and today almost 90 percent of new cars are Flex-Fuel and 40 percent of the country's non-diesel transportation fuel usage is ethanol.

The U.S. government decided during the Carter administration to subsidize the production of alternative fuels. In 1978 the Energy Tax Act represented this change in the direction of Federal energy legislation. For the first time instead of promoting oil and gas, the Act lent support to fuel from renewable resources. The subsidy was $0.40 per gallon of ethanol blended into gasoline at a rate of at least 10 percent and used as a motor fuel.

The Tax Reform Act of 1984 set the tax credit at $0.40 per gallon of ethanol and gradually increased the credits to its current level of $0.51 per gallon. Both of the 1978 and 1984 Acts might have seemed to be created for the development of renewable fuels, but in fact the motivations for creating ethanol subsidies are less than clear because the oil companies were being forced to phase out tetraethyl lead in leaded gasoline and needed to add ethanol to unleaded gasoline to help prevent engine knock.

Ethanol received a further boost when the 1990 Clean Air Act Amendments mandated a minimum of two percent oxygen content in gasoline to control carbon emissions. The purpose of oxygenates was to have oxygen in the fuel to permit the exhaust-catalyst systems to achieve simultaneous control of oxides of nitrogen (NOx) and unburned hydrocarbons and carbon monoxide (CO). The first oxygenates that were used was methyl tertiary butyl ether (MTBE)— but this substance was found to cause ground water contamination and was banned. The oil companies had no choice but to look to ethanol and it quickly gained widespread acceptance as a fuel additive. Meanwhile, a $0.54 tariff on imported ethanol kept major alcohol producers like Brazil from importing ethanol to the U.S.

Then the Energy Policy Act of 2005 established a Renewable Fuel Standard (RFS). This required that 4 billion gallons of ethanol would be blended into gasoline in 2006 and then raised by 700 million gallon increments each year until 2012. The Renewable Fuel Standard was restructured by the Energy Independence and Security Act of 2007 which set the renewable fuel volume mandate for 2008 at 9 billion gallons with annual increases to attain a volume of 36 billion gallons in 2022.

One of the charges leveled against ethanol as a fuel, and particularly ethanol made from corn relates to its "net energy." In the 1990s, a paper from Cornell University stated that a gallon of ethanol required more energy to produce than could be obtained from burning it in an engine, stating that ethanol produced a negative net energy. The method in the analyses added together energy usage from a variety of sources including diesel fuel to run the farm equipment, natural gas consumed to make nitrogen fertilizer, coal to produce the electricity consumed in the ethanol plant, and so on. This information was treated as big news as the idea that more energy was consumed than was returned was considered a death knell for the ethanol business.

Subsequent study by a large number of researchers have dispelled the notion that ethanol has a negative energy balance. The biggest criticism of the Cornell study is that it used obsolete data and ignored the energy contribution that comes from the use of byproducts such as DDG as a valuable animal feed. Iowa State University in 2008, using the latest data for inputs for agricultural activities, feedstock transport, production of the ethanol and transporting it to the pump came up with a value of 728,205 BTU to produce 1 million BTU's of energy, or a net energy efficiency of 1.22. More easily stated, a gallon of ethanol returns 22 percent more energy than it takes to make it. This number is well in line with more than a half-dozen other studies on the return of energy from ethanol.

The net energy return of corn ethanol seems modest until you compare it to that of gasoline. The Iowa State study found that the fossil energy required to remove 1 million BTUs of energy in the form of crude oil from the ground, refine it and then transport it to a gasoline station required an addition of about 225,641 BTUs to the return of 1 million BTUs. Thus, the total energy needed to use a million BTUs in an automobile is 1,225,641 BTUs of energy. In other words, the net energy efficiency for gasoline is 0.78, or every gallon of gasoline returns about –22 percent of the energy required to produce it.

The idea of a negative return on an energy investment shouldn't be surprising. Turning a lump of coal into electricity and then transporting that electrical energy over transmission lines is enormously inefficient. A traditional coal-fired electrical power plant is about 30-35 percent efficient. Transmission losses are about 6-8 percent. Yet we don't complain about massively negative net energy balance when we turn on a light bulb.

In reality, the concept of net energy has a serious flaw when it comes to the energy returned from a fuel. In the net energy analysis, each form of fossil energy, coal, natural gas, and oil is solely based upon the number of BTUs of each material that is used. A million BTUs from the burning of coal has significantly different value in the real world than a million BTUs coming from natural gas or oil. Don't believe me? The price of a million BTUs of coal is $1.73 while the cost of a million BTUs coming from natural gas is $9.25 and from gasoline is $21.08, using 2009 Energy Information Administration data. Energy from petroleum is much more versatile and valuable than energy from coal and so we pay significantly more for it.

A better way to look at the energy value of ethanol is to examine how much fossil energy can be displaced by its usage. Remember my pickup truck? I could go 285 miles on the 2.85 gallons of gasoline in my nineteen gallon gasoline tank. Admittedly, some of the remaining 16.15 gallons of ethanol in the tank needed some fossil fuel to grow corn, ferment it, and to distill and distribute the alcohol (remember that ethanol returns 22 percent more energy than it takes to make it, but only part of the input energy is from petroleum). Putting E85, with 85 percent alcohol and only 15 percent gasoline in my tank means that I can go a long way while only using up a small amount of fossil fuels.

Perhaps the most controversial aspect of using corn for fuel is the idea that corn is first and foremost a food product. The issue was brought sharply into focus at the end of 2007 and into 2008 when six things happened:

- The U.S. corn crop came in at a record 13 billion bushels
- The U.S. produced a record 5.9 billion gallons of ethanol from corn
- Corn prices rose from $2.50 a bushel to nearly $4.00 a bushel
- Oil prices went from $60 a barrel to nearly $100 a barrel
- The Food Consumer Price Index (CPI) went up 4.9 percent, the highest rise since 1990
- In 2008, a worldwide food shortage caused riots in places like Egypt and Haiti

The average yearly rise in Food CPI is 2.96 percent so clearly something was affecting food prices during 2007. Because 54 percent of U.S. corn production goes to feeding cows, pigs, and chickens, there was a quick flurry of news stories blaming the diversion of 20 percent of the corn crop to ethanol production as the reason for the rise in the cost of food. Beef prices were up 4.5 percent, pork up 1.4 percent, poultry up 6.3 percent, dairy went up 13.4 percent and eggs up a whopping 32.6 percent. Wheat and soybean prices were also way up, attributed to the takeover of farmland by corn. The case against ethanol from corn seemed like a slam dunk. Except the price of other food commodities, like tomatoes up 18.9 percent, fresh fruit up 5.8 percent and sugar up 3.6 percent didn't fit the model. None of these foods use corn or other grains, and fruit orchards in California weren't being displaced by corn fields. What was going on?

Remember our friendly farmer Brian Kreps? Almost everything

he does including planting, fertilizing, and harvesting involves the use of energy obtained from petroleum. His trucks, tractors, and combine all run on diesel fuel and the nitrogen fertilizer he uses comes from natural gas. In good years, when corn prices are high, the costs of energy in growing the corn is covered. In lean years? Well, farmers can always count on the farm subsidy.

In 2007, oil prices rose more than 66 percent, and corn prices went up 60 percent. According to the USDA, only 19 percent of the price we pay for food is actually the cost of growing the food. Fully 24 percent is a category that the USDA calls "Marketing" and it includes packaging, transport, advertising and profits. The USDA also says that transportation accounts for 11 percent of the total energy used in the food system and that transportation and energy combined account for 7.5 percent of the costs of food. If oil prices went up 66 percent and oil accounts for 7.5 percent of the cost of food, wouldn't it be rational to expect a 5 percent increase in the cost of food across the board?

The huge percentage increases in eggs and tomatoes bothered me. Why should they be so expensive? It's true that egg exports were way up in 2006 and 2007, causing a reduction in the number available for the U.S. market. I went to my refrigerator to look at my eggs and tomatoes. In my refrigerator. Eggs and tomatoes are shipped in refrigerator trucks or rail cars and must be kept cold to keep from spoiling. Refrigeration takes energy and energy costs were big in 2007. If you want thing shipped cold, you have to pay.

Not convinced? How about this? There are fifty-six pounds of corn in a bushel. At $2.50 a bushel, that corn costs $0.05 a pound. At $4.00 a bushel the corn costs $0.07 a pound. It takes two-point-six pounds of corn to produce 1 pound of beef (cows aren't very efficient,) or about $0.10 of corn that costs $2.50 a bushel. If corn prices rise to

$4.00, it costs about $0.18 to produce that 1 pound of beef, resulting in a rise of about eight cents a pound in the price of beef in the past year. Likewise, for the two pounds of corn it takes to raise a pound of chicken, the increase from $2.50 to $4.00 in corn prices resulted in an increased cost of 6 cents per pound of chicken. Food prices are up as a result of using corn to make ethanol, but not by the dramatic amounts that have been reported. The cost of energy, most particularly petroleum is the most likely culprit.

If turning 20 percent of the 81 million acres of corn crop into 5.9 billion gallons of ethanol had only a small effect on food prices, what will happen when ethanol production is expected to reach 15.2 billion gallons by 2012, requiring 97 million acres to be planted in corn? I asked Amani Elobeid that question. Dr. Elobeid is an agricultural economist at the Center for Agricultural and Rural Development (CARD) at Iowa State and the co-author of a 2007 study of the effect of corn ethanol production on food prices. "Oil penetrates every stage of the process," she said. "Much higher ethanol production will result in higher corn, soybean, and wheat prices. But the response by other countries such as Brazil and Argentina as food prices go up can mitigate the rise. You may see lower food exports from the U.S.," said Dr. Elobeid. In 2007, Argentina's fragile economy was boosted by a huge soybean crop, much of which was exported for hard currency. "If you are a producer then it's great; if you are a consumer, you are negatively impacted," added Elobeid.

Despite the diversion of 20 percent of the U.S. corn crop to the production of ethanol in 2007, the U.S. still exported 2.25 billion bushels of corn, 19 percent of U.S. production, 6 percent more than in 2006, and the highest amounts since 1990. In the period from October 2007- February 2008, the U.S. exported 5.5 million more metric tones of corn than the same period the year before, an increase of almost 25 percent.

During 2007 however, China drastically reduced its exports of corn and the country has gone from a major corn exporter to a significant corn importer. Most corn in China now goes to feed livestock, not humans. This is due to an increase in meat production (mostly pork) as increasingly more affluent Chinese are turning away from their traditional vegetable-based diets. Just as China's quest for more oil has helped to drive oil prices higher, its newfound need to import corn, palm oil, soybeans, and other foodstuffs has increased commodity prices across the board. This is not bad if you are Argentina, as that country's resurgent economy is largely based upon soybean exports to China, but it's a real problem if you live in sub-Saharan Africa. Add 2007 crop failures in the Ukraine and Australia to China's appetite for imported corn, and it's not hard to see where a food shortage is coming from.

Another negative impact comes from the possible contributions to global warming due to greenhouse gases released when former forest and prairie become farmland to support an increase in the amount of land needed to support ethanol produced from corn. It's pretty straight-forward: if you rip down old growth forests, you release carbon that was sequestered over many decades as the trees were growing. The trees decay and release their $CO_2$ and the ground releases some of the carbon that has been sequestered. This implies that land use must be carefully watched and the amount of ethanol available from corn sources needs to be studied from a variety of positions, including its impact on food and on the creation of new farmland.

Even in a perfect world, corn ethanol isn't the best long-term solution to replacing gasoline. It uses a great deal of water, a resource that is becoming scarce in many parts of the world. It requires large amounts of fertilizer, which when applied to excess washes down our rivers and forms hypoxic dead zones in critical estuaries and in the Gulf of Mexico. At current corn ethanol production levels, the issue of food is not yet critical, but as the amount of ethanol production dramatically increases, the impact on food prices and corn available for export will be more deeply felt. Other issues like using corn as a monocrop and overuse of soils are also problems that we face if we use corn as our sole source of biomaterial to produce ethanol fuel.

The real value in corn ethanol is that it allows us to build an infrastructure to support much greater quantities of ethanol in the future. Having an opportunity to learn how to produce, transport, and dispense a fuel that is new to the infrastructure cannot be overstated. Likewise, building a fleet of E85 flex fuel vehicles will produce a demand for ethanol that will be met when the next step comes along. That next step? Second-generation ethanol from a wide range of plants, grasses, weeds, and even algae that are just now being recognized for their value in the battle to replace petroleum.

# Chapter 7
# The Energy Alchemists

World War II in the Pacific was tough. Intense and desperate fighting, a long often unreliable supply route, debilitating tropical diseases, and acute shortages of even basic necessities made conditions miserable for the troops. To make matters worse, shortly after arriving in the warm damp environment of tropical and sub-tropical islands, GI's found that their canvas tents, ropes, sandbags, and cotton uniforms began to disintegrate before their eyes. Often such equipment was ruined before it could even be unpacked. They called it "jungle rot" and it quickly became one more woe to add to their litany of miseries. The Army Quartermaster Corps set out to find the reason for the decay.

Elwyn Thomas Reese was a PhD student at Pennsylvania State University during the war and worked initially on efforts to grow fungus for the production of penicillin, but soon moved to the Quartermaster's Laboratories in Philadelphia to look into the jungle rot problem. Elwyn Reese was born in 1912 in Scranton, PA and his father had been a coal miner in Wales before moving to the United States. Reese quickly determined that the decay of cotton and canvas materials was due to a fungus found in the Pacific Islands. In 1946, after the war ended, Reese received his doctorate in biology from Penn State—his dissertation topic dealt with degradation of cellulose materials—and continued his work with the Army Quartermaster Corps. The mild-mannered biologist and fungus and mushroom expert would work for the Army for the rest of his life.

Working with Dr. Mary Mandels at the Natick Army Laboratories in a suburb of Boston, Massachusetts, Dr. Reese managed to isolate the most active fungus, called *Trichoderma viride*, from a decaying WWII pup tent that had been sent back from Bougainville, in the Solomon Islands. The fungus secreted enzymes that would attack the cellulose materials in canvas, cotton, and rope and dissolve them into sugars that could be further broken down and consumed by the fungus for energy. The Army wanted to find a way to kill the fungus, but Dr, Reese felt certain that there was a commercial application for an organism that could break down insoluble cellulose into soluble and digestible sugars.

For the rest of his career, Reese worked on *T. viride*, elucidating the mechanism of its processes and using irradiation with high-energy electrons and ultraviolet light to mutate the dark-green fungus, creating an organism that produced even greater amounts of the mixture of cellulase enzymes that broke down the cellulose fibers. He hinted in his work that his discoveries might someday provide the building blocks for a new source of fuel, but oil was cheap and plentiful and interest in alternatives to petroleum was minimal.

In the early 1970s, during the first energy crisis, his research suddenly took on greater importance as the federal government began to look for an alternative to gasoline fuels. Dr. Reese's fungus could break down plant cellulose into sugars that could then be fermented to produce ethanol as a substitute for gasoline. Dr. Reese officially retired in 1972 and his long-time colleague Dr. Mandels took over the studies, but he remained active, going to the laboratory almost every day to continue his research. In 1977, the fungus used in the effort to produce ethanol was renamed *Trichoderma reesei* in his honor. In 1980, the Department of Energy (DOE) took over Reese's research into ethanol from waste materials. In the mid-1980s, fuel prices fell and the DOE lost interest in the alcohol fuel project, but by then several commercial applications for *T. reesei* had developed, including using the enzymes to create a faded-denim look in "stone-washed" jeans. Dr. Elwyn Reese died in 1993, survived by his wife of fifty years, two daughters, and five grandchildren, and was buried in Scranton, Pennsylvania. He was largely unknown outside of his own narrow field that included biologists and mushroom aficionados. His entire career had been spent studying one organism—a fungus that he felt sure might provide the key to sustainable energy.

"We don't really have an energy supply problem. What we have is an energy capture and distribution problem," said Bruce Dale, a Professor of Chemistry at Michigan State University who has been working on the production of ethanol from the cellulose of plants since 1976. I visited Dr. Dale in his laboratory on the Lansing campus of the University. "Our annual consumption of energy is supplied by the sun [to the earth's surface] every hour. In one and half days, the sun delivers to the earth the energy equivalent of all of the estimated recoverable oil. Among the ways that solar energy is captured and stored in the biosphere, plant matter is one of the more obvious." Plants convert a few percent of the solar energy that hits them into carbohydrates and other sugars and they store this solar energy as structures of the plant.

Dr. Dale realized from an early age that the world was constantly changing. "I grew up in a small copper mining town in the mountains of eastern Nevada, a town called Ruth. My dad was

a mining engineer for Kennecott Copper Corporation. I think it was
the summer when I turned twelve. He was the engineer in charge
of developing the mine so he knew where the ore was, or more
specifically where it wasn't. He came home and said that the mine
didn't have much longer, seven or eight more years, and we need to
leave. So he moved us—about a year later we were in Arizona and
sure enough eight years later the mine was closed. The little town I
grew up in, about 700 people, a couple thousand dogs, a neat little
town, is gone—it's a ghost town. We are doing the same thing with
oil as we did with copper only with oil its worse—we burn it up and
it's gone for millions of years—at least with copper we can recover it
from wires and generators if we need to. Our whole society is built on
mining oil. We are burning it up by the billions of barrels and it's not
being regenerated. Our society is headed toward the same sort of ghost
town unless we are careful about our choices from here on."

About 70 percent of the mass of a plant is sugar—tied up in
cellulose and hemi-cellulose, the stuff that makes up the plant cell
walls. These are long polymer chains made up of sugars laid down
to give the plant rigidity and that also provide the tubes from roots to
the leaves to move water and nutrients. Breaking down those polymer
chains and getting at those sugars is difficult. To break apart the plant
structures you must treat then chemically, physically and with heat to
open up the plant cell walls. That's called pre-treatment and has been
the major focus of Dr. Dale's laboratory work. "What I have been
working on for thirty-plus years is to get at the sugars that are locked
up in plant cell walls."

Once the plant fibers have been pretreated to make the
cellulose and hemi-cellulose accessible, they must be further broken
down into sugars. "There are three basic platforms for making ethanol

from cellulosic materials," said Dr. Dale. "One is the thermal or syngas platform. It's been known for a long time that you can burn plant materials at high temperature in the presence of little or no oxygen to make syngas, which is a mixture of carbon monoxide and hydrogen. Both carbon monoxide and hydrogen are reactive molecules—you can process them chemically—not involving biological processes using metal catalysts to build the carbon and hydrogen into various types of alcohols."

A second platform is to heat the biomass at lower temperatures (300°-600° C) without air under what is called pyrolysis. The biomass is deconstructed into a mixture of char, gas and "bio-oils." The bio-oil produced is the cheapest liquid biofuel on the market, perhaps less than $0.50 a gallon, but is extremely poor in quality compared to petroleum products. It is highly acidic, not soluble with petroleum-based fuels and has half the energy content as gasoline. However, they can be converted into a usable fuel and using catalysts to improve the rate of the process, these bio-oils might potentially be upgraded into gasoline and diesel fuels.

The last process is a biological approach using organisms that secrete enzymes to attack the cellulose and break it into sugars. This an approach that Dr. Reese pioneered with biological molecules that go after long chains and break them down to make sugars. The approach that works the best depends upon what kinds of materials are used as feedstocks. "I think the thermal platform will be used more for woods—particularly soft woods [conifers such as pines spruces] and so forth because they are very difficult to convert biologically," said Dr. Dale. "I think we will end up converting straws, hays and grasses using the sugar platform. I think it will be feedstock determined."
The choice of grasses for use as a feedstock, although important from

the viewpoint of tweaking the proper enzymes, is fairly wide open. "Literally there are hundreds if not thousands of candidate species that might be grown across the country. Switchgrass is an attractive one. It doesn't need a lot of water, doesn't need much fertilizer, it's drought resistant and it's native throughout much of the country," said Dr. Dale.

When the sugars are broken out of the cellulose polymer chains, the fermentation process to produce ethanol can proceed in a way similar to that used to make ethanol from corn or sugar cane. "It turns out that the fermentation where microorganisms take sugar and make ethanol out of it is very efficient in conserving the energy content in the sugar—95-98 percent of the energy value in the sugar ends up in the ethanol after the fermentation. Now you've converted this solid material—sugar from the plant cell walls into a very nice liquid fuel—something you can burn very well in an internal combustion engine." Once you have the sugars you actually have a variety of products that can be made using microbes. Isobutanol for example, an alcohol that also burns well in engines and doesn't absorb water as readily as ethanol, has been discussed as a possible motor fuel. Its production by fermentation however has thus far not been too promising as in concentrations greater than 1.5 percent it tends to poison the fermentation organisms bringing the process to a halt.

Actually, there is a another method to remove the sugars from cellulose. In the early 1900s the Russians and Germans developed a process using strong acids to convert cellulose and hemi-cellulose into sugars. Both countries used this process to make alcohols from wood to use as a fuel and to produce other products. Germany found the acid hydrolysis process particularly helpful during World War II to supplement its fuel supplies. After the war acid hydrolysis fell out of use, but in the 1970s was revived as the U.S. government searched for alternatives to gasoline. Since 2003 a southern California company, Blue Fire Ethanol, has operated a pilot plant in that state that converts waste materials into ethanol using this process.

For those who see boosting ethanol production as a matter of national security, using cellulosic materials has some advantages. "If you can release these sugars at high enough yield at low enough cost you now have an essentially inexhaustible fuel source— on the order of 100 billion tons of cellulose material are captured in the biosphere every year—that number is roughly ten times the total energy that all people use and twenty-five times the amount petroleum energy used, in rough numbers," said Dr. Dale. "The opportunity for regional and rural economic development is also significant. Instead of having the wealth of the fuel industry concentrated in a few places in the world, you spread out the wealth where this fuel that we all need and want is produced by a much larger cross section of our population."

If cellulosic ethanol is so promising, and has been around for so long, why isn't it available at the pumps now? "It's been an under-funded field. If we had put the effort into developing cellulosic ethanol back then, during the oil embargoes and oil shocks in the 1970s, if we made a sustained commitment to developing these alternatives, we wouldn't be in the damned pickle we are now," said Dr. Dale.

With the 2007 Energy Independence and Security Act requiring ethanol production levels of 36 billion gallons by 2022, and corn ethanol unable to reach those levels, clearly cellulosic ethanol is going to need begin its ramp-up soon. "I think it will happen in several parallel paths—depending upon what the raw material is," said Dr. Dale. For example, I think the people who are using the trash to ethanol approach—Blue Fire Ethanol— will be successful. That's kind of brute force technology, but it works. It's valuable but its scale is limited. I think we will see some plants being built or expanded for thermal conversion—I think that platform will work particularly with wood construction debris, which is not really good candidate for biological conversion. The other place I see a lot of growth in the immediate future? The cellulosic ethanol industry will get launched where we have an existing corn ethanol industry. We'll learn how to use that existing infrastructure and learn how to make cellulosic ethanol in existing corn ethanol plants."

The fermentation part of the process is similar to that used for corn ethanol, so currently existing corn ethanol plants would need to modify only the front end of the facilities. After working for more than thirty years in the field, Dr. Dale is optimistic. "Within four to five years we will know that we can make ethanol cheaply. Once it is proven that the economics are competitive, then the lid is going to blow off. We have this great big investment opportunity— there is no apparent market limit for these fuels, we know the technology works, and we have all the societal things going for it. They will be built as rapidly as they can get the financing together and establish the supply chains. In fact, we are more likely to be limited by supply chain development than we are by conversion technology"

There are several companies that are busy trying to prove that economic case. One of them is Iogen, located in the capital of Canada, Ottawa. Iogen has actually been in the enzyme business for years, and has always had an eye on making alternative fuels from plants. It started with Patrick Foody, a Canadian engineer who built grain elevators and silos. He had this idea in the seventies when the Club of Rome came out with its report that the world was going to run out of food. Foody asked himself how he could take wood and break it down to become cattle feed? That was the genesis of Iogen. After working on a process using commercially available enzymes, he was able to create cattle feed from wood fibers. But, it turns out that although cattle would eat his enzyme treated wood that had been broken down, there was no fat in the wood so that the meat tasted like shoe-leather.

Dr. Dale had sent me to Ottawa on a snowy winter's day to visit Iogen's research laboratories and its demo plant—the world's only operating enzyme hydrolysis plant. "Very early in Iogen's days we were actually working very closely with some of the people who were first involved in the Natick laboratories studies where they isolated the strains," said Heather Pikor, Iogen's Research manager. The strain she is talking about is our old friend, *Trichoderma reesei*, the cause of jungle rot that was discovered by Elwyn Reese. "Their goal was of course to destroy them, but they realized they had this hyper-secreting strain of organism that is secreting cellulase—could those be advantageous in a different way?"

*T. reesei* actually makes a complement of five enzymes that are together called cellulase. Those five are require to complete the hydrolysis or breakdown of an insoluble molecule of cellulose into soluble sugar molecules. Each enzyme is specific in its action and you need all of those enzymes to break up cellulose.

Pikor, a biologist by training, began working at Iogen in 1980, just after college. She was the company's eighth employee. "Pat Foody Sr. had a vision for making ethanol for cars from the day I joined the company in 1980," said Pikor. "As part of it we got into developing our own enzymes and that's how we got into the enzyme business. Enzymes can be very expensive. Your enzymes have to be very good at what they do and they have to be made in a concentration that doesn't cost you too much. The cost comes from needing to have a strain, which secretes a high amount of enzyme, one that's really potent in the application. You need to have a really superior strain making a superior enzyme, and then, obviously, you need to have cost effective manufacturing as well." Pikor's group is working to improve the *T. reesei* strain and a recent DOE project that sequenced the genome of the fungus has been helpful.

Pikor walked me through the process of making the enzymes from *T. reesei* that would turn plant cellulose into sugar and eventually into ethanol. It all starts out with a smudge of blue green in the center of a Petri dish. "That Petri dish is pure culture of a strain," she explained. "What you are looking at are spores—a state at which the organism is alive but not requiring a lot of nutrients to grow. It's not doing anything, but it's alive." During my Iogen plant tour, I had seen banks of glass flasks. "What you do is scrape those spores into a sterile Erlenmeyer flask that contains a media which is a nutrient solution— some salts and minerals and some sugar—because *Trichoderma reesei* eats sugar." The fungus in the flask now has the right temperature and it has food, so it grows.

The little spore grows with hundreds of branches creating a viscous biomass that is brownish yellow and that is mostly opaque. After growing overnight in the flask, the biomass is transferred into a 2,000 liter fermenter and it grows for another day. "We only feed it enough to keep it alive—but not enough to have sufficient nutrients," said Pikor. What the organism does in response is to secrete more enzymes—it's natures way, secreting its enzymes while in this semi-starvation state in a search for more cellulose to dissolve and eat. "By about twenty-four hours we have built a reasonable biomass and then we control the concentration based upon the amount of food that it is given. Cut back food, enzymes go up." At some point *T. reesei* begins to die after the enzyme level has reached its peak. The enzymes are filtered from the dead fungus and water is removed to concentrate the enzyme. It's a batch process and takes a bit less than ten days from the Petri dish to the concentrated enzyme.

"In the 80s and 90s we graduated into pilot plants where we were using 400 gallon tanks in a batch process. Each of those probably cost us $7 to $8 million and we did two pilots—one in the 80s and one in the 90s." Jeff Passmore, a Vice President at Iogen is explaining how the company's cellulosic ethanol production has ramped up over the years. "You cannot leapfrog from pilot to commercial and this is where some firms have had difficulty because they haven't taken the interim step which is to build a demo plant." Iogen's demo plant is located in southern Ottawa on the edge of the airport and adjacent to the company's laboratories.

"In a demo plant, instead of 500 gallon tanks, you have 50,000 gallon tanks and it's not batch process anymore, but it's a continuous process," said Passmore. "We built a demo plant in 2000 through 2003 and started operating in 2004 so we are the only firm with that kind of operating experience at a demo plant. The purpose of a demo plant is to teach what works and what doesn't and what is scalable and what's not. It is on a small commercial scale—this is the real life situation and we bring in big tractor-trailer loads of 1,000 pound bales of straw from farmer's fields every week. It's not a controlled feedstock. The bales are full of stones, and dirt, and dead mice, and all kinds of inhibitors that you would find in an industrial application." The process has helped Iogen fine-tune its enzymes. "The enzymes that might have worked really well in a lab or pilot scale suddenly, with real word situations and a huge tank, their performance goes down."

The company keeps designing more robust enzymes while it

simultaneously engineers a more forgiving less aggressive process. "It's very iterative. You have to design the enzyme around the process and the process around the enzyme. That's what we've been able to do here, learning from real-world applications."

Passmore tells me that the two biggest cost components for cellulosic ethanol are the cost of the enzymes and cost of feedstocks, the raw material from which the ethanol is made. You don't want to truck straw feedstock more than 100 miles to get to the ethanol plant as the transportation costs quickly become prohibitive. A variety of feedstocks can be used with Iogen's mix of enzymes. "We focused initially on wheat straw or other cereal straws because in western Canada there is a lot of wheat," said Passmore. "Typically in some parts of Canada farmers have trouble disposing of the wheat straw." The amount of straw removed from the field and turned into ethanol depends upon the type of soil the farmer has. "You would not remove the straw from clay farm zones where farmers plow the straw back into the land. In black soil zones, if you can remove the straw, the farmer can think about no-till processes. You have to be conscious of the soil zones because it has to be done in a sustainable way. About 50 percent of the farmers want to part with 50 percent of their material."

Because wheat straw is only available during part of the year, a cellulosic ethanol plant will need significant feedstock storage capacity. The first commercial-scale plant that Iogen is planning will use 750 tons of straw a day, about 300,000 tons a year to produce 20 million gallons of ethanol. Those kinds of volumes will require both at-plant and on-farm storage—farmers can stack big bales of straw at side of their field and deliver it as needed. "Straw purchases of those volumes will bring $10-12 million of revenue into an area, at $50-60 a ton for straw," said Passmore.

When the cellulose enters the plant it will go into the kind of pretreatment processing that Michigan State's Dr. Bruce Dale has been researching. "The idea of pre-treatment is to explode the biomass so that you've maximized the surface area for the enzymes to attack," said Passmore. It is a high temperature cook in a low-level acid at about 200° C. "Cellulose is cellulose, the main difference is not enzymes but the pre-treatment," said Passmore. Pretreatment alters physical structure that makes cellulose more susceptible to enzymes. If it's too harsh, it can destroy some of the carbohydrates that would be turned into sugar and alcohol. You can also overcook sugars so that they dehydrate into compound that will not turn into ethanol. Dr. Dale has been working with a lower temperature (about 100° C) pretreatment process that uses ammonia instead of acid to avoid these sugar destruction reactions.

After Iogen's pre-treatment reactor the cellulose looks like mud, but all of the components of the plant are still there. It then goes into a series of four large tanks where enzymes created from *T. reesei* turns cellulose to glucose. By the time the solution gets to tank four, it consists of glucose with lignin floating on top of it. The glucose is filtered leaving behind the lignin, which looks like a moist chocolate cake after it is pressed out. For most feedstocks, about 65 percent is carbohydrates and 20-25 percent lignin. The rest is ash and metallic elements present in straw. The glucose goes off to be fermented, in Iogen's case using yeast developed by Purdue University that converts glucose and several other more complex sugars that are produced into alcohol. Lignin is a highly-polymerized impervious mesh or wrap that protects plants from attack and helps trees and grasses to stand up straight. Lignin can't be broken down by the enzymes, which means it can't be made into sugar and thus into alcohol fuel, but lignin has about 80 percent of the heating value of regular thermal coal, making it fine for burning in boilers for power generation. "Last year's plants are turned into this year's energy and next year's plants store the carbon that is released from this years plants. You are just recycling the carbon on an annual basis," said Passmore.

The first thing most Americans ever heard of switchgrass was during President Bush's 2006 State of the Union Address where he called for the prairie grass to become a new source of renewable energy. The grass has been the subject of intense scrutiny in the cellulosic ethanol field. "Switchgrass is a perfect feedstock," said Passmore. "It's a native prairie grass that used to grow back in the days when the buffalo roamed. It is drought resistant because its sends its root system down about six feet, it's a perennial crop so you mow like you mow your lawn every fall. The yield per acre is much higher than the yield per acre from corn stover. We've grown a couple hundred acres of switchgrass just up the Ottawa Valley here to see how it would grow—it is literally six and half feet tall and so dense you can't walk through it. But farmers are not going to grow switchgrass on spec with the hope that an ethanol plant will be built up the road—so initially we see that we will be building plants to operate on agricultural residues."

Corn ethanol also has a role to play in the creation of second-generation biofuels. "The thing about corn is it's what's going to get us to the second generation. You have to understand, thanks to corn ethanol, cellulose does not have to sell car companies, oil companies, and consumers on the fact that ethanol is a reliable fuel that they can recommend. Oil companies feel comfortable blending it because they've been doing it. Car companies warrant [mixtures in gasoline of up to] 10 percent and consumers don't pull up to the pump wondering if they can put ethanol fuel in their car. We are making the same molecule, it just happens to come from a non-food source."

There are a lot of people who are carefully watching Iogen to see how well the company can manage the development of its enzyme cellulosic process. "The lineup to be first to be second is longer than the lineup to be first," noted Passmore. Still, the company has been visited by representatives of governments from around the world. "There seems to be three policy drivers why governments around the world are interested in second generation renewable fuels," said Passmore. "Everyone interested is how can they take advantage of cellulosic ethanol opportunity. The greenhouse gas environmental reason, the energy security domestic source of energy reason, and new economic opportunity for agriculture. Depending which country you are in, each of those three moves to the top of the list. We can offer solutions in all three areas."

Iogen isn't ready to talk about the cost or amount of water it will take to make cellulosic ethanol. "The market is going to expect that because we are making the same molecule, cellulose ethanol is going have to be cost competitive with corn ethanol," said Passmore. "This is our model for the first half dozen plants, but who knows what will happen—look at the evolution that the corn ethanol industry has gone through how much more efficient they've become compared to ten years ago and how much less water and piping they use," said Passmore. The company is sensitive to the water use issue. "We don't want to have an environmental solution that causes other environmental problems—so one of the things we are being conscious of as we design the plant is water use and recycling and making sure that we can recycle the water. We are conscious of that."

There is a company working on cellulosic ethanol that has announced its projected cost and water use numbers almost from its startup. Coskata is located in Warrenville, Illinois, a suburb of Chicago. The company made waves in early 2008 when it announced that it was partnering with General Motors and would be able to produce ethanol from municipal waste at a cost of a dollar per gallon, with almost no water used in its process. It seemed almost too good to be true, so I went to Warrenville to find out more.

The Coskata facility in Warrenville, about 40 miles southwest of Chicago is nondescript—it doesn't look like someplace where game-changing technology is being developed. From the outside, it could easily be mistaken for the branch offices of a large insurance company. Coskata actually was formed in 2006 at nearby Argonne National Laboratories, which serves as an incubator for high-tech startups, and moved to its Warrenville offices in 2007. When I arrive, I am met by Richard Tobey, who is the Vice President of Research, Development and Engineering at Coskata. His background includes a degree in Chemical Engineering from Michigan Technological University and he started working for Coskata in early 2007, after a 28-year career at Dow Chemical Company. Tobey drives a tan-colored hybrid Toyota Prius and is the kind of pragmatic engineer who likes to explain difficult concepts with everyday analogies.

"If you watch wood burn in a fireplace the flame isn't really actually on the surface of the wood, it's separated from it because the gases coming out mix with the air and you get the flame front—so burning wood in a fireplace is ultimately gasification in an open air form," explained Tobey. "What you do in gasification to get synthesis gas is much what like they did to get town gas in the early 1900s where you heat up organic matter in the absence of oxygen and it will produce town gas, also known as synthesis gas—a mixture of carbon monoxide and hydrogen." As far back as the 1920s, syngas was used to produce transportation fuels through a process invented by Franz Fischer and Hans Tropsch at the Kaiser Wilhelm Institute in Germany. The Fischer-Tropsch process used metal catalysts to synthesize syngas into a variety of hydrocarbon materials, including alcohol fuels. The problem is that the process is difficult to control and instead of ending up with a pure stream of ethanol, the result is often a whole range of alcohols and paraffin. At best you can expect to get about 80 percent ethanol and 20 percent other alcohols. "If you want to make wax, Fischer-Tropsch is perfect," said Tobey.

A variety of feedstocks can be used to make syngas using gasification. In addition to plants and agricultural waste, you can use municipal waste, and even coal. "We see that as a big advantage to the Coskata process," said Tobey. "We can take plastics, wood, shredded tires—gasification is brutally indiscriminate—it takes everything down to carbon monoxide and hydrogen." The gasification process is mildly endothermic, meaning you need to add an additional 7 percent of energy to keep the producing carbon monoxide and hydrogen from the feedstocks.

One of Coskata's founders, Todd Kimmel, began looking at ways that syngas might be processed to produce just ethanol. "What about using the gasification of the thermal chemical front end in conjunction with a biological back end? That would be a novel approach," said Tobey, describing Kimmel's reasoning. "Then you could use bacteria, which aren't relying on the temperature of the reaction and a catalyst system, but are using enzymatic processes which lower the reactions down to the temperature of life. Now you don't have all that energy cranked in that makes all those other alcohols, but you can stop it right at ethanol."

The mixed thermal and biological approach had another

advantage, especially when using agricultural waste or other plants as a feedstock. "The challenge is that the biomass is about 70 percent cellulose and hemi-cellulose and 30 percent lignin, for which there is no process for today. Ultimately, it is limited by the fact that 30 percent of the feedstock cannot be converted to ethanol. There is just no fermentation process known to man that converts lignin to ethanol. So there was an opportunity to go after 30 percent of the feedstock [that is lignin]," said Tobey.

Kimmel found out that a bacterium had been isolated by Ralph Tanner at Oklahoma State University that could change syngas into ethanol. These particular bacteria produce ethanol or acetic acids from the gases produced deep in sediments and swamps from rotting and decaying organic matter. The bacteria take in gases and secrete acetic acid or ethanol, in the process locking carbon into a chain that other bacteria can use. "These guys live at the fringe of the energy cycle," said Tobey. "They live in these extreme conditions and squeaking out an existence by processing those gases."

Just as humans need air to breathe, the bacteria need a mixture of hydrocarbons to produce energy. "Ethanol to them is like carbon dioxide is to us. The way we get our energy is through oxygen going to the carbon that we have eaten to produce $CO_2$. The way the bacteria get their energy is through carbon monoxide and hydrogen going to ethanol. When we exhale $CO_2$ it's because we are working. The bacteria make ethanol the same way. The harder they are working, the more ethanol they are making. That's what you need to do to maximize the efficiency of the process." The bacteria work deep in mud and muck and are anaerobic; they can't survive in the presence of oxygen. "They like oxygen almost exactly the same amount that we like carbon monoxide. At a couple hundred parts per million of oxygen they are dying," said Tobey.

Part of Coskata's proprietary process involves introducing the syngas to the bacteria, which are suspended in water. You could simply bubble the gas to them, but Coskata has found more efficient ways of providing the gas to the bacteria that Tobey declines to discuss. "The advantage of a traditional ethanol processes, and in fact even the cellulosic approaches in the second-generation ethanols is that you are doing a yeast fermentation of soluble sugars in solution—man's been doing that for thousands of years, mostly to drink," said Tobey. However, Coskata's process doesn't ferment sugars into alcohols. "We get 100 percent access to all of the carbon, but the challenge with this process is that the syngas isn't very soluble in water so it's difficult to get the gas into solution so that it can be accessed by the ethanol making bacteria," said Tobey.

The next step is to separate ethanol from broth. This takes place in a continuous process. If the alcohol level in the broth were to rise to 19 percent it would poison the bacteria and stop the process, so there is a tradeoff of ethanol production and productivity. "Our process runs lower ethanol levels so that we don't poison the bugs," said Tobey. Once the alcohol is removed it can be distilled using industrial processes or can be concentrated using membrane vapor permeation of ethanol with membranes that act like kidneys to filter out the alcohol. The permeation method uses less than half the energy that distillation, but Tobey expects commercialization will begin with proven distillation technology.

Tobey claims that the process uses less than a gallon of water per gallon of ethanol produced and in fact that one byproduct of the biochemical process is water molecules. Depending upon the moisture content of the feedstocks, additional water can be liberated to the atmosphere during the process. Coskata also claims that 90 percent of the chemical energy in the syngas is recovered into the ethanol that is produced. The remaining 10 percent is biomass that can be recycled to release its energy. This extremely high efficiency and the low cost of the feedstocks that can include municipal wastes is the reason that Coskata estimates that it can produce ethanol at a price approaching a dollar a gallon.

The biological processes that occur do create carbon dioxide as a byproduct. In fact, by weight, 55 percent of the carbon that goes into the process comes out as ethanol while the remaining 45 percent comes out as $CO_2$. Even so, Argonne Labs analyzed the Coskata process and found an 84 percent reduction in greenhouse gas emissions was possible burning the company's cellulosic ethanol versus gasoline if the 7 percent external energy required comes from outside source like coal or natural gas. Using biomass itself to add the 7 percent energy needed results in a 90 percent reduction in greenhouse gas. This compared to a 30 percent improvement that was calculated for corn-based ethanol.

The bacteria are under constant development and its genome has been sequenced to aid in genetic manipulations. Coskata's plans are to license the technology for the biological processes, after building several full-scale plants to prove the concept. The company has built a demonstration facility near Pittsburgh that will be capable of producing 40,000 gallons per year of ethanol. From there Tobey predicts a linear scale-up to a commercial 100-million gallon plant should be possible by 2011. The price of oil has an effect on these plans. "Unless the price of oil is above $50, it's hard for other technologies to compete. Everything north of there makes things better and better." Dr. Dale's analyses confirms Coskata's numbers and shows that when oil is $25 a barrel, the biomass cost alone makes cellulosic ethanol from plants uncompetitive with conventional fuels from crude oil.

In late 2008, Coskata announced an agreement with U.S. Sugar to build a 100 million gallon-a-year ethanol plant in Clewiston, Florida, near the Everglades. The plant will gasify bagasse—the leaves, plant tops and crushed stems of sugar cane that is left over after sugar production—and then put its bacteria to work to make ethanol. By placing the ethanol plant close to the sugar-making operations, the cost of transporting the sugarcane feedstock will be kept low.

Because of the wide variety of feedstocks that are possible, and unlike corn ethanol or even enzymatic ethanol plants that must be located within a 100-mile radius of their agricultural feedstocks, Coskata's plants can be spread across the country, producing local ethanol for local consumption. "We don't view that there is going to be a Standard Oil of alternative energy that comes out of this," said Tobey. If you look at all the studies, it's going to come from lots of different places—there's not a Prudhoe Bay biomass basin. The industry will be segmented and diversified—a PC computer model rather than the mainframe computer model that the petroleum industry is today."

To move things forward, in 2007, the U.S. Department of Energy (DOE) selected six biorefinery projects into which it would invest up to $385 million for a four-year period. The six included companies that proposed using feedstock made from corn stover, wheat straw, yard and wood wastes, switchgrass, rice straw, and wood based energy crops. BlueFire Ethanol in California was on the DOE list, as was Iogen with a plan to build a plant in Idaho. Since the announcement, Iogen and a company called Alico from Florida have decided not to continue with the DOE funding; Alico decided it was too risky to go into the ethanol field, and Iogen preferring to build its plant in Saskatchewan with help from a $500 million cellulosic ethanol incentive package from the Canadian government.

Corn ethanol and upcoming cellulosic ethanol aren't the only commercially available biofuels in the U.S. today. Biodiesel has been available to motorists in Europe since the mid 1990s, and in the U.S. since the early 2000s. In 1900, Rudolph Diesel had demonstrated that his compression-ignition engine could run on peanut oil (strictly speaking a biofuel, but not biodiesel) at the World's Fair in Paris and he was intensely interested in plant-based fuels. In a 1912 speech, Diesel said, "the use of vegetable oils for engine fuels may seem insignificant today, but such oils may become, in the course of time, as important as petroleum and the coal-tar products of the present time."

Diesel automobiles that operated on petroleum-based fuels were pioneered by Mercedes-Benz, Hanomag and Citroen in the mid 1930s and European manufacturers have found the diesel engine to be robust, reliable and particularly fuel-efficient. European manufacturers spent the 1990s perfecting turbocharged direct injection diesel technology so that it could produce incredible fuel economy figures while dramatically reducing exhaust emissions. Further research brought to the passenger-car segment urea-injection technology, which had pioneered on European heavy trucks, making these engines nearly as clean as the cleanest gasoline offerings. The diesel was so successful in Europe, few manufacturers there had any interest in hybrid technology. Why should European manufacturers place two drive systems in a hybrid vehicle to attain thirty to forty miles-per-gallon when they could get the same results using a single modern direct injection diesel engine? The engineers at many European carmakers simple scratched their heads when you asked them why they weren't building a hybrid.

The problem, of course, was the North American market. Because of the poor performance, clouds of soot and general disrepute of early diesel cars from the 1970s and 80's, Americans have had trouble accepting the idea that a diesel engine could be clean and powerful. Although Audi's formidable victories at Sebring and Le Mans and Volkswagen's excellent TDI powerplants have turned the enthusiasts' heads, most of the driving public thinks of diesels as smelly, smoky and slow and look at hybrids as clean, efficient and hip. Until recently, Europe's manufacturers have steadfastly held their positions that a new modern diesel is a better solution than a hybrid.

Instead of hybrids, the emphasis in Europe has been in finding better fuels and more sustainable for diesel applications. This is where biodiesel comes in. Biodiesel refers to a non-petroleum-based diesel fuel made by transesterification of vegetable oil or animal fat, which can be used alone, or blended with conventional petroleum-based diesel fuel. Transesterification, in organic chemistry, is the process of exchanging an alcohol group in an ester (such as vegetable oil) with another alcohol to produce a different ester (biodiesel). Biodiesel refineries can produce biodiesel fuel from soybeans, palm oils, vegetable oils, recycled cooking grease and other waste materials. The process was used before World War II in South Africa to produce diesel fuel and during the war by the U.S. in order to obtain a byproduct of the process, glycerin, which was used to make explosives. Biodiesel can be used as a blend (B5=5% biodiesel, B20=20% biodiesel) up to about 20 percent biodiesel in unmodified engines, or in pure 100 percent B100 form with some engine recalibrations required. The energy content of a gallon of B100 is about 86 percent that of a gallon of petroleum-derived diesel fuel.

The world produced a total of 135 million tons of vegetable oils in 2007, and about 10 million tons were used for biodiesel production, or about 7.5 percent of the total plant oil production. In the U.S., we produced 450 million gallons of biodiesel in 2007, up eighty percent from 2006. In 2006, 90 percent of all U.S. domestic biodiesel was made from soybeans, but thanks to rapidly rising commodities prices, that number is closer to 60 percent now as biodiesel producers have turned to lower cost animal fats and waste vegetable oils for their feedstocks. An acre of soybeans can produce about 60 gallons of biodiesel each year. Like corn, soy is a food source for both animals and humans and the same arguments against using food as fuel is often applied to soy-based biodiesel.

Fortunately, there are wide varieties of plants that can be used to make biodiesel. This is both a blessing and a curse. There is at least one plant species that can be grown to make biodiesel in almost any part of the world, but the rush to produce the fuel has resulted in the destruction of jungles and old-growth ecosystems to replace them with biofuel crops. When farmers knock down carbon-absorbing forests and replace them with fields of soybeans, or palm trees, aside from losing important and sometimes irreplaceable habitats, the greenhouse gas benefits of the biofuels grown on the land can be delayed for centuries. Brazil is losing millions of acres of tropical Amazon rainforests to grow soybeans while Malaysia, which grows 80 percent of the world's palm oil, is converting forests into even larger palm oil farms in search of the profits that come from selling biodiesel fuel to European countries. In 2007, an arm of the European Union (EU) had set a target to replace 10 percent of its gasoline and diesel fuel usage with biofuels by 2020.

Other plants are under study, such as jatropha, a sub-tropical shrub that grows quickly and that produces seeds with up to 40 percent oil content. Best of all, jatropha isn't edible and so doesn't compete as a food source. Malaysian growers currently plan to have as much land dedicated to jatropha as are currently used for palm oil.

Waste cooking oil can also be used to produce biodiesel fuel, and the process is simple enough that community newspapers seemed filled with accounts of locals who collect fry grease from their neighborhood restaurants, convert it in vats in their garages, and then drive around town in diesel cars that have been converted to operate on the stuff. Invariably, there is a reference to the exhaust smell of "French fires" somewhere in the story. The process is straightforward transesterification, but the sources of free waste oil are beginning to dry up as restaurant owners have begun to realize that used grease has value, and several larger companies have gotten into the waste oil to biodiesel business.

Then there is pond scum. It almost sounds too good to be true. The plan is to grow millions of acres of algae in large open ponds filled with wastewater and then to harvest oil from the algae and turn it into biodiesel fuel. Energy crisis solved. Global warming eliminated. Energy security ensured. What could be simpler?

Not that algae is anything new. Commercially, algae have been used for centuries as a fertilizer to grow crops and condition soil. Algae is used as animal feed and also, especially in China and other parts of Asia, as a food source. It can be used to soak up nitrogen fertilizer from fields and as a pigment and in cosmetics. It's pretty useful stuff, and, as nearly 30,000 different species of algae and hundreds of thousands of different types have been identified, more uses are found almost daily.

Algae have been around pretty much since day one of life on earth and, if you remember from Chapter 2, is in fact the source of the oil that we refine into oil and gasoline. If we had time we could wait around for tens of millions of years as today's algae slowly changed into petroleum. Too impatient? How about speeding things up? It turns out that some of the hundreds of thousands of different types of algae contain up to 75 percent oil.

In 1978-1996, the Department of Energy (DOE) funded a program with the National Renewable Energy Laboratory (NREL) called the "Aquatic Species Program." The program's initial focus was to sequester carbon dioxide emissions from coal-fired power plants, but when researchers discovered that some algae had high oil contents the emphasis shifted to growing algae to produce biodiesel. Because of their extremely fast growth rates and high oil content, NREL suggested that 7.5 billion gallons of diesel fuel could be produced from roughly a half-million acres of algae grown in desert land covered with algae ponds. More recent research has suggested that around 15,000 gallons of oil can be obtained annually from an acre of land cultivated with algae, compared with about twenty gallons of oil if that acre were planted with corn that was then processed into biodiesel fuel. If that were true, we would need an area of about 9.5 million acres— an area roughly the size of Maryland—to grow enough algae to replace our current oil consumption.

Great! Let's do it! Except, even though we've had more than a dozen years of continuing research since the end of the NREL program, making oil from algae isn't quite ready for prime time yet. Finding the right strains of algae, learning how to grow them and stress them so that they produce the maximum amount of oil and learning how to extract that oil has taken significant research, but is fairly well understood in the laboratory. The problem comes in scaling things up. Questions like how deep to make the ponds (light only penetrates about six inches in an algae filled pond), how many different strains of algae, how to avoid contamination by bacteria or invasive species and how to keep your oil-producing algae from escaping and invading the local environment are all details that need to be worked out.

"None of this makes any sense until we get to the farm level," according to Clayton McNeff, Chief Science Officer for Ever Cat Fuels, a Minnesota company that is building a prototype processing plant that will harvest oil from algae. "It's the scale-up," he added. "A lot more research needs to go into the area—we need more funding. We need to go out of the laboratory do some larger scale ponds with the ideas that we currently have and see if they work on a larger scale." McNeff indicates that they will be doing this work in the next few years, but there is a lot of work that still needs to be accomplished. "It depends how much resources are put into it. If we have the willpower, I think it can be done in the next ten years." Growing the algae, developing the commercial systems, figuring out the best methods of extraction all need to be worked out. As with so many promising alternatives to fossil fuels, despite what you might have heard or read, fuel made from algae isn't quite ready for prime time yet.

In 2005, the US Department of Agriculture (USDA) and the Department of Energy (DOE) produced the "Billion Ton Study." It had been estimated that displacing 30 percent or more of the country's petroleum energy demands with energy from plants would require 1 billion tons of biomass per year. Looking at forest and agricultural land, the study concluded that 1.3-billion tons of biomass was available each year, while still meeting food, feed and export demands. This was backed up by the 2007 National Renewable Energy

Laboratory's (NREL) Assessment of the 30X30 Scenario which confirmed that 30 percent of the nations energy needs could be met with biofuels by 2030, but only if the necessary research was initiated and policies and incentives were in place to promote investment in a new carbon future.

New uses for old carbon are being developed everyday. Some of them aren't even that new. For a long time, natural gas was considered a nuisance. This combination of mostly methane and a few other hydrocarbon gases was often flared off at oil wells. Eventually, natural gas found a niche as a heating fuel and, as welding techniques and the ability to make leak proof pipe couplings improved, it was sent through pipelines that soon crisscrossed the country. In the 1930s, experiments using natural gas as a transportation fuel were successful, but with the low cost of oil, there wasn't a lot of interest. Natural gas did find a niche in vehicles like forklifts and commercial vehicles. The United States has vast natural gas reserves, and in the 1970s and 80s, compressed natural gas (CNG) was examined as a way to avoid importing oil and also as a cleaner, less polluting fuel than gasoline. Automakers began developing cars, trucks and buses that could use CNG in the 1990s, although their use was limited primarily to fleet sales and commercial purposes. There are presently about 9 million natural gas vehicles in the world, and about 130,000 in use in the United States. There are also about 1,200 natural gas fueling stations in this country.

Detroit's carmakers eventually became more interested in hydrogen and hybrid vehicles and have pulled away from CNG. Other makers, notably Honda, have embraced the fuel. Honda's Civic GX sedan (in production since 1998) uses natural gas and also has a home-fueling system that allows owners to refill their car's natural gas fuel tank overnight from the same gas that is piped into the home for heating. CNG fans point to the 20 percent lower greenhouse emissions that result from burning natural gas when compared to gasoline as a strong reason that more vehicles should use the gaseous fuel.

Natural gas got a strong boost in 2008, when oil man T. Boone Pickens suggested that the nation's power companies should stop relying on natural gas burned in turbines to handle peak loads at electricity generating plants and instead should use wind power to generate electricity (see Chapter 4). "Back in 1988 when I first started selling this [natural gas], my big pitch was 'it's cleaner, it's cheaper, and it's domestic'. I said someday cleaner and domestic is going to be worth something…," said Pickens. The oilman says that his plan will free up huge amounts of natural gas that could then be used as a transportation fuel, particularly for heavy-duty over-the-road trucking, and that that would reduce our oil imports. "If you move 22 percent [the amount of power generated using natural gas in the U.S. today] out of power generation into transportation fuel, it will reduce your imports [of foreign oil] by 38 percent," said Pickens.

Natural gas has other uses, beyond energy production. Many plastic products begin as methane molecules that are engineered to create long chains of polymers to make the plastics upon which the world depends. Although plastics have their own environmental issues, it has been argued that burning natural gas to obtain its energy is a waste of a resource that could be better served in making a useful product.

According to the EIA, the U.S. has a proven natural gas reserve of more than 211 trillion cubic feet. It has been suggested that this is a supply that could last more than 100 years. In the U.S., natural gas is found alongside oil in places like the Gulf of Mexico, and in vast shale deposits located around the U.S. Natural gas is a fossil fuel however, and like oil, its supply in not inexhaustible. Natural gas is a hydrocarbon fuel that produces carbon dioxide as it is burned, and so its use does add to the amounts of greenhouse gases released into the atmosphere. Natural gas can also require large amounts of water to produce during the drilling and recovery process.

Methane, the gas that makes up most of natural gas, is also found in an unusual form in places like the arctic and deep under the ocean. Methane gas hydrates occur when methane gas molecules are trapped into ice structures. When the water ice melts, the methane is released. These flammable chunks of ice were first examined in the mid-1960s by Russian scientists who found them interesting, but without any real application. More recently, a joint effort between BP, the United States Geological Survey (USGS) and the Department of Energy (DOE) has begun to drill the vast deposits of hydrates that are present on the edges of the Alaska permafrost. The methane gas hydrates are incredibly abundant, located domestically in Alaska and the arctic as well us deep under the Gulf of Mexico, and spread around the world. Previous wild estimates that there could be more hydrocarbons locked up in methane hydrates than in all other fossil fuels combined have been discounted of late, but if the test wells prove out, this burning ice could prove a huge source of natural gas.

Natural gas can also be turned into a liquid fuel through a process called Gas-to-Liquids (GTL). This can be accomplished after creating syngas, using the Fischer-Tropsch process we have already discussed. GTL has been suggested as a way to keep the world moving using liquid fuels after oil supplies begin to dry up. Because it uses a carbon-rich feedstock, and produces carbon dioxide, both in its production and also when it is burned as fuel, GTL is not considered friendly to global climate change.

Coal can also be converted into liquid fuels—either gasoline or diesel fuel. The coal can be converted into a syngas and then processed using Fischer-Tropsch, or, in the Bergius process can be mixed with hydrogen gas and heated until it liquefies. This was the process used by oil companies in South Africa. There is also a lower-temperature process in which coal tars are produced when coal is heated between 450° and 700° C. All of these coal-to-liquid (CTL) processes release far more carbon dioxide than is created by the refining of petroleum into gasoline or diesel. The only hope for CTL might be the development of effective carbon sequestration technology (see Chapter 5).

For many in the energy and transportation industry, the big advantage of natural gas is not so much its use as a long-term fuel source, or in GTL, but rather that it builds the infrastructure and gets the public ready for hydrogen. There has probably been more misinformation, hype, hope, and fantasy written about hydrogen than any other transportation fuel. Literally billions of dollars have been spent on research into using the simplest and most abundant element in the universe to power our vehicles of the future.

Hydrogen as a fuel has the potential to store and release a lot of energy. When we talk about the energy content of fuel, what we are really talking about is its enthalpy of combustion, that is the fuel's chemical reaction with oxygen. The energy contained in hydrogen is released when it is combined with oxygen to form water vapor. The amount of energy released when a pound of hydrogen is combined with oxygen has more than three times the energy than a pound of gasoline. This is misleading however. Hydrogen is an extremely small molecule giving the gas an extremely low density. Consequently hydrogen takes up a lot of space. Even when hydrogen is liquefied at extremely low temperatures, a gallon of gasoline has almost four times the energy that is contained in a gallon of liquid hydrogen.

Energy must be used to create gaseous hydrogen from other compounds, typically either by electrolysis of water or by breaking down some other hydrocarbon such as natural gas. For this reason, Hydrogen is often thought of as an energy carrier, rather than a source of energy like fossil fuels that come out of the ground. Electrolysis uses huge amounts of electricity and electrodes that split the hydrogen atoms away from the oxygen atoms in water. The gases produced must be kept separate as hydrogen is extremely combustible. If you have access to large amounts of renewable electric power, for example Norway with its numerous hydroelectric dams or Iceland with its geothermal power stations, creating hydrogen in this way is clean and produces no greenhouse emissions. It has been suggested that producing hydrogen from excess wind generation capacity or from solar electricity or nuclear power sources might also be possible. If you have to make hydrogen using electricity made from coal, you are still producing significant greenhouse gas emissions.

Hydrogen can also be produced through a variety of industrial processes where hydrogen is split off of hydrocarbons such as natural gas. Most industrial hydrogen is produced in oil refineries by heating natural gas with steam in the presence of a catalyst. This is how 95 percent of hydrogen is produced in the U.S. Oil refiners use hydrogen to break down heavy grades of crude into lighter ones that are easier to refine in a process called hydrocracking. About half the hydrogen produced every year goes to oil refining, while the other half goes into the production of ammonia ($NH_3$) that is further processed into fertilizer.

The energy carried in hydrogen can be extracted either by combustion or by using complicated electrochemistry. Ford and BMW explored the combustion of hydrogen in modified internal combustion (IC) engines in the 1970s, and in 2007, BMW demonstrated a dual fuel hydrogen and gasoline version of its 7-Series sedan called the H7 that would operate by burning hydrogen in its V-12 engine. The advantages of using hydrogen as fuel in a conventional IC engine are primarily one of cost and simplicity. Hydrogen acts much like natural gas in this case, but because there is no carbon in the fuel, there are no emissions of carbon dioxide greenhouse gas. The primary emission is water vapor, however some oxides of nitrogen (which are also greenhouse gases) are also produced, but can be removed using existing technology.

Modifications to the engine included the need to revise the sealing provided by the piston rings to avoid letting hydrogen leak past and into the crankcase, which could cause an explosion when the hydrogen mixes with the engine's motor oil. The BMW H7 uses a ten gallon cryogenic liquid hydrogen storage tank that keeps the fuel at -253° C, although after nine days a half full tank of hydrogen fuel will have evaporated completely away. The V-12 engine makes 265-horsepower and has a range of 125 miles on hydrogen.

The other way to extract energy from hydrogen is to combine it with oxygen in a controlled way to produce electricity and water vapor. This is done in device known as a fuel cell. NASA used alkali fuel cells in its manned space flights in the 1960s and 70s, combining hydrogen and oxygen from onboard tanks to produce the electricity needed to travel to the moon and back. These cells operated at 300-400° F, offered efficiencies approaching 70 percent, and flew on all of the Apollo moon missions as well as on the Space Shuttle. Alkali fuel cells are bulky, require extremely pure hydrogen gas with no carbon dioxide impurities, and they are extremely expensive due primarily to the large amounts of platinum metal catalyst that they require. For use in a road vehicle, something potentially less expensive and more robust was needed. The leading candidate is a fuel cell using a Proton Exchange Membrane (PEM).

Proton Exchange Membrane (PEM) technology got its start at General Electric in the early 1960s. PEM fuel cells can generate electricity without any moving parts. The heart of the system is a thin, permeable sheet of polymer plastic. Hydrogen atoms are stripped of their electrons at the anode electrode and these hydrogen protons migrate through the porous membrane to the cathode electrode. The PEM will only allow protons to pass, but prohibit the passage of electrons and gaseous hydrogen. The left-over electrons at the anode are siphoned off, passing through wires to whatever electrical device is to be powered, and finally ending up back at the cathode, where the electrons, hydrogen protons, and oxygen from the air combine to form water vapor.

Each PEM cell produces just a small amount of electricity, so groups of cells must be connected together to produce a stack with enough energy to power larger devices. PEM fuel cell efficiencies of 40 to 50 percent have been realized. To speed up the reaction a platinum catalyst is used on each side of the membrane. A conventional automotive fuel cell stack as presently envisioned would contain up to 100 grams of platinum, worth more than $3,000 on the current market. Platinum is an extremely scarce resource, 30 times less common than gold. About 80 percent of the world's platinum comes from South Africa, with the majority of the remaining coming from mines in Russia and Canada. A small deposit of platinum is mined in the U.S. in Montana.

PEM technology found its way into vehicle applications in the 1990s. A Canadian company, Ballard Power Systems tested PEM cells in buses in Vancouver and quickly became one of the technology leaders in the field. The company signed development contracts with DaimlerChrysler and Ford Motor Co., both companies pumping hundreds of millions of dollars into Ballard. GM and Toyota combined forces on their own fuel cell experiments, but bought PEM fuel cells from Ballard, as did Honda, Nissan and Volkswagen.

Hydrogen was quickly becoming the embodiment of the holy grail of automotive technology. DaimlerChrysler demonstrated its NECar fuel cell concepts, beginning with a van full of equipment in 1994. By the time the NECar 4 was shown in 1999, the system fit into a small five-passenger Mercedes-Benz A-Class hatchback, running on cryogenically (-250° C) stored compressed hydrogen powering a 320 fuel cell stack and capable of 90-mph and a 280-mile range. I drove the NECar 4 at a 1999 event for the media in Washington D.C. and found the car easy to operate. On powering up the vehicle, there were some initially loud compressor noises, but after selecting drive, the car was responsive to its "throttle" pedal and quite useful and unobtrusive. At the time, DaimlerChrysler officials said that the fuel cell powerplant alone would cost more than $30,000 and admitted that it would need to cost a tenth of that before the company could consider production. DaimlerChrysler vowed to start selling fuel cell vehicles by 2004, Honda claiming that its car would be on the market in 2003. Ford, GM, Honda and BMW all said that they hoped to have fuel cell vehicles ready in time to compete with DaimlerChrysler. Ballard admitted that the cost of the PEM fuel cells was still eight to fifteen times higher than it would need to be to compete with the IC engine, but hydrogen fans were convinced that volume manufacturing would bring down the prices.

At the end of 2007, Ballard sold its automotive fuel cell research operation to Ford and Daimler in an all-stock deal. Ballard said that the automotive research was draining $15 million per year from its profits and that the company wanted to concentrate on stationary fuel cell power sources. The company also noted that it didn't see the retail prospects for a fuel cell vehicle developing any time soon.

In 2008, Honda introduced the first "production" fuel cell vehicle into the California market. Called the FCX Clarity, the four-passenger four-door sedan weighed 3,600 pounds and could travel from zero to sixty in twelve-point-five seconds. A single forty-five gallon tank behind the rear seats stores gaseous hydrogen at 5,000 psi and can power the car for 270 miles on a fill up. The company made just 200 of the FCX Clarity vehicles and none of them are for sale; customers lease them for $600 per month for a fixed three year contract. Five hydrogen fueling stations are open to the public in the Los Angeles area to facilitate fueling the Hondas.

In 2008, General Motors deployed 100 Equinox fuel-cell cars for trials with customers in New York and Los Angeles. These vehicles were not for sale or lease, but were lent to potential customers to get their impressions and ideas about hydrogen vehicles. Depending upon the pressure of hydrogen used to refuel the Equinox, it has a range of between eighty at 5,000 psi and 160 miles at 10,000 psi on a tank of compressed hydrogen. GM claims to have spent more than $1.2 billion on hydrogen research and development and remains a staunch supporter of hydrogen as the fuel of the future. Larry Burns, GM's Vice President of Research and Development and Strategic Planning said in a keynote address at a Las Vegas Alternative Fuels conference, "These challenges are solvable—the technology exists to meet these challenges. It's going to take collective willpower to pull it off—it's going to take solutions that thrive in a market economy because we are working with some pretty big numbers when you realize that we are approaching a billion vehicles on the planet."

There are four miracles that need to occur for hydrogen to become a viable transportation fuel. As we have already seen, fuel cells are extremely expensive and use materials (platinum) that are hard to find and expensive. Work is underway to find ways to reduce the amounts of platinum required, or eliminate it entirely, but for now PEM fuel cells are at NASA levels of expense and not ready for mass production. Producing hydrogen also presents a major obstacle. Making hydrogen from a hydrocarbon, like natural gas, releases greenhouse gases into the atmosphere and reduce the advantage of using hydrogen in the first place. If you have to make hydrogen from natural gas, why not just burn natural gas in your vehicle and not bother with an expensive fuel cell? Until there is an environmentally friendly and reliable way to produce vast quantities of hydrogen, it's hard to see the real advantage.

Distributing hydrogen is less of a miracle, but difficult none-the-less. Most hydrogen today is produced where it is needed in a fertilizer plant or oil refinery. Honda has demonstrated a Home Energy Station that makes hydrogen from natural gas right in an owner's garage, but this still releases greenhouse gases into the atmosphere. Hydrogen that is transported usually goes by truck as compressed gas in cylinders on trailers. This burns diesel fuel and is inefficient. It has been calculated that a forty-four ton truck that can carry enough gasoline to fuel 800 cars can only carry enough hydrogen to fuel eighty vehicles. It is also possible to send hydrogen through pipelines, but they must be coated on the inside to prevent hydrogen embrittlement and subsequent cracking of the metal and leaks in the pipeline. The world's longest hydrogen pipeline goes between Belgium and France and covers 250 miles.

Having made and distributed hydrogen, the next step is to store it on a vehicle. Remember the BMW H7 and its loss of half of its tank of hydrogen in just nine days? Cryogenic tanks for liquid hydrogen are expensive, but the alternatives are tanks with hydrogen compressed to 5,000 or 10,000 psi, which seems astonishingly high for vehicles traveling on city streets. Still, GM's and Honda's test vehicles have adopted this storage method for real-world testing. Hydrogen can also be combined with other materials to become compounds rich in hydrogen. "There are products around that have a lot of hydrogen that at slight pressure can become liquids," Bill Reinert, Toyota's alternative energy told me in Detroit. "I'm thinking of things like common ammonia—$NH_3$—lots of hydrogen, we make tons of it, know how to store it, and its so cheap that when they put it in the ground as fertilizer only two percent is taken up—the rest is wasted," said Reinert. He envisions an on-board reformer that uses simple ammonia as a source for hydrogen used in the fuel cell. "On a per kilogram basis, $NH_3$ has more hydrogen than liquid hydrogen does. So you start thinking about that and it's pretty interesting—I'm just saying…"

Does all of this mean that hydrogen has no future? It comes down to a chicken and egg question. Most experts argue that without a hydrogen infrastructure, consumers won't want to buy vehicles if they can't find fueling stations. Other experts argue that energy companies won't build a network of fueling stations unless there are enough cars on the road to make it profitable. In California, Governor

Swartzenegger had promised a hydrogen highway with 200 fueling stations open in the state by 2010. To date, there are only thirty-three. GM has outlined a plan where forty refueling stations spread over three counties in the Los Angeles would put drivers consistently within three-point-five miles of refueling. The company says a network of 12,000 stations across the U.S. would put 70 percent of the population (those living in the 100 largest cities) within two miles of a refueling spot.

If hydrogen cars, and in particular hydrogen fuel cell vehicles do live up to their promise, we can expect them to roll out slowly. Barring any materials miracles, due to the extreme cost of the fuel cell stack, these first hydrogen cars will probably be small, allowing for smaller, less powerful, and less expensive fuel cells and smaller requirements for on-board storage of pressurized hydrogen. Such a vehicle would most probably be an urban commuter vehicle, one that stays close to home to ensure proximity to a fueling station network. It's hard to imagine even such a modest vehicle on the market before 2030.

The exception to this small-car scenario might be hydrogen-powered buses or heavy trucks. If you have a vehicle that travels the same route everyday, carrying roughly the same loads, you can design the fuel capacity of the vehicle and build hydrogen refueling stations in strategic places to make sure you always have fuel when you need it. Bigger vehicles can also accommodate bigger hydrogen fuel tanks. These vehicles can either combust hydrogen in a modified diesel engine or use fuel cells to power electric motors. We might see some limited application of hydrogen fuels in buses and trucks by 2020.

During most of the mania for hydrogen cars exhibited by carmakers, the emphasis has been on having a high-technology vehicle that carmakers could bring to Washington to show off to Congress how far thinking they are. Because nobody has any expectations for a hydrogen car in the near future, showing the car and talking in generalities was often enough to convince lawmakers and the general public that a hydrogen economy was just around the corner. The bloom is off the hydrogen rose. Moving to hydrogen will be long and protracted and the transition will still be taking place long after 2050. By then, we will have hopefully developed a new and better way of traveling from place to place.

# Chapter 8
# Deep Mobility

I've just traveled a typical commuter trip from the suburbs to downtown, getting an equivalent of forty-eight miles per $3 gallon of gasoline and producing almost no pollution in the process. Was I in an electric car? A fuel-cell vehicle? Some sort of hybrid? No, I was riding the rails on the Hiawatha Light Rail system, a commuter train in Minneapolis, Minnesota.

Prior to World War II, it was common to take the train when traveling any significant distance between major cities, while streetcar lines and subways carried people across town. After the war the growth of the airline industry for intercity travel, the explosion in automobile ownership, and the cheaper economics of city buses resulted in a reduction of rail travel of all kinds by passenger trains and streetcars. Freight service on many railroad lines began to take priority over passenger service, limiting schedules for commuters and travelers. In addition, it was expensive to maintain the railroad track bed for first class passenger service, and the reduction in the quality of the railroad experience convinced many passengers to look for alternatives. With the construction of the Interstate Highway System beginning in 1956, the railroad's passenger service continued to decline.

In the 1990s, looking for ways to reduce congestion and cut

commuting costs for lower income groups, light rail projects started showing up in major metropolitan areas. Federal money was available to build the systems in many cities. Light rail differs from traditional railroads in that the cars are smaller and usually motorized, and the system frequently follows a closed loop whose tracks are dedicated only to light rail use.

The vast expense involved in light rail construction and its infrastructure proved irresistible to pork barrel politicians and the potential to reduce pollution and provide equitable access has made the idea of such systems popular among environmentalists and social activists.

The Hiawatha Light Rail (HLR) system in Minneapolis follows Hiawatha Avenue, going from the Mall of America, to the Minneapolis-St. Paul Airport and then through eleven neighborhoods to the eventual northernmost station in the warehouse district in the heart of Minneapolis. Construction began in 2001 and a total of seventeen stations were built on the twelve-mile rail route. The cost of construction was $715 million and the system was opened in 2004.

The HLR uses rail cars built by Bombardier in Canada. They are ninety-four feet long and can carry sixty-six seated and 120 standing passengers. The cars usually run connected together as a pair, and up to eight trains operate on the rail line at any one time. The cars are powered by electric cables suspended sixteen feet above the track surface. Top speed is fifty-five miles per hour, but in service top speed is limited to about forty miles per hour. Tickets are purchased at automated kiosks at the stations and cost $1.50 ($0.50 for seniors and students) and $2.00 during rush hours for a two and a half hour riding period. There is no ticket taker, but instead random checks are made on the trains. Get caught without a ticket and you'll be charged with

*Riding the Hiawatha Light Rail (HLR) in Minneapoolis*

a misdemeanor crime and fined $180.

I caught a train at 9:10 am on a Tuesday morning at the Mall of America. For the first few stops I was the only person in my car. Although the train corners as if on rails (because it is), my automotive journalist colleagues, used to the luxury accommodations of a Lexus or Audi, would complain that the seats are as hard as boards and have little lateral support. The electrically operated trains are quiet and have large windows to view the world as it passes by. The tracks have welded joints so the ride is exceptionally smooth. I arrived in downtown Minneapolis at 9:51 a.m. and immediately hopped a train back in the other direction. My fellow riders were mostly old and young people, including two people who used the free bike racks to bring their two-wheelers with them. The ride back took just about the same amount of time. Trains pull into the stations about every eight to ten minutes and run from 4:00 a.m. until 2:00 a.m., so the schedule doesn't give any excuses for not using this facility.

The average commute is about twelve miles to get to work. If you have an Audi A6, getting twenty miles per gallon, your round trip commute will cost you one-point-two gallons of gasoline, or $3.60 if gasoline is three bucks a gallon. Except that the current estimates for car ownership, including wear-and-tear, maintenance and insurance put the costs at forty-eight cents per mile. This means our twenty-four mile commute to and from work each day is costing $11.52 plus $3.60 for gas or a total of slightly more than $15 a day.

Now, compare that to the HLR. The cost, during rush hours is $2.00 for a ride, or $4.00 for the day—about what you'd spend for gas for your Audi. Except you don't have parking, wear and maintenance to worry about.

The Hiawatha line carries approximately 19,300 passengers daily. It works well, but only if you lived along the Hiawatha line and need to get someplace also served by the train system. The HLR does coordinate with the city bus schedule.

There are hidden costs that the taxpayer must bear. The HLR costs $19.85 million a year to operate. Despite a ridership that is 65 percent higher than expected, the light rail system only brings in $7.2 million from fares. The balance is made up by tax money. Proponents of the system point to higher property values in the neighborhoods through which the train travels, lower traffic congestion and improved air pollution as reasons why the system is working. But electricity has to be generated somewhere and vehicle traffic must wait at light rail crossing gates, making some areas actually more congested if you aren't riding the HLR. In any case, light rail fever has caught on enough so that an additional line between Minneapolis and St. Paul is planned for 2013.

If I had to commute to downtown each day, would I ride a light rail commuter line? The financial incentives are significant and not having to fight traffic would be a real plus. But only if I happened to live nearby a light rail station. As it happens, I don't so using light rail wouldn't be an option. That's the real limitation of the concept—one that won't be solved without a network of light rail systems. With

the operating costs so high, what city could afford such an extensive
system?

Ironically, the Twin Cities could once afford just such an
extensive public transit system. Minneapolis and St. Paul had a 524
mile network of electric streetcars that served the entire metropolitan
area from the early 1900s until the early 1950s. Commuters could ride
from the southernmost reaches of the Minneapolis suburbs as far north
as White Bear Lake, at the northern extreme of the metro area, and
just about anywhere in between. During World War II, ridership was
especially heavy, but after the war the greater flexibility of scheduling
and economy of buses, along with the push to put everyone into an
automobile, killed off the streetcars, the last route closing down in
1954. As with street car and public transit systems in so many cities in
the United States, most of the streetcars in the Twin Cities were burned
and the rails were pulled up and sold for scrap. By the end of the
1950s, street railways operated in fewer than a dozen U.S. cities. The
personal automobile was the future.

Although automobiles have been around for more than 100
years, it is the past sixty years that have seen the largest wholesale
change in personal mobility in the United States. Fueled by cheap and
abundant fossil fuels, the widespread ownership of private vehicles
has made it possible for workers to live in suburban and rural areas
and commute long distances to their jobs. Before the wide scale
adoption of the automobile for personal mobility, nearly all cities had
a dense "downtown" business center that was usually close to water
or rail transportation. Public transportation catered to these business
districts, providing a way for commuters to travel to and from work.
This changed after the turn of the twentieth century, and by the 1920s,
automobile transportation and truck freight provided access from

outside of this zone, and cities began to sprawl.

After World War Two the concept of the suburb really took hold as GI's returned home and started families—the beginning of the baby boom. It was helped by Abraham Levitt and his sons who began construction of 2,000 mass-produced rental homes for returning GI's. They called it Levittown and it was built in a potato farm on Long Island. The homes were built on slabs, all lumber came from a lumber yard owned by Levitt and was pre-cut and delivered by rail. By July, 1948, Levitt was able to build thirty houses a day. Even at this pace, they couldn't keep up with the demand. By 1951, Levittown had grown to more than 17,000 homes and shopping centers, schools, playgrounds, and a community center had been added to serve the new home owners and renters. The Long Island Levittown became the most famous and others were developed in Pennsylvania, New Jersey (which was renamed Willingboro), and Puerto Rico.

The concept of sprawling suburbs caught on around the country. With jobs readily available and the post-war economy on the move, there were plenty of new families to buy those homes, often on credit. Americans had done without during the war years and they weren't shy about buying the latest electric gadgets for the wife to use in the kitchen, a new black and white television for the family, and a shiny new car for dad. Detroit's automakers were more than happy to convert their production facilities back to civilian automobile production, with easy financing terms for anybody who wanted to buy a car.

In 1956, President Dwight D. Eisenhower signed the Interstate Highway and Defense Highways Act that would create America's Interstate Highway System. Although primarily designed to promote national defense by easing the movement of troops and material during a war, the Interstate system soon bridged the distances between the cities and towns. Unlike most of Europe, America is blessed with wide open spaces and Detroit became adept at building large luxurious automobiles powered by lazy V-8 engines that could gobble up miles. Such cars were not fuel efficient, but gasoline was cheap and the car companies learned how to market ownership of those big and shiny automobiles as the essential right of every American citizen. To be a success meant to own a car and nobody wanted to ride a bus or a streetcar if they didn't have to.

Growth was the key; both for the automakers and for the nation in general. Everything was predicated on an ever increasing Gross Domestic Product (GDP) and substantial returns on every investment. The automakers quickly found a way to ensure that their business would increase every year: Growth's handmaiden, planned obsolescence. By changing the styling and features of their automobile every year, Detroit's carmakers were able to convince buyers that driving last year's model was for losers. A robust economy, easy credit and financing terms and the social push to keep ahead of one's neighbors in the suburbs kept the factories humming.

Growth is a funny thing. With a seemingly modest growth rate of just 3.46 percent, the quantity of something will double in just twenty years. Similarly, a more robust growth rate of 6.93 percent will result in a doubling every ten years.

The population of the earth in 1950 was about 2.5 billion people with an annual growth rate of 1.47 percent. Twenty years later, the global population had risen to 3.7 billion and the population growth rate was 2.07. In 1990, the earth held 5.3 billion people and was it was beginning to feel a bit crowded, despite a drop in growth rate to 1.56, close to the rate in 1950.

By 2010, we will have 6.8 billion people inhabiting our small planet. There are already twenty-five megacities—urban areas with more than 10 million residents. By 2015, it is projected that we will have at least thirty-five cities with a population of 10 million or more, putting an ever-increasing strain on resources like water and energy. All of this growth is expected to take place in developing countries, principally in Asia, Africa, and South America. Coincidentally, these are areas in the coming decades that are expected to be hardest hit by drought and the effects of global climate change. By 2050, the population is expected to reach 9.3 billion people. We keep growing, but can the earth continue to support us?

Researchers have been trying to answer that question for decades. Carrying capacity is defined as the ability of an environment, the earth in this case, to support organisms (humans) in a sustainable way. Carrying capacity estimates vary all over the board, from as few as 1 billion people to as many as 40 billion people. Most estimates seem to fall between 2 to 5 billion people as a population that is sustainable for our planet. Then how can we support the current population of more than 6 billion people? By extracting resources and energy from the earth in a non-sustainable way, something we have been doing for more than 250 years, since the beginning of the industrial revolution.

We have been using up the capital provided by our planet instead of living off the interest. Cheap energy in the form of coal, oil and natural gas along with technological innovation that allows us to exploit that energy has allowed us to grow more food, reallocate water resources, and control illness and disease. These are all good things, but they often occur with an unaccounted cost of air and water pollution, destruction of ecosystems, extinction of species, and changing our global climate. Unfortunately, the process of burning through our capital is changing the earth: China's food production is decreasing as deserts encroach upon what used to be productive farmland, water resources are dwindling, species of animals are disappearing at alarming rates and there are only a finite number of mountain tops in West Virginia that can be removed in the search for more coal.

Over a short period of time we have built a world based upon technology and growth. Consider that in 1950, worldwide production of vehicles was 8 million per year. By 1970, that number had jumped to 22 million, and by 1980 to 29 million. In 1990, vehicle production was up to 36 million, in 2000 it was running at 41 million, a level it stayed at until 2003. By 2006 that number had jumped to 49 million, and by 2007 more than 73 million vehicles were built. This included roughly 53 million passenger cars and 20 million commercial vehicles.

What happened? China came on board as a vehicle manufacturer. Of the vehicles built in 2007, more than 8.8 million of them were made in China, which has seen more than 20 percent growth per year as an automotive manufacturer. Even with 2008's global economic slowdown factored in, within ten years the worldwide number may reach 100 million vehicles built every year, thanks to emerging countries like India, Thailand, Malaysia and the former Soviet Republics.

China is moving into the mainstream and is no longer content with its third world status. Moving up requires energy and resources: the energy to build an automobile for example is as much as 20 percent of the total energy it will consume in its lifetime. If you build a lot of cars, you need a lot of energy.

But China isn't just building cars. The country's average rate of economic growth for the past twenty-eight years is 9.5 percent, more than four times the rate of other first world economies. A much quoted statistic indicating the level of this growth is that China is building the equivalent of two new coal-fired power plants every week to meet its electricity and energy demands. Building a power plant requires vast amounts of steel and concrete and other critical materials and China's boom has made them one of the world's biggest consumer of construction resources.

When I drove west-to-east through China in 2000, I noticed a significant amount of road-building and huge new gasoline stations dotting the landscape, each with thirty to forty gas pumps, none with any cars filling up with fuel. China was getting ready for the onslaught of automobiles. When I drove through the country again in 2007, traffic was heavy and all of those gasoline pumps were needed to keep cars moving down the road. China now has more than 23,000 miles of highways, that's more than double what was there in 2001, and second only to the U.S. road network. In 2000, there were roughly 6 million passenger cars in China, by 2008, that number had reached 41.7 million private passenger cars, according to China's public security ministry.

China and its citizens see no reason why they shouldn't enjoy the same standard of living as other first world countries. Who are we to tell them they can't? China's middle class alone is forecast to double in size to over 40 percent of the population by 2020 to 520 million people, which is almost double the size of the total U.S. population. As of the early part of the twenty-first century, China's consumption of grain, meat, coal, steel, fertilizer, cellular phones, TV sets, refrigerators, and cement has surpassed that of the U.S. and keeps growing. If the consumption per person were to reach U.S. levels,

China would consume 67 percent of the current world grain harvest, 80 percent of the world meat production, 110 percent of world's yearly coal use, 120 percent of world's yearly oil production and twice the world's annual paper production. If things continue the way they are going, we will need another planet filled with the earth's resources just to support China's growth. That's just China; other countries in the region, notably India, whose population is expected to surpass China's by 2030, continue to grow and demand their piece of the resources and energy pie. The problem is we don't have another planet.

The idea that sometimes growth can be counterproductive to the betterment of mankind is not new. Between 1798 and 1826, Thomas Robert Malthus published six editions of his treatise *An Essay on the Principles of Population*, in which he noted that increasing numbers of humans on the planet called for new ways "to increase yields while preserving natural habitats and biodiversity." John Stuart Mill, whose *Principles of Political Economy,* written in 1848 and considered one of the cornerstones of modern economics, discussed in one chapter what he called the "stationary state" without growth as an ideal condition for society.

Growth often has unexpected and unintended consequences. Rachel Carson's 1962 book *Silent Spring* decried the excessive applications of synthetic pesticides to increase crop production as the population continued to grow, and their unexpected effects on insects, birds, and every other part of the ecosystem of the entire planet. Her book is often cited as the beginning of the modern environmental movement. In the 1960s a geochemist named Clair C. Patterson, who had trained at the University of Chicago and had worked on the Manhattan project during the war, discovered a dramatic increase in atmospheric lead had occurred just about the time that the use of tetraethyl lead became widespread in gasoline in the 1920s.

Patterson published his results and then, unlike many lead industry researchers who depended upon the lead industry for their research grants, continued to pursue the truth about the detrimental effects of atmospheric lead, especially in children. Leaded gasoline had allowed Detroit to build ever larger and more powerful automobiles— a big selling point in the age of planned obsolescence. Lead was a well-known neurotoxin, but the oil companies and automakers weren't about to let that stand in the way of the growth of their industries.

Toward the end of the 1960s and into the 70s, the environmental movement started to take hold and people began to wonder who was really controlling their destiny. Paul R. Ehrlich's *The Population Bomb*, written in 1968, suggests that death and famine would be the result of uncontrolled population growth beyond the earth's carrying capacity. This was followed in 1972 by a book commissioned by an academic group called The Club of Rome. The book, titled *Limits to Growth,* used newly-developed computer models to examine the consequences of a rapidly growing population in a world of finite resources, including energy. Its results didn't look too promising for mankind, but were quickly rejected by those who ran industry.

To my mind, the most interesting book sounding a warning about unsustainable growth was E.F. Schumacher's *Small is Beautiful*, which appeared in 1973. This book, whose subtitle was "Economics as if People Mattered" was particularly interesting because Schumacher was one of *them*; he came from the ranks of the economists, having worked for more than two decades for the UK National Coal Board. Schumacher argued that the modern economy was unsustainable and that fossil fuels were finite and nonrenewable and needed to be viewed as capital rather than expendable income. He also believed that the earth's ability to resist pollution was limited and that governments should concentrate on achieving sustainable development. Because the most money then and now resided in the hands of those who are willing to exploit the earth's nonrenewable resources, Schumacher's theories and warnings were also largely ignored by big business and social-scientists.

About the same time (1974), M. King Hubbert, whose accurate predictions of U.S. peak oil we have already discussed in Chapter 2, presented testimony before a House of Representatives subcommittee on the regulation of the national growth rate of energy usage. Among the other things the then seventy-one-year-old geophysicist explained to the representatives that in the history of mankind, stretching back for 5,000 years and forward perhaps for another 5,000 years, fossil fuels are a blip. He called it a "Washington Monument-like spike" and his graphs showed the time span from the early use of coal in 1750, to the last drop of petroleum is consumed sometime after the year 2100 will have only lasted little more than 350 years.

"On such a time scale," he testified, "it is seen that the epoch of the fossil fuel can be but an ephemeral and transitory event— an event, nonetheless, that has exercised the most dramatic influence so far experienced by the human species during its entire biological existence." He also observed that the population during the period before 1750 was largely static but that since that time our population has exploded in an exponential way, all due, according to Hubbert to the ready availability of cheap fossil energy.

In 1973, the Norwegian philosopher and mountaineer Arne Naess had introduced the term "deep ecology." The term referred to a growing understanding among some environmentalists that simply adding additional air filters or a new set of laws wasn't having the desired effects of making a cleaner and safer world. Deep ecology asked more profound questions about choices that people make everyday in their lives. People in the movement realized that society cannot continue with the industrialized world's "business-as-usual" without eventually destroying the nature of biological and human diversity. Instead of trying to fit more filters to a factory smokestack, they asked why the products from the factory needed to be made in the first place. Deep ecology has always attracted the fringe elements of the ecology movement and something more acceptably mainstream was needed. In 1987, the field of Ecological Economics got its start. Ecological economists look for sustainability and social equity and understand that, more often than not, global economic growth "has resulted in increased extraction of natural resources and increased waste and emissions."

This idea of going "deep" was further explored by writer and environmental activist Bill McKibben in his 2007 book *Deep Economy*. In addition to examining resource depletion and global climate change, McKibben noted, "New research from many quarters has started to show that even when growth does make us wealthier, the greater wealth no longer makes us happy."

Faced with a continuing reduction of fossil fuels, a planet that is rapidly becoming overcrowded, an economic system focused on what we now know to be unsustainable growth and that will be unable to adapt to a slower economy, and a changing global climate, how can we create our own "deep mobility" to chart a course through the minefields of business-as-usual? Or, more simply, can we build a deep mobility transportation system that doesn't depend upon the sales of more than 70 million private automobiles every year for it to succeed?

It turns out, within an emerging framework of "New Mobility," there are innovative business, governments, and non-governmental organizations (NGO's) all over the world who are doing just that. One such center for New Mobility is SMART, Sustainable Mobility & Accessibility Research and Transformation at the University of Michigan. Its managing director is Susan Zielinski, a transplanted Canadian who happens to drive a first-generation Honda Insight hybrid (but mostly walks and rides a bike) and who emphasizes both a complex systems and a market approach to new mobility. I spent eight months at the University of Michigan as a journalism fellow studying energy and transportation and Zielinski was one of my advisors. We spent many hours together in college coffee shops, discussing how to save the world by developing more sophisticated, elegant, and practical systems...

What is new mobility? "It's the moving of goods, moving people and moving less—and it's also moving minds," said Zielinski. She notes that soon two-thirds of the world's population will be living in and around cities and that transportation systems need to become more sophisticated, more innovative and better connected in order to respond to the urbanization trend. In the U.S., the average driver wastes twenty-seven hours a year waiting in traffic delays. One only needs to sit in traffic in Los Angeles, or watch half-full commuter trains rush past while stranded by rush hour on the Chicago 'expressways" to know that something is terribly wrong with our present automobile-based transportation system and that it needs to change.

It is the interconnectedness of New Mobility that Zielinski stresses over new types of fuels or electric propulsion, ideas that, though an important part of the overall equation, end up keeping us in our same single occupancy automobiles. "There is a tendency to think of new fuel technologies as the silver bullet. But biofuels don't address the bigger picture problem—their use still keeps us in our often over-sized individual cars, adding to congestion, and making accessibility a problem for much of the world's population," said Zielinski. "Even if every car in the world ran on alternative fuels, we would still be faced with increasing problems of safety, sprawl, inadequate and inequitable infrastructure, and congestion."

Congestion is becoming a pressing problem. There are more than 900 million cars on the road in the world today and that number could reach 2 billion by the middle of the century. More vehicles are crowding onto limited road networks and the resulting congestion creates pollution, reduces fuel efficiency, wastes time, and sets up for inequitable access to daily needs dividing those with cars from those without.

One solution that SMART is developing and has piloted for getting people out of their private cars is the New Mobility Hub Network system. Just as the cell phone, personal digital assistant (PDA), and laptop has allowed us a variety of telecommunications choices, so too should our mobility needs be met with a variety of interrelated technologies, modes, and services. It's akin to our personalized, customized IT portfolios that link a cell phone to a laptop to a camera to an internet search engine—a multi-faceted system that today's kids are making mainstream. Transportation is going the same way.

It's elegant in its simplicity. "Imagine a day," said Zielinksi as she described the concept, "when steps from your door, or even from inside your home or office, you could enter a network of New Mobility Hubs, places near you that connect a whole range of transport amenities including buses, trains, streetcars, clean fuel taxis, car share that could be plug in hybrids, and bike share vehicles, and in some cases day care, satellite offices, cafes, shops and entertainment. This is all brought together by a cell phone or PDA that offers real-time information on arrival and departure times and availability, as well as access to information on local restaurants, shops, services, maps and guides. The PDA or cellphone also allows you to quickly and easily pay for these affordable modes and services with just a single wave past the reader." The beauty of the Hub network described by Zielinski is that you can transfer seamlessly from one mode of transportation to the other (including a car if needed), using the best mode for the purpose—going from a train to a waiting car share at one Hub, dropping it off at another to pick up a waiting bus. "This system, which doesn't pit mode against mode, but rather optimizes the best mode for the purpose, is easy, it's convenient, it's affordable, and it's twenty-first century," exhorts my former advisor.

How soon might we begin to see these Mobility Hubs around the globe? Sooner than you might think. The integrated fare payment underpinnings of it are in Hong Kong. The Octopus card system is a rechargeable electronic smart card that can be used to make payments and on the city's transportation system. It was launched in 1997, primarily to pay fares on the mass transit system, but since has branched into other areas of commerce such as restaurants, gas stations, parking meters, grocery stores, and vending machines.

Cape Town, South Africa will host the 2010 World Cup soccer games and is using that event to upgrade its aging taxi, bus, and rail systems. Part of this plan includes the establishment of as many as ten connected New Mobility Hubs in time for the World Cup. The Cape Town Hubs will link buses, metro trains, taxis, car shares, and bike shares. Some of the Hubs will also include restaurants and shops, and travelers will use cell phones to obtain real-time traveler information. The plan is to build a transportation infrastructure based on New Mobility, a good preparation for when the city increasingly restricts private transportation into the city to improve congestion and air quality as it has have already started to do. Other cities around the world that are involved in New Mobility projects include Bremen, Germany, Toronto, Canada, Bogotá, Columbia, Curitiba, Brazil, Paris France, Washington D.C. and Portland, Oregon.

In France, although the Paris Metro is already an efficient way of getting from one part of the city to another, bicycles (also an important part of New Mobility hub networks) are more efficient to get to the places that are between the Metro stops (an early iteration of hub networks). A bicycle rental program, called *Vélib,* (for *vélo,* bicycle, and *liberté,* freedom) started in 2007. More than 20,000 heavy gray bicycles are distributed around the city and can be rented for 1 euro per day or for five euro per week. There is slight additional charge for bikes rented for longer periods than thirty minutes. Users can rent bikes online, or can rent them directly at any of the 750 bike stations around the city, all the while reducing vehicle congestion and greenhouse gas emissions. Some American cities like Washington D.C., Chapel Hill, North Carolina and Ft. Collins, Colorado have similar bike sharing programs up and running. However, according to health organizations, two thirds of American adults are considered overweight and almost a third are considered obese, making it hard to imagine how bicycles will become a major part of the New Mobility transportation system in the U.S.

The whole idea of giving up one's car and riding a bicycle, or "sharing" a car doesn't come easy to many Americans. But the concept is not to have to give up one's car, just use it differently and to use other things. Saying you will give up your car in order to use car share or bikes is like saying you have to give up your laptop in order to use your cell phone. One project that has been successfully changing the mood in the U.S. since 1999 is Zipcar. When I met Zipcar's founder Robin Chase at a 2008 New Mobility conference, she explained where the idea came from. "In the Fall of 1999, I had just come back from a Sloan [MIT Business School] reunion and everyone was doing startups. The talk was everywhere was wireless—what's the wireless innovation of the future. The Internet was going strong and I had three kids and one car that would sit at an office park, far away and inaccessible to me. What I saw was what wireless technology and the Internet was made for—I could see the need and the moment for the technology." With her German business partner, Chase quickly developed a plan. "Zipcar is an idea from Europe. We didn't think of the idea, we just did it much better."

The idea is elegant in its simplicity. You join Zipcar online or by phone and receive an electronic zip card. Then when you need to use a car, you reserve one online or by phone for the times you need it. The cars are parked in special parking spots around the city. Walk up to your car, hold the zip card near a sensor on the windshield and the doors unlock, giving you access to your car. "If I as a business am going to rent cars by the hour, the cost of that transaction has to be close to zero, whereas in the car rental industry it was costing them $10-12 a transaction to process renting the car and doing all that stuff that goes around it," said Chase. "I knew as a consumer that I was never going to rent a car for an hour if I had to go stand in line and fill out paperwork and go miles to the place where the car was, so that this really required these wireless technologies and Internet access to make it happen."

The startup was modest, but well thought out. "I knew we needed to brand it as the smart, urban, hip, cool thing to do, nothing to do with environmental anything and that we needed to use cool cars and distinguish ourselves from car rental in every way possible," said Chase. "Anything that had the word 'share' in it was very negatively perceived by about forty percent of the population because sharing meant 'hippie', 'co-op', 'I have to wait my turn' and 'I don't like sharing.' Today we speak about car-sharing but in those days, for the first three years I banned those words from my staff's mouths. Hotels could be called bed-sharing—would that make you interested?"

Zipcar quickly became a phenomenon, growing month to month by 7 to 21 percent. "We launched in Boston—people had this impression that it would be all college students and I fought that impression tooth and nail," said Chase. "We saw that I was correct and the members were twenty-one to eighty years old, male and female, all income groups and the only predictor was a college education." Zipcars are now in ten major U.S. cities, seven university towns with 180,000 members and more than 5,000 cars available.

When my friend Charlie Partridge, whose day job is with the BBC in England, came to the U.S. for four months, I convinced him to try Zipcar. Afterward, he told me, "Zipcars are cool! They have nice models that look good and are fun to drive. I found the Zipcar to be an ideal compromise." Partridge found it easy to reserve a car when he needed one. "I needed a car, but I did not need one all the time. Zipcars are easy to book online for the trip to the supermarket or that cross town visit. I used them a lot and never had a problem." For longer trips, Partridge thought that conventional rentals were a better deal. "I wouldn't use a Zipcar for a long trip or for more than a day: a conventional hire worked out to be cheaper."

Robin Chase says that car sharing via Zipcar makes sense in a lot of ways. "The idea, from an individual's perspective is that in cities, if you don't need a car to get to work, it means your own personal car is sitting there idle for five days a week. Yet it's costing you about $25 a day. They are paying high parking rates and high insurance costs and are using the cars infrequently so those individuals can figure out that this is a crummy deal. Once they join they find that there are all of these other benefits that beat out personal ownership. Those benefits are that you have a car that meets your particular need for that particular errand for that phase in your life. If you are a Zipcar member you can get the pickup truck when you go to Home Depot you can get the fancy BMW when you want to drive your client around. A ton of people have joined because of Mini Coopers, to go on dates and propose to people in a Mini Cooper. You're able to choose the car that fits your need."

In 2003, Chase left Zipcar to start up a ride sharing company called GoLoco. "Today the average American spends 18 percent of their income on their car, and everything I know about transportation says that's going to go to 25 percent no matter what because of rising fossil fuel prices, increasing use of road tolls and user fees on roads, we'll have congestion charging and hopefully having carbon taxes, which will inexorably move us up. The economics of car ownership in the model we have today, the impacts to individuals in a household level will never work. Yet, they are living in places with no mass transit alternative. I do believe the major trends will be car sharing and ride sharing will become the norm. We have social networks so you can get over the stranger anxiety, we can do the money sharing online using PayPal, you don't have to discuss money in the car so it's not embarrassing, and we all are walking around with these wireless devices in our hand so we can do this realtime. GoLoco is in that market as an early mover of ridesharing," explained Chase. GoLoco isn't the only ridesharing company in the U.S. and the concept is growing in different parts of the world.

Most personal travel takes place between urban and suburban areas that are also highly dependent upon local motor transport systems for their supply of food, energy, raw materials, and finished goods. The mobility system that has developed for people and goods, particularly in the United States, is highly energy intensive and makes a significant contribution to atmospheric greenhouse gases such as carbon dioxide. Remember, worldwide the transport sector (including land, aircraft and sea sources) accounts for 23 percent of the total CO2 emissions from the combustion of fossil fuels. Our urban transport system is almost entirely dependent upon oil in the form of gasoline and diesel fuel.

In addition to its role in contributing to global climate change, the transportation system we have developed is particularly susceptible to the results of changes in the global climate. Sea level rise for example, can inundate tunnels and roadways in low-lying coastal areas. Higher temperatures in summer months can cause buckling of steel railroad tracks and softening of road surfaces, resulting in greater damage from traffic. More frequent severe weather events can result in localized flooding, causing road infrastructure and bridges to collapse as they deal with water flow rates beyond their designed capacity. Although there will be some positive aspects to a warmer planet (e.g., less snow removal in Northern areas, the possibility of an open sea route through the Northwest passage from the Atlantic to the Pacific oceans), global climate change will, in general, present significant challenges to the transportation infrastructure and needs to be a prime consideration in future plans.

New Mobility promises a transportation system to provide personal and freight transportation. Our deep mobility system that avoids the business-as-usual model must:

- Establish a transportation system that alleviates congestion and crowding in urban areas while providing equitable access for affordable mobility
- Develop new energy technologies and a transportation infrastructure that drastically reduces the greenhouse gas emissions from personal vehicles, buses, trucks and aircraft
- Creates new sources of liquid or gaseous fuels that reduce the demand for oil
- Find ways to reduce the use of or eliminate personal vehicles from daily commutes and transportation requirements
- Evaluate and modify existing and create new infrastructure that takes into account possible disruptions caused by future global climate change events and their consequences

The New Mobility Hub Newtork system uses a variety of interconnected, technology enhanced transportation modes services (like Zipcar and bike sharing), based upon travel schedules, destinations, and the ability to reduce greenhouse gas emissions. While each of these transportation modes will compliment one another and will be used together, how do they stack up when compared to one another? Let's look at each on its own and compare its range and usefulness, its ability to reduce oil usage, its susceptibility to global climate change and its ability to reduce urban congestion and integrate into a new mobility transportation network:

**Walking**

Walking would appear to be the ideal replacement for an energy intensive transportation infrastructure. Most people walk for at least a part of their daily commute, even if only to travel from the parking lot to their office or workplace. At a pace of three miles per hour, a walker in reasonably good condition could be expected to walk one mile during a reasonable twenty minute timeframe, limiting the practical commuting distance as a primary transportation mode. Weather also has a significant effect on commuting by walking as rain, storms, snow, or excessive heat can limit or even cancel it as an option. For several decades, walkers were largely ignored when designing transportation infrastructure, and as a result many U.S. cities are not walker friendly. Street-level sidewalks, pedestrian walkways, highway overpasses and covered paths between buildings all enhance a city's ability to be walked through.

Walking is susceptible to future global climate change due to increased fatigue and stress caused by increased temperatures, and as low-lying infrastructure (sidewalks and pedestrian walkways) become inundated by rising sea levels. Walking is incredibly adaptive to change as it requires the least amount of dedicated infrastructure.

Walking would seem to be greenhouse gas neutral, as the carbon dioxide exhaled by an exercising human being was originally sequestered by a living plant before being consumed and returned to the atmosphere through human metabolic activity Approximately ninety-four kCals of energy are required to walk a mile at a three mile per hour pace. According to the U.S. Department of Agriculture (USDA), the average human being requires 2,000 kCals (calories of food energy) for general metabolism each day, but many in western society consume significantly more calories (more than 2,700 kCals) each day. The Center for Disease Control (CDC) reports the average calorie intake for a U.S. male is 2,693 kCals. If no additional food calories are consumed to offset the extra energy output from walking, then commuting a mile by walking does not add additional carbon dioxide to the atmosphere.

If the energy required for walking a mile is offset by consumption of additional food calories, the $CO_2$ output picture changes. Our modern food infrastructure adds significantly to the carbon dioxide levels released to produce food energy. A person eating a typical American diet releases zero-point-three nine pounds of $CO_2$ while burning the 94 kCals needed to walk a mile. This $CO_2$ is not exhaled by the walker of course, but was emitted in the process of creating the food from which the walker obtains energy. A large amount of the food's $CO_2$ comes from the use of petroleum in farm operations, for fertilizer, for packaging and food processing and for transportation to the grocer's shelves.

Dietary choices dramatically alter the amount of $CO_2$ generated by a person. Foods such as beef add significantly to $CO_2$ emissions and are an inefficient way to generate food calories. It is estimated however that a vegan diet (particularly using locally grown vegetables that don't require much transportation) will result in approximately zero-point-zero eight pounds of $CO_2$ per mile walked.

The impact of the foods a person eats on the carbon dioxide emissions of the transportation mode highlights the importance of a system's approach to the study of future personal mobility. It isn't simply about changes to the transportation infrastructure, but a holistic examination of how the world works.

**Bicycling**

Bicycles multiply a human's work, allowing for greater

efficiency. Whereas walking a mile requires ninety-four kCals at three miles per hour, riding a bicycle requires only thirty-four kCals per mile while traveling at ten miles per hour. This greatly expands the range possible for a twenty to thirty minute commute, while reducing the energy expenditure of the commuter when compared to walking. Bicycles frequently share the road with automobiles, buses and other transportation systems; and this can pose safety problems unless special bike lanes are created. Bicyclists face many of the same weather related limitations as walking commuters, and the consequences of sea level rise and global temperature increases are also similar.

Because bicycling requires significantly less energy per mile when compared to walking, the $CO_2$ generated in the creation of this food energy is also less at about zero-point-one four pounds of $CO_2$ per mile for a typical U.S. diet. A vegan diet reduces $CO_2$ output to an almost negligible 0.03 pounds per mile for a bicycling commuter. This analysis neglects the amount of $CO_2$ generated when the bicycle is manufactured.

**Personal vehicles (gasoline)**

The reality in the U.S. is that people don't commute by walking or bicycling; they get to work by driving a gasoline powered automobile. According to a 2006 U.S. Census Bureau survey, eighty-six-point-seven percent of all U.S. commuting is done by the personal car, light truck or sport utility vehicle (SUV).

Commuting by automobile became popular in the 1950s and 60s as families moved to suburbs and farther from the workplace. The average commute in the U.S. is sixteen miles and takes twenty-five minutes, although cities like Los Angeles are known for average commutes that can be an hour or longer.

One gallon of gasoline contains 31,500 kCals of energy and about 2,421 grams of carbon. $CO_2$ emissions from gasoline total nineteen-point-four pounds/gallon. Thus, it is easy to calculate that when gasoline is burned in a typical automobile in the U.S., achieving twenty miles per gallon, approximately zero-point-nine seven pounds of $CO_2$ are released for each mile traveled. The fuel economy of a personal vehicle affects the amount of $CO_2$ released per mile. A sport utility vehicle or full-sized pickup truck achieving fifteen miles per gallon, for example will release one-point-twenty-nine pounds of $CO_2$ per mile, while an economy car getting thirty-five miles per gallon will release zero-point-fifty-five pounds of $CO_2$ per mile traveled. These analyses neglect the greenhouse gas emissions generated in the manufacture and disposal of the vehicles. Reducing travel also has a positive effect of greenhouse gas emissions. In 2007, Americans traveled 3 trillion miles by car, but in the first half of 2008, travel by car was down 2.1 percent according to the U.S. Department of Transportation, in large part due to the price of gasoline, which has risen dramatically to more than $4.00 per gallon. When gasoline prices dropped to less than half that after the economic crisis at the end of 2008, travel by car in the U.S. crept back upward again.

Although personal vehicles contribute to global climate change, the effects of warming and subsequent sea level rise also affect them. Road infrastructure in low-lying costal areas is particularly susceptible to flooding and to being washed away during storm-surge. Higher average temperatures can soften road materials, causing damage by highway traffic and reducing a road's life expectancy. In Northern areas, higher average temperatures may result in more or less snow, depending upon moisture levels and weather patterns, either increasing or decreasing the costs associated with snow-removal and highway maintenance.

**Motorcycles/scooters**

In many parts of the world, motorcycles and motor-driven scooters are viable means of transportation for commuters. Where the climate is moderate, year-around commuting on two-wheels is a possibility, while in the northern parts of the country, such commuting is more seasonal. Commuting by motorcycle or scooter limits the amount of cargo that can be carried and increases the need for both weather protection and protective clothing to reduce injury in the event of a fall or collision with another vehicle. Riding a scooter or motorcycle safely also requires a certain level of attention, physical coordination, and proficiency that not all of the general commuting public may wish to achieve. A typical small motorcycle or scooter (200-cc or smaller) can get fifty-five miles per gallon of gasoline, resulting in a $CO_2$ emission of zero-point-three pounds per mile. Two-wheeled vehicles are best when used for commuting in urban settings where their small size, maneuverability and ease in parking make them a viable choice, at least during good weather. Because they share the road with other personal and commercial vehicles, two-wheel vehicles are subject to the same effects global climate change as these vehicles.

**Personal vehicles (diesel)**

In Europe and Asia, diesel automobiles and sport utility vehicles are common, while in the U.S. they are relatively rare. One gallon of diesel fuel contains 34,950 kCals of energy and 2,778 grams of carbon, and burning a gallon of diesel fuel produces twenty-two-point-two pounds of $CO_2$ ( about 14 percent more than gasoline). At equal fuel economies, a diesel engine produces about 15.25 % more $CO_2$ per mile, or about one-point-twelve pounds per mile for a vehicle achieving twenty miles per gallon on diesel fuel. Because diesel engines are more efficient due to higher compression ratios and no throttle plate, and because they burn a higher energy fuel than gasoline engines, they can achieve 20 percent or more improved fuel economy figures and thus can actually reduce the amount of $CO_2$ per mile emitted. Diesel fuel cost nearly $5.00 in mid-2008, economics that cooled the interest in diesel passenger vehicles in the U.S.

**Personal gasoline/ethanol fueled vehicles**

Ethyl alcohol, or ethanol, has existed as an automotive fuel since the early 1900s. By the mid-1970s, Brazil had switched an entire fleet of cars from gasoline to biofuel ethanol made from sugar cane. In the U.S., ethanol is principally made from corn and is mixed as a 10 percent blend with gasoline as an anti-knock additive. Ethanol can also be blended with gasoline to produce E85, an 85 percent mixture of ethanol. To use this fuel in vehicles requires some modification to the fuel system to create a Flex-Fuel Vehicle (FFV) that can operate on a range of ethanol and gasoline mixtures. There are approximately 6 million Flex-Fuel vehicles on the road in the U.S., and the number is increasing. In 2007, the U.S. produced 5.9 billion gallons of ethanol from corn, and The Energy Independence and Security Act of 2007 has mandated that 36 billion gallons of renewable fuel (of which 21 billion is required to be biofuel) be a part of the fuel mix by 2022 with at least 15 billion gallons of ethanol produced yearly by 2015.

Ethanol produced from corn can be relatively energy intensive. Processing corn uses fossil fuels to produce fertilizers, operate diesel farm machinery and to convert the corn into ethanol. Future ethanol production from cellulosic materials such as hay, wood chips or specifically grown biofuel crops promises higher ethanol yields per acre at lower energy investments. Ethanol contains less energy per gallon than does gasoline (21,270 kCals), but engines can run more efficiently with the higher compression ratios allowed by ethanol's anti-knock properties. The following table gives an indication of the amount of $CO_2$ per mile emitted by ethanol biofuels for a 20 mile per gallon vehicle:

**TABLE 2: CARBON DIOXIDE PER MILE FOR BIOFUELS**

| Fuel | Pounds of $CO_2$ per mile |
|------|---------------------------|
| Gasoline | 0.97 |
| Corn Ethanol | 0.76 |
| Sugar Cane Ethanol | 0.43 |
| Cellulosic Ethanol | 0.09 |

The feedstock and the process by which ethanol is produced and the way that land is used to grow the feedstock have great impact on its viability to reduce greenhouse gas emissions.

**Electric and hybrid vehicles**

Electric cars were popular in the early 1900s. They were excellent for use around town, were quiet, produced no pollution and were easy to operate. The electric car's biggest problem was its limited range caused by the amount of charge that its battery was capable of carrying. Gasoline engines, whose range was limited only by the amount of gasoline carried on-board, eventually replaced the electric car. In an effort to reduce exhaust emissions in the 1990s, the State of California mandated that a percentage of vehicles sold by manufacturers had to be electric vehicles. California backed away from this mandate when it became clear that battery technology still wouldn't allow an acceptable range for most consumers. The electric car was replaced by the hybrid vehicle.

The concept of a gasoline hybrid electric vehicle has been around for more than a hundred years, but it wasn't until the beginning of the twenty-first century that such vehicles became commercially available. Honda and Toyota (with its successful Prius) have dominated the market, although GM and Ford have recently produced several hybrid models. The technical details vary with different models, but the objective is to use an electric motor and battery to augment a regular gasoline engine to improve fuel economy and reduce the $CO_2$ emissions from the vehicle. By 2010, a new form of plug-in hybrid will be available from GM (Volt) and Toyota (Prius) that will allow charging from the electric power grid and provide electric-only operation for a limited range before the gasoline engine kicks in to extend the range of the vehicle to acceptable levels.

Hybrid vehicles can be expected to achieve fuel economy levels of at least fifty miles per gallon, at which point $CO_2$ emissions will be zero-point-thirty-eight pounds per mile or better. The carbon dioxide missions from plug-in hybrid and electric vehicles depend dramatically upon the source of electricity to the power grid. A plug-in hybrid operating with electricity generated from a typical coal-fired plant results in a $CO_2$ level of zero-point-seven pound per mile. If the electricity comes from a nuclear plant or from wind or solar energy, the $CO_2$ levels drop to zero-point-thirty-three pounds per mile or less, depending upon how much gasoline operation is required.

**Personal vehicles using other fuels**

Several other fuels show promise for the future. Liquefied Petroleum Gas (LPG) and Compressed Natural Gas (CNG) are fossil fuels that burn slightly cleaner than gasoline and diesel. They require a different fuel system than is currently in use but have been well-proven to operate with a minimum of problems. As with other fossil fuels, their availability will also be limited over time.

Hydrogen has been proposed as a solution to both limited future petroleum supplies and to greenhouse gas emissions. Hydrogen can be burned in an internal combustion engine or used in a fuel cell to produce electricity. Either process is extremely clean and produces no carbon dioxide. Unfortunately, current commercial processes to produce hydrogen use natural gas as a feedstock and produce significant quantities of $CO_2$ as a by-product.

Coal-to-Liquids (CTL) is a process by which coal is converted into a petroleum substitute. Gasoline or diesel fuel can be synthesized through such a process. Huge amounts of carbon dioxide are created through the CTL process, and capturing and sequestering the $CO_2$ in geologic storage is the only realistic way in which this process can be viable. Unfortunately, there is currently no feasible process by which this amount of $CO_2$ can be sequestered.

### TABLE 3: POUNDS OF CARBON DIOXIDE PER MILE FOR OTHER FUELS

| Fuel Type | Pounds of $CO_2$ per mile |
|---|---|
| Gasoline (20 mpg) | 0.97 |
| Liquefied Petroleum Gas (LPG) | 0.78 |
| Compressed Natural Gas (CNG) | 0.69 |
| Hydrogen Gas | 0.57 |
| Liquid Hydrogen | 1.03 |
| Coal-to-Liquid with sequestration | 1.01 |
| Coal-to-Liquid w/o sequestration | 2.12 |

Reference EPA 2007

## Transit Bus

Carbon dioxide emissions from public transportation are particularly hard to estimate. Local city buses, for example, vary widely in their ridership. A bus is empty as it leaves the bus barn until it picks up its first passengers for the day. During rush hour, buses may be filled to capacity, but during slow times the bus may have just a few passengers. For a city bus the $CO_2$ emissions are estimated to be zero-point-seventy-one pounds per passenger mile.

Because buses travel on regular roadways (or sometimes on special bus lanes adjacent to roadways) they are susceptible to the same effects from global climate change and sea level rise as are other road users. The advantage of buses over other public transportation is their adaptability; buses can be rerouted or new routes can be created as road and social conditions change, providing advantageous flexibility.

## Commuter rail/subway

Like buses, ridership of commuter rails varies greatly with the time of day and the route. Commuter rails and subways are huge public works projects that require years to design and build and which can greatly disrupt other transportation infrastructure during their construction. Carbon dioxide emissions per person depend greatly upon ridership. For a subway or light commuter rail the $CO_2$ emissions are estimated at zero-point-thirty-six pounds per passenger mile.

More than any other transportation system, rail cars and subways will be effected by global climate change. Underground tunnels near costal areas will be endangered by sea-level rise, and existing rail bridges and infrastructure will be threatened by storm water flow amounts exceeding their design parameters. Increased ambient temperatures can contribute to rail buckling, causing accidents and requiring additional maintenance. As conditions change, rail and subway lines will prove to be less adaptable to meet new requirements.

New Mobility systems that include a variety of transportation modes must consider the emission of greenhouse gases such as carbon dioxide and how such emissions can be minimized for the greatest number of commuters, while still attaining other goals such as reduced congestion, optimized travel time, and equable access. In addition, transportation is susceptible to change and disruption as a consequence of global climate change and these changes must be a part of planning for the future. The complexities of developing this new infrastructure will require a systems approach that goes beyond simply examining transportation systems to include the entire social fabric of modern and emerging societies.

The real question about New Mobility is, after building an infrastructure of Hubs and a variety of transportation modes, will people be willing to give up their personal automobiles and the perceived advantages that they provide (anonymity and freedom) to embrace a new system whose advantage largely benefit society (reduced congestion, more equitable access, reduction of greenhouse gas emissions and pollution)? It could be a hard sell, but if we don't take drastic steps our overtaxed transportation infrastructure soon won't support the increasing demands we are making of it. As Susan Zielinski said, it's about moving minds…

# Chapter 9
# A Brighter Future

In researching this book, I have covered more than 10,000
miles. Many were crooked miles, with zigs and zags that would lead
me to people and places that, beforehand, I never knew existed. I
crisscrossed North America, meeting people who are on the front lines
to make our world a better place. There is some irony that for most of
the journeys, I did not use public transportation, buses, light rail, car
sharing, or ride sharing. I traveled the American way—by personal
automobile. Aside from airlines, our automobiles make up the only
real system of accessible mobility that we have in this country and the
only real choice that I had for most of my travels. I used renewable
E85 ethanol when I could find it for my old flex-fuel Ford Ranger
pickup, but most of the time, I burned non-renewable, fossilized, old
carbon in the form of regular unleaded gasoline.

Along the way, I spoke with engineers, scientists, geologists,
technicians, visionaries, pragmatists, skeptics, fanatics, and farmers,
all of whom had reason to dread the future. Many of them have a clear
view of the problems we are facing, problems that the general public
are just beginning to comprehend. Yet most of them are optimistic
that we are up to the challenges that face us, that our innovative spirit
and technological abilities will help us solve the problems we have

generated. Is their optimism misplaced?

First, let's review what we have learned. Petroleum fuels more than 95 percent of our transportation needs in the United States. Petroleum is old carbon, the fossilized remains of algae, processed over millions of years deep within the earth. Access to cheap energy from petroleum has allowed Americans to achieve a high standard of living and helped foster the formation of suburbs. Suburban living, in turn, results in the need for workers to commute to their jobs; and they generally do this in personal automobiles. The resulting congestion is inefficient as it wastes both time and fuel.

Petroleum from conventional oil wells is becoming harder to find. This will drive the price of motor fuels higher and has resulted in exploitation of unconventional sources including deep sea and arctic environments, tar sands, and eventually the processing of oil shales. There is evidence that the procurement of oil from the earth and accessible by conventional means has peaked or will peak in the none-too-distant future. For Americans, a peak in global availability of oil may occur because of geopolitical factors beyond our immediate control. In addition, rising demand in countries such as China and India puts an ever-increasing strain on the world supply of oil.

Burning old carbon in the form of fossil fuels returns to the atmosphere the carbon dioxide that was stored millions of years ago in living organisms. Before the industrial age, the amount of carbon dioxide in the atmosphere was in the mid-200 parts-per-million (ppm). Because of the burning of high carbon fossil fuels like coal, oil and natural gas, the level of carbon dioxide in the atmosphere is increasing, to a current level today of about 385 ppm.

Carbon dioxide, along with methane, and water vapor is a greenhouse gas; they trap the energy of the sun close to the earth's surface, causing a gradual warming. The average temperature of the earth has warmed about 1.5° F over the past 100 years, attributable in large part to the increase in carbon dioxide levels caused by the burning of fossil fuels and returning carbon back into the atmosphere. The temperature rise, although small, has already begun to show its effects in the Arctic and Antarctic regions, where glacial melt and the breakup of sea ice and ice shelves is the most noticeable result. Glacial melt is especially disconcerting as it can result in a rise in sea level which could threaten coastal regions during the next century. The warming effects of carbon dioxide in the atmosphere will continue to increase, as once the gas is released into the atmosphere it can remain there for decades or longer. Carbon dioxide mixes completely around the globe, which takes some time so emissions made today won't take effect for some time to come. As the global average temperature continues to increase, the effect on the earth's climate will become more significant. The only solution is to reduce the levels of greenhouse gas emissions.

Given the huge amounts of petroleum we use every day in the U.S., finding substitutes for oil poses a challenge. Changing from oil to natural gas as a transportation fuel is one possibility. Natural gas is a lower carbon fuel and produces less carbon dioxide than oil when burned. The U.S. has a vast supply of natural gas, but processing it from subsurface shale can be water intensive, and water is rapidly becoming a critical resource.

Motor fuels can also be made from plants. For the past thirty years, this has been done in Brazil by producing ethanol from sugar cane. In the U.S., 20 percent of the nation's corn crop is used to produce ethanol, which is mixed with gasoline in quantities of 10 percent as a gasoline additive and 85 percent (E85) as an alternative fuel. When ethanol is used in amounts higher than 10 percent, vehicles must be modified slightly to maintain efficient operation. About 8 billion gallons of corn ethanol are produced annually in the U.S., and we have the potential to reach 13-15 billion gallons a year. The argument that corn ethanol takes more energy to produce than it releases is not correct; it returns about 22 percent more energy than it takes to produce. Because corn is a food source, primarily for animals, the diversion of animal feed to fuel vehicles has been a topic of intense debate.

Ethanol can also be produced from woody plant materials and agricultural waste such as corn stover (leftover stalks and leaves). This is called cellulosic ethanol because it breaks down a plant's cellulose and changes it into ethanol. The cellulose is insoluble in water and must be broken down into a sugar that can then be fermented into ethyl alcohol (ethanol). There are several ways to do this, including a thermal process, a biological process, and a combination of both. Using plant cellulose is the only way that we will ever reach the U.S. government's target of 30 billion gallons of biofuels to be produced annually by 2030.

Other biofuels include biodiesel, a fuel made from plant oils or from oils harvested from algae. Palm oil is used to make biodiesel, and destruction of tropical forests to plant more palm trees is having a negative effect on reductions of greenhouse gases. Algae have potential, especially when grown in areas with large amounts of sunlight, such as the American Southwest. The advantage of biofuels is that they are renewable, whereas oil is a finite resource.

Another proposed motor fuel is hydrogen, but there are significant hurdles to implementation. It takes significant energy to produce hydrogen, it is difficult to store and transport, and both the fuel and the fuel cell to convert hydrogen into electricity are very expensive. Hydrogen can be burned in a modified car engine, or it can be used in a fuel cell to produce electricity that powers an electric motor. The only emission from a fuel cell equipped vehicle is water vapor. This makes hydrogen quite attractive, at least in the abstract. Hydrogen may begin to show up by the mid 2030s in smaller vehicles but may find applications before then in buses, heavy trucks, or other vehicles which have set routes and can be refueled at more predictable locations.

Regardless of the fuel used, vehicles must become more efficient. Automakers have started this process, making internal combustion engines that burn gasoline more efficiently and installing transmissions with more gear ratios to keep the engine operating in its most optimal speed range. Unfortunately, the efficient drivetrains have been used as a marketing tool to increase vehicle performance rather than to enhance fuel economy. Vehicles have become heavier over the past decades with the incorporation of mandatory safety systems such as air bags and comfort features such as high-end stereo systems and electrically controlled windows, door locks and seats on even entry-level automobiles. The preference for light trucks and sport utility vehicles has also pushed the average weight of vehicles higher. Heavier vehicles require more fuel than lighter ones, and most of the improvements in engine and drivetrain efficiency have gone into moving heavier vehicles.

The average car only uses 25-30 percent of the energy in its gasoline fuel to move the car, the rest is lost in friction and heat. To make vehicles more efficient, carmakers have begun to develop hybrid vehicles, using an electric motor to augment the gasoline engine. This allows the engine to be smaller and more fuel-efficient. The disadvantage of hybrids is the cost and complexity of carrying two complete drive systems and the weight penalty imposed by carrying electric storage batteries. Battery technology is improving, especially with the development of new lithium-ion batteries, but the weight is still significant.

Because most people drive less than thirty miles a day, plug-in hybrid vehicles under development will charge a battery system at night and allow an all-electric range of thirty to forty miles. If this range is exceeded, a small gasoline engine will engage to charge the batteries and "extend" the range of the vehicle. The cost and weight of the battery package is the biggest challenge such vehicles face.

Electric plug-in hybrid vehicles must obtain power from the existing grid. The system of interconnected coal, nuclear, hydroelectric, and alternative energy sources needs a major overhaul before it will be capable of supplying electricity to hundreds of thousands of hybrid vehicles. Coal is a particularly dirty fuel, emitting heavy metals such as mercury and arsenic as well as copious amounts of carbon dioxide. Coal, especially when mined by mountain top removal, is also environmentally destructive. Technologies to capture and sequester underground the billions of tons of carbon dioxide produced by coal-fired power plants are in their infancy and are at least two decades away.

Electrified vehicles require lithium for their battery packs and rare-earth elements for the permanent magnets in their electric drive motors. China is a huge producer of lithium and the source of more than 95 percent of commercial rare-earth elements. The only U.S. lithium mine still operating is a small operation in Nevada, owned by a German company. The only U.S. source for rare-earth elements, a mine in California, has been closed for more than a decade.

Ultimately, an alternative to the use of personal vehicles for every trip needs to be found. Alternative fuels and hybrid vehicles don't change the paradigm which we have created. Americans love the freedom represented by personal vehicle ownership and, with the exception of small urban pockets well-served by public transit options, we are notoriously reluctant to use mass transit systems. In other parts of the world, new mobility systems are taking shape, combining walking, bicycles, personal vehicles, car sharing, ride sharing, buses, light rail, and rail systems. Communication technology promotes ease of use by allowing commuters to check schedules and pay for transportation.

As I have demonstrated in this book, we are running out of access to cheap fuel, and we need to do something about the greenhouse gases our transportation system emits if we are to reduce manmade global climate change. Many people point to the development of increasingly more complex forms of technology as our salvation. Some have suggested that our response to our present energy crisis should be similar to the 1960s moon shot in its commitment; a ten-year, technology-based endeavor that the whole country can rally behind and support. Others claim that the Manhattan Project, the four-year scramble to create the first atomic weapon during World War II, is a better model to solve our energy dilemma as it implies the same level of response to a threat to our national security. Both projects involved billions of dollars, innovation on an almost unimaginable scale, and the mobilization of hundreds of thousands of scientists, engineers, technologists and skilled labor, to achieve a single goal.

Maybe there is a better model for big-scale projects. Indianapolis businessman, Carl Fisher, and his investors built the Indianapolis Motor Speedway and held the first 500-mile race there in 1911. Fisher's experiences and his realization that the American automobile industry was on the brink of an explosion of growth led to his dream of a transcontinental highway. His position within the youthful automotive industry gave him credibility among other industry leaders. Fisher began a letter writing campaign and formed a planning group to solicit support for the idea. Fisher had no faith that the government could handle such a project, so he decided to independently find financing for the highway. In the first thirty days, more than a million dollars of private money had been pledged to build the road across the continent. In 1913, the newly incorporated Lincoln Highway Association held its first official meeting.

The Lincoln Highway Association used the money it raised to survey a route, to build so-called "seedling miles" which were mile-long sections of rural paved roads that would demonstrate the concept to a sometimes skeptical public, and to provide materials and know-how to state and local officials so that road construction could begin. The Lincoln Highway Association sparked a demand from the public for all-weather hard-surface roads, and in 1916, the federal government passed a bill requiring states to establish highway departments and providing matching funds for state highway projects.

The Lincoln Highway project got a boost in 1919 when an Army convoy of seventy-nine vehicles crossed the country and proved a need for new and better roads to support military operations. One young officer on the convoy was Dwight D. Eisenhower who, when he later became the thirty-fourth president, signed the Interstate Highway and Defense Highways Act in 1956 that would create America's Interstate Highway System.

Eisenhower's Interstate Highway system would eventually supplant secondary roads, making long-distance travel even easier and allowing people to work in the city, yet live in the suburbs, completely changing the American way of life.

Carl Fisher died on July 15, 1939 and never imagined Eisenhower's Interstate System, despite the pivotal role the Lincoln Highway had in its creation. President Eisenhower died on March 28, 1969, twenty-two years before the Interstate Highway System was declared completed on September 15, 1991. Building the Interstate System had taken thirty-five years at a cost of $114 billion.

To address our energy problems today we need this type of long-term view. Rather than the flash of a space program or atom bomb project, we need the decades-long commitment of innovative and farseeing individuals such as Carl Fisher, who engaged the private sector to create a network of roads that served the public. Private industry and entrepreneurs cannot do it all on their own. We need the resources of a federal government that recognizes problems and solutions, one with the courage to embark on enormous projects like the Interstate Highway System, knowing that it will be our children and grandchildren who will benefit from our foresight. The private sector and federal, state, and local governments must work together to find solutions that the planet can live with, avoiding the petty arguments that arise when we leave important decisions to short-sighted politicians whose horizon extends only until the next election cycle. If we can learn anything from our history, it is that we have to have the patience and bravery to think and act on a large scale and to work for the future, even if we never personally see the end result.

At the end of 2008, several significant events occurred which have the potential to change both our quest for energy, and our ability to address global climate change. Perhaps the most significant was the sudden and nearly complete collapse of the global financial system.

Almost overnight, major banks, investment firms, and insurance
companies suffered liquidity crises that threatened their survival.
Governments around the world stepped in with hundreds of billions
of dollars to help shore up financial institutions. The resulting
credit pinch had a huge effect of the already beleaguered U.S. auto
industry, such that General Motors and Chrysler were forced to go to
Washington to seek loans to prevent bankruptcy and stay afloat. Ford,
which had already accomplished some restructuring, looked for a
line of credit in the event that slow auto sales would continue into the
future. By the end of 2008, the U.S. industry annualized sales rate fell
to 10.5 million cars, which is fewer than 12 million or so cars that are
scrapped in the U.S. every year.

U.S. carmakers were not doing well before the 2008 crisis.
Hemorrhaging tens of billions of dollars per year, while claiming that
they were building the sport utility vehicles (SUVs) and light trucks
that the public wanted, their product mix paid no attention to the
looming realities of the end of cheap energy and the need for curbing
greenhouse gas emissions. Instead of trying to get ahead of the curve,
they were trying to wring every last dollar from the inefficient and
overweight SUVs and trucks leaving their factories. GM, Ford and
Chrysler all have fine engineers who understand global priorities and
realities and who have the ability to innovate and provide real world
solutions to real problems. Management can be blamed for not being
able to see beyond the next quarterly sales numbers. Their persistent
lack of vision did not allow them to formulate a viable plan for a
changing planet.

Even while GM has been working on its much-ballyhooed
Chevrolet Volt plug-in hybrid, it introduced a 6.2-liter, 556-horsepower
Cadillac CTS-V model with a supercharged V-8 engine that could go

from zero to sixty miles per hour in three-point-nine seconds. This was in addition to the Chevrolet Corvette ZR-1 model with a 638-horsepower supercharged V-8 engine and a top speed of almost 200-mph. Did GM really need two supercars? Given its stark financial position, did it need even one?

Don't get me wrong. The car-guy part of me is all in favor of mega-horsepower performance cars capable of incredible racetrack performance. When times are good and you are flush with cash, it is impressive to see what talented and dedicated automotive engineers are capable of building. These are not those times. When resources are scarce and the problems that we face on a global scale are looming on our event horizon, the very clever engineers need to be mobilized to solve real problems, not to find another tenth of a second at the racetrack.

Although the big-three car companies prostrated themselves before Congress at the end of 2008, in the end a loan guarantee by the Bush White House used bailout money intended for financial institutions to rescue the automakers. The executives of the car companies were forced to promise that they would restructure and reinvent themselves. Politicians, meanwhile, pronounced that plug-in hybrids would be the green cars of the future, reducing greenhouse gases and ensuring our national energy security.

What will the cars of the future look like, and who will build them? The general assumption is that they will be built by the current big players: General Motors, Ford, Honda, and Toyota to name a few. Today's cars are built in an energy intensive way out of materials like steel and aluminum that require massive amounts of energy and infrastructure to create. Huge expenditures of capital are required for research into new technologies and to meet various regulations.

These factors make it extremely difficult for a newcomer to enter the automotive field.

If we look back to the 1970s, the model of an industry dominated by a few lumbering giants was also true for the computer manufacturers. This model was disrupted by small, nimble companies like Apple, Commodore, Radio Shack, and Compaq whose personal computers were able to leap over established companies like IBM and Honeywell to create innovative, adaptable and less expensive options to the traditional mainframe computer.

Building vehicles out of lightweight composite materials such as carbon fiber doesn't require the huge investments in infrastructure; and off-the-shelf electric propulsion motors, battery packs, and electronic controllers are just about ready to hit primetime. Who knows from where the next great idea will come? The biggest obstacle for a nimble new player in the automotive world is the myriad of regulations every new car must meet. It's been said that if you could design and develop something that did everything a car does, without *looking* like a car to lawyers and regulators, you could be the next Apple.

Cars in the future will need to be smaller and lighter. This will be accomplished using lighter weight materials and smarter designs. For decades U.S. automakers have claimed that they cannot make money on small cars. This will need to change. Boosting efficiency will become all-important, leading to the increasing application of plug-in hybrid technology, although the weight of batteries (even using lithium-ion chemistries) and their cost will necessitate a shorter range than the 40 miles that has been designed into the Chevrolet Volt. The gasoline or diesel engine in the hybrids will cycle on and off frequently, and they must be designed for maximum efficiency while running and during startup. Biofuels, specifically ethanol made from agricultural and municipal waste, and dedicated biofuel crops such as switchgrass must become a significant part of our fuel portfolio; and every non-diesel car or light truck needs to be designed to operate on an E85 blend of gasoline and alcohol. In addition to conservation and increased efficiency, these are the only ways in which we can extend our remaining oil. The transition must begin now.

Cars designed around these simple goals could be made reliable and durable enough to last for ten years or more, much like the old Volkswagen Beetle. It successfully eschewed designed obsolescence and retained its basic design for decades. Such cars need not be boring to drive or to look at, and many automotive stylists and designers are already working on innovative ideas for future small cars.

Vehicles in the future will need to be more specialized. If you want a sports car, why not a full electric with a limited range but extremely high performance for high-speed fun on the race track? If you need a light truck, how about buying a high-efficiency biofuel diesel or natural gas-powered vehicle? If you only need to haul things occasionally, trucks could be available through a car-sharing company like Zipcar. A high-speed rail system would be a good choice for longer trips.

The future is fascinating to think about, but what can you do now to make a difference? In terms of your personal vehicle, take some tips from hyper-milers, the high mileage enthusiasts who stretch fuel economy to astounding levels. Make sure that your tires are properly inflated, that your air-cleaner is not dirty, and that you use a synthetic (more slippery) motor oil in your engine. Many SUVs have rooftop luggage racks that can be removed when you are not using it to reduce aerodynamic drag.

Few people want to hear it, but the largest gain you can make in fuel economy comes from how you drive. Keep your speed below 60 mph on the freeway, look far down the road and slow down gradually so that you don't have to use your brakes as much, anticipate the changing of traffic lights so you can avoid coming to a complete stop, and avoid hard acceleration. These suggestions will also make you a safer driver. Avoiding extra trips saves gas; and combining stops, starting with the farthest away first will let your engine warm up more fully, saving some additional fuel.

At least 20 percent of the energy used by a vehicle in its lifetime comes from manufacturing it, so keep your car well maintained and keep it for a long time. The argument used to be that we needed to get older high-polluting models off the road, but any car built since the late 1990s has all of the modern technology it needs to be reasonably clean so the recommendation is not valid. We need to break people of the idea that everyone needs a new car every three years; it might as well start with you.

I would love to say that you should take public transportation, but with very few exceptions, public transportation in the United States is almost useless. Why does this have to be the case? If we agreed to allow a bus or train to be an acceptable means of getting from place to place, our elected officials could become supportive of public transit and less enthralled with building new roads and parking lots. New Mobility Hubs, combining various modes of transportation like car sharing, buses, light rail and pedestrian walkways may help make public transit more palatable.

As dire as the 2008 financial meltdown was for Wall Street, it actually is providing an enormous opportunity for real change. Without the collapse, it would be far too easy to push for a business-as-usual approach, arguing that anything else would threaten the financial stability of the country's economy. With the stability disrupted, it is clear that attempting to return to the old system, one that doesn't account for true costs and risks, would be foolish. We can no longer let Wall Street act irresponsibly.

One downside to the financial situation has been reduced investment in alternative energy programs. Venture capitalists and large corporations alike are reluctant to invest in projects with a small potential for short-term success. To balance this, President Obama has announced a $150 billion overhaul of U.S. industry to set it on a low-carbon path. The investment is designed to revive the economy by creating millions of jobs targeted at projects in the renewable energy industry.

The election of President Obama was certainly a significant event of 2008. His announced intention to implement a carbon cap and trade system to account for the cost of carbon in our fossil fuels, his position on global climate change (backed by his choice of Steven Chu to head the Department of Energy and Harvard professor of environmental policy, John Holdren, to be the President's chief science advisor) bode well for a forward-looking U.S. government. His goal of 1 million plug-in hybrids on the road by 2015, his requirement of 60 billion gallons of advanced biofuels to be phased into our fuel supply by 2030, and his intent to reduce greenhouse gas emissions by 80 percent by 2050 cannot just be campaign promises. The key will be to hold the Obama administration and all of its high-profile members accountable to the promises that were made. The massive grassroots organization created for the election of Obama to the presidency has the potential to be an agent for change if it can be put to proper use.

If we are to attain any goal of significant numbers of plug-in hybrid vehicles, the first priority for infrastructure improvement must be a complete revamping of the electric power grid. The system we have now is an antiquated relic dating back to the 1930s. New transmission lines, the seamless incorporation of alternative energy generation systems such as wind and solar, and smart metering to allow the transfer of information between the grid and millions of vehicles will be needed to allow smooth functioning of the system. As important as bridges and roadways are for the present transportation network, a fully functioning electric power grid is the key to our transportation future.

Generating electricity for this grid in a way that reduces greenhouse gas emissions becomes problematic. Coal is the most abundant—yet dirtiest—fuel that we have to generate electricity. A plug-in electric vehicle is really running on coal. Capture and geologic sequestration of the carbon dioxide generated from coal-fired plants is decades away; and hydroelectric, solar, and wind power cannot supply all of our needs. The only other viable power source is nuclear energy; we need to get over our fears and agree that the dangers inherent in an expanded nuclear industry are far less than the consequences of runaway global climate change.

If we are serious about biofuels, we need to level the playing field by removing the tariffs on imported ethanol, the subsidies provided to framers to grow corn, and subsidies to the oil companies to blend ethanol with gasoline. By accounting for the true cost of carbon in our fuel sources through a carbon tax or a cap-and-trade system the advantage of biofuels over gasoline and diesel fuel will become apparent.

The problem with these plans is that they do not get us out of our cars and into more efficient modes of public transportation. Public transportation and decreased use of personal automobiles is something that the Obama administration hasn't discussed. It is a topic avoided by politicians as it may be interpreted as a move to diminish the independence of the American public. The transition to alternative forms of transportation will require a completely different mindset for our society. If we are to meet the goals of reducing our greenhouse gas emissions by 80 percent in the next 40 years, we can't keep driving to work alone. We need a better system than one person driving to work in a 6,000-pound SUV, and we need it soon.

Will biofuels, hybrid cars, and public transit be enough to ensure a brighter future? In a word, no. Our problems won't be solved by government programs and legislated solutions. We need to become an informed citizenry and to hold our government and business institutions accountable to us, to our well-being, and to our long-term goals. Endemic in the present system is a push to maintain the status quo. It is a business-as-usual approach that keeps politicians in office and highly compensated corporate CEOs in charge of their business empires. For the fortunate few who profit disproportionately within the current system, instituting the long-term changes we need is not in their personal best interest. It would be unrealistic to expect the president of a coal company, the CEO of an oil company, the politicians they help elect, or the lobbyists who represent them to support a wholesale change to alternative energies. There is no short-term profit for them or for shareholders; but we need to seriously reconsider whether these special interest groups should have the ability to negatively impact our world's future.

They are a savvy group. We can expect to be bombarded with schemes and ideas that will help "ensure our energy independence."

There will be many bad proposals that will promise to help solve all of our problems but few solutions that address both energy and the environment in a positive way. We need to keep sight of long-term goals and objectives, even when we are told that they can't be done or that they won't be profitable.

There is a perception that Americans won't accept change or inconvenience. Many politicians are more than willing to stand against offshore oil drilling or coal-fired power plants, but the first time a rolling power blackout occurs in their district, or motorists are forced to sit in line for gasoline, they will vote in favor of whatever is perceived to make the problem quickly go away. Americans are resilient and intelligent, and our politicians need to be reminded that we have shown that we can and will do what is necessary to reach our goals. As citizens, we need to have the strength to support visionary and principled politicians who are capable of making tough choices.

We are heading toward a dramatically different world. If we continue with business-as-usual and allow special interests, corporations, and politicians to continue to make shortsighted decisions, the world may end up a particularly unpleasant place, especially for those who live in poor nations. The developing world cannot compete for energy, has minimal resources to put toward infrastructure, and is most threatened by the negative effects of global climate change. For humanitarian and security reasons, we cannot ignore the threat that climate change poses. Is this the world in which we want to live?

Just as I observed in Beijing with the Chinese in 2000, we do have a chance to do something different. We can change how we manage energy and infrastructure to benefit the world's people, to control the effects of climate change, and to mitigate the effects before they overwhelm us. The Chinese were unable to resist following the Western model of constant growth and resource exploitation. Will we be able to shake off more than 100 years of hidebound tradition, greed, and public apathy to make real change? Our opportunity to make the best changes won't be easy for two reasons; it will require us to become involved, and it will require some sacrifices in our way of life.

If you grew up in the 1960s, you know that the civil rights movement was one of the century's most important triumphs. It is easy, looking back, to assume that people of all races and backgrounds were involved in some way in that struggle. Of course this is not true. Most people, black or white, weren't involved at all. Some were involved at the fringe or were quietly supportive. Only a small number of committed and vocal people made a difference. Despite the dangers and the difficulty they did it for a simple reason: it was the right thing to do.

We need the same grassroots action and resolve to help solve the problems that we currently face. More accurately, young people today need to take over the fight and make energy and global climate change their issues. For the rest of their lives, these will be their problems, and they will be the ones who need to solve them. As difficult as it is for me to admit it, I am now middle-aged; and although I want to be a part of the battle, the real heroes in this fight are currently in elementary, middle, and high school. They are the ones who we need to engage because they will decide what kind of world in which they will live.

There is an odd resonance here. Members of the baby-boom generation will remember the phrase "don't trust anyone over 30," attributed to 24-year-old student Jack Weinberg in 1965 when he was the head of the Free Speech Movement in Berkeley, California. Those young adults of the 60s grew up to transform society by exposing political corruption, enhancing societal equality, and recognizing an obligation to the environment. Unfortunately, we also dropped the ball, becoming profligate consumers of energy, connoisseurs of conspicuous consumption, and vastly increasing the level of greenhouse gases in the atmosphere. It's not too late for us to undo some of the damage we have caused. Our generation can help by getting things started, by not losing sight of what we owe our children, and by not passing to them a hopeless situation. If we do nothing or if we don't act intelligently on climate change and renewable sources of energy, we may turn a difficult situation into an impossible one.

The millennial generation, the 76 million Americans born between roughly 1980 and 2000, are especially well suited to the challenges that they are facing. Technology has helped this generation become socially connected in ways that were unimaginable just ten years ago. They are the first generation to be completely immersed in a digital and internet-driven world. Electronically connected to one another, their social networks allow them to cross between the virtual and actual worlds with ease. Although it is argued that such networking creates alienation, the coming generation is not only socially connected, they are also interested in civic action of the sort that will make the kind of changes that we will need possible. While baby-boomers and Generation Xers showed a marked decrease in volunteerism and community involvement when compared to previous generations, the opposite is proving true for the millennial generation.

The millennial generation is built largely upon horizontal communications among their peers, rather than intergenerational vertical communication. They are more trusting of each other than of authority figures. This may be of enormous benefit when it comes to solving the future's problems. Although it seems strange, what we don't need right now is experience—the world is changing so quickly that the actions taken just ten years ago to solve a problem might be exactly the wrong thing to do today. They used to say that experience is the best teacher—today and in the future, it might be more a liability.

The next generation is made up of consensus builders, and this will be a much more useful world-view than total reliance on potentially irrelevant experience. We should expect great things from our next generation—they are our only hope. Look at the success of the Obama presidential campaign as an indication of what can happen when a large group is mobilized into action at a grassroots level. We will need the same sort of leverage if we are going to beat the status quo.

The idea of sacrifice is never popular. If you work hard and get ahead, you feel as if you deserve the luxuries and comforts that your hard work has brought to you. Yet, if we are to get a handle on climate change and energy limits, we will need to change our behaviors in some profound ways. It doesn't mean that we will have to give up our private cars, for example, but it does mean that we will need to use them in different ways. If you live in a city or a suburb, you shouldn't need a car to get from place to place; some form of new mobility transportation should be able to move you where you want to go. If you need to travel between cities, there should be a rail system that can accomplish that cheaper and cleaner than you can go by private automobile. You can still use your car to go to places that simply can't be served by other means of transportation (we live in a very large country), but there should be viable alternatives.

It is important to think of the consequences of your actions rather than focusing on the sacrifices you are making. It is easy to become accustomed to small luxuries that can be wasteful and unnecessary. The flat-screen plasma television in your home uses a large amount of energy in standby mode, just so you can have a picture appear instantly when you switch it on. Would it really be such a hardship to wait for 30 seconds for your television to light up, and in the process saving significant electric energy? In everything you do, you should ask questions. When I turn on the light, from where does the electricity come? How is it generated? Where did the coal come from? How was it mined? How much extra carbon dioxide is spewing out of a plant because I forget to turn off that light? When I fill my tank with gasoline, how much of it came from the tar sands in Canada, and what does my driving an extra twenty miles have to do with the ongoing pollution problems in Saskatchewan? We need to go deep. Instead of asking the price of gasoline, we need to ask if a trip to the market is really necessary at this moment. Could it be combined with another trip tomorrow? If I were to telecommute one day a week, could I consume 20 percent less gas?

It is easier to ignore the realities of a wasteful society than to have to consider uncomfortable questions, but the payoff for the "sacrifice" will be cleaner air, less congestion, and a more responsible role in preventing flooding disasters in low-lying areas of the world. Are these things worth not driving your car to work everyday, or giving up a 500-horsepower SUV in favor of something smaller and more environmentally friendly? Who knows, with fewer cars on the roadways, and smaller lighter cars, driving might just become fun again, instead of the drudgery that commuting in rush hour has become.

During the course of writing this book, I have met a range of very bright people who have been and are working on a better future. They are specialists; most of them are unaware of what the others are doing and some have worked for decades in their laboratories in obscurity. Often their work has been an uphill battle against financial realities that don't reward forward thinkers as much as short-term risk-takers. Like the builders of a medieval cathedral that took centuries to complete, few of these intelligent and dedicated individuals will ever see the true fruit of their labors. Yet they come to work each day, fired with the enthusiasm that they are doing the right thing. If we want to make a difference in the world, if we want the future to be a brighter place, we need to support these people and their work. They are real people working on the real solutions to the problems our children will face.

I started out this book as a car guy, addicted to oil, and with gasoline running through my veins. I still like cars; I probably always will. My love of cars has provided me with a livelihood and a sense of freedom and some truly extraordinary adventures. By keeping my eyes shut, I was able to pretend that the oil-soaked world of the automobile would last forever. Thanks to the many extraordinary people I have met, my eyes are open. I know now that cars, energy, infrastructure, and the world is going to change. I want it to change for the better. As difficult as it will be to alter our habits and our society, we can do it. Not through government mandates and regulation and edicts, but one person at a time. One person can make a difference and each of us can be that person.

We have traveled down a lot of crooked miles to reach this point in history. We are facing many challenges. But the good news in finding the answers is that we are not starting from zero. Good people have been working on solutions far longer than most of us have been aware that we are in trouble. As we have seen in the preceding pages of this book, they continue to do so. You can help them in their quest for a brighter future.

Make sure that our best and brightest become scientists, engineers, and policy makers and make sure that they have what they need to continue their work. Be informed. Question everything. Don't trust the special interests, no matter how appealing their promises. Speak up. Make your needs known. Speak for those who have no voice. Do not let the power of the people slip away or allow it to be sold off to the highest corporate bidder. The planet is ours.

# APPENDIX 1

## Pounds of Carbon Dioxide per mile by transportation mode

| Transportation Mode | Pounds of $CO_2$ per mile |
|---|---|
| Walking | |
| U.S. diet | 0.39 |
| Vegan diet | 0.08 |
| Bicycling | |
| U.S. diet | 0.14 |
| Vegan diet | 0.03 |
| Passenger Vehicle | |
| Gasoline (20 mpg) | 0.97 |
| Gasoline compact (35 mpg) | 0.55 |
| Gasoline SUV (15 mpg) | 1.29 |
| Diesel (20 mpg) | 1.12 |
| Passenger Vehicle- Ethanol (20 mpg) | |
| Corn | 0.76 |
| Sugar cane | 0.43 |
| Cellulosic | 0.09 |
| Motorcycle/Scooter (55 mpg) | 0.30 |
| Passenger vehicle- hybrid (50 mpg) | 0.38 |
| Bus (per passenger mile) | 0.71 |
| Trains/subway | 0.36 |
| Passenger vehicle (20 mpg) | |
| Hydrogen gas | 0.57 |
| Liquid Hydrogen | 1.03 |
| LPG | 0.78 |
| CNG | 0.69 |
| Coal-to-Liquid with sequestration | 1.01 |
| Coal-to-Liquid w/o sequestration | 2.12 |

# ACKNOWLEDGMENTS

Much of the research that led to the writing of this book took place while I was a part of the Knight Wallace Journalism Fellowship at the University of Michigan during 2007-2008. The Fellowship, directed by Charles Eisendrath, provides an opportunity for mid-career journalists to spend time in an academic setting, attending classes, working with professors and undertaking research. I am deeply indebted to Charles and to my fellow Fellows in the Knight Wallace program for their support and encouragement with helpful ideas, intelligent conversation, and their vast experience in telling a compelling story.

Susan Zielinski, the Managing Director of the center for Sustainable Mobility & Accessibility Research and Transformation (SMART) at the University of Michigan acted as one of my advisors during my time there. Our long conversations about New Mobility and the future of transportation helped me understand the work that is taking place to make transportation more equitable and sustainable around the world. David Cole, chairman for the Center for Automotive Research in Ann Arbor, Michigan, also provided guidance regarding the intersection of alternative fuels and hybrid vehicles, suggesting that the automotive future will lie in this direction.

While at the University of Michigan I had many opportunities to discuss topics as diverse as energy, infrastructure, vehicle technology, and geology with a number of experts, and their assistance is greatly appreciated. Professor Carl Simon, the director for the Center for the Study of Complex Systems was particularly helpful in pointing me in the right directions. One person to whom he introduced me was Dr. Irv Salmeen, Research Scientist at the Center for the Study of Complex Systems. After spending a career at Ford Motor Company, Dr. Salmeen is now studying the complex interactions between physics and society, particularly as they relate to the transportation field. Aside from the numerous face-to-face discussions and conversations, and scores of e-mails, I am most grateful for the time he took to review the manuscript for *The Crooked Mile* prior to its publication. Any errors or lack of clarity in the final work is my fault entirely, as his suggestions in every case made the book stronger and easier to understand for a wide-ranging audience.

Because so much of *The Crooked Mile* is comprised from interviews with leading scientists and engineers who are working today on the challenges we face in the future, I am especially grateful to the individuals who took time to meet with me, explain their work to me, and help me put together the elements that created this story. Their generosity made this book possible.

I am also especially grateful to my wife for her support, her critical eye as an editor, and her insistence that *The Crooked Mile* tells a story that is both timely and important. The additional ongoing support and encouragement from Stephany Evans of FinePrint Literary Management is appreciated.

This book carries the words *iunctus populi* on the front pages. This translates to "the people united" and it is to that spirit of universal cooperation that I dedicate this book.

# Notes and References

## Chapter 1

Barzini, Luigi. *Peking to Paris.*
New York: Mitchell Kennerley ©1908.
Lake Elmo, Minnesota: Demontreville Press, Inc. ©2007.

International Energy Agency (IEA), *China Statistics 2006*
http://www.iea.org/Textbase/stats/electricitydata.asp?COUNTRY_
CODE=CN

IPCC, 2007: Summary for Policymakers. In: *Climate Change 2007: The
Physical Science Basis. Contribution of Working Group I to the Fourth
Assessment Report of the Intergovernmental Panel on Climate Change*
[Solomon, S., D. Qin, M. Manning,
Z. Chen, M. Marquis, K.B. Averyt, M.Tignor and H.L. Miller (eds.)].
Cambridge University Press, Cambridge, United Kingdom and New York,
NY, USA.

HR6: *Energy Independence and Security Act of 2007* http://www.govtrack.
us/congress/bill.xpd?bill=h110-6

*How to Avoid Dangerous Climate Change: A Target for U.S. Emissions
Reductions*
[Luers, Amy L., Mastrandrea, Michael D., Hayhoe, Katharine, Frumhoff,
Peter C.] Union of Concerned Scientists, September, 2007.

## Chapter 2

Giddens, Paul H. *Pennsylvania Petroleum 1750-1872: A Documentary
History.*
Pennsylvania Historical and Museum Commission ©1947.
Margaret Anne Mong ©2000.

Tarbell, Ida M. *The History of the Standard Oil Company.*
New York: The Macmillan Company ©1904.
Mineola, New York: Dover Publications ©2003.

Yergin, Daniel. *The Prize: the Epic Quest For Oil, Money & Power.*
New York: Free Press ©1992.

Margonelli, Lisa. *Oil On The Brain: Adventures From The Pump To The Pipeline.*
New York: Nan A. Talese/ Doubleday ©2007.

"Grant in Pennsylvania," *New York Times*, September 18, 1871, p. 5.

Bray, Richard, President of Sohio. *Oil Industry Quotes.*
http://www.geohelp.net/membermquotes.html

Hutton, Frederick Remsen, *The Gas Engine: A treatise on the Internal Combustion Engine.* New York: John Wiley and Sons ©1903

Musselman, M.M. *Get A Horse! The Story of the Automobile in America.*
New York: J.B. Lippincott Company ©1950.

Ickx, Jacques. *Ainsi naquit l'automobile.*
Switzerland: Edita S.A. Lausanne ©1971.

"Motor Experts Study Fuel Supply Problem" *New York Times*, August 31, 1919, pg. 50.

Kettering, C.F. *The Fuel Problem*
Kettering University Archives, Flint, Michigan, Dated 1921

Unpublished statement by Thomas Midgley, Jr., Vice President and General Manager of the Ethyl Gasoline Corporation. Probable release date April, 1925. Kettering University Archives, Flint, Michigan

"Knockless Gas On The Market" *Los Angeles Times*, October 21, 1923, pg. V18.

"Another Man Dies From Insanity Gas" *New York Times*, October 28, 1924, pg. 25.

"Bar Ethyl Gasoline As 5th Victim Dies" *New York Times*, October 31, 1924, pg. 1.

"Death Gas Mixture Danger Exaggerated, Says Expert" *Los Angeles Times*, November 23, 1924, pg. G3.

"Declares Ethyl Gasoline As Safe as Straight Fuel" *The Washington Post*, November 23, 1924, pg. A3.

"Sees Deadly Gas A Peril In Streets" *New York Times*, April 22, 1925, pg. 25.

"Inquiry To Fix Ethyl Gasoline Health Hazard" *Chicago Daily Tribune*, May 21, 1925, pg. 25.

"Shift Ethyl Inquiry To Surgeon General" *New York Times*, May 21, 1925, pg. 7.

"Seven Experts Named To Study Ethyl Gas" *New York Times*, June 7, 1925, pg. 2.

"Find Lead In Gasoline Not Hazard" *Los Angeles Times*, January 20, 1926, pg. 4.

"Tetraethyl Lead Is Effective Foe of Engine 'Knock'" *The Washington Post*, June 12, 1927, pg. A3.

"Experimental Studies on the Effects of Ethyl Gasoline and its Combustion Products" [Sayers, R.R., Fieldner, A.C., Yart, W.P., Thomas, B.G.H.] Department of the Interior, Bureau of Mines, 1927.

"Proceedings of a Conference to Determine Whether or Not There Is a Public Health Question in the Manufacture, Distribution, or Use of Tetraethyl Lead Gasoline." Department of Health Bulletin No. 158, August 1925.

Boyd, T.A. *The Early History of Ethyl Gasoline* Report OC-83, Project #11-3, Research Laboratory Division, General Motors Corporation, Detroit, Michigan (unpublished) June 8, 1943. Kettering University Archives, Flint Michigan.

Hamilton, Alice *Exploring Dangerous Trades: The Autobiography of Alice Hamilton, MD.* Boston: Northeastern University Press ©1943, (reprinted 1985).

"Caltech Scientist Tells of Lead Poison Damage" Getze, George. *Los Angeles Times*, September 12, 1965 pg. B.

"Warning Issued on Lead Poisoning" Sullivan, Walter. *New York Times*, September 12, 1965, pg. 71.

"E.P.A. Ban On Lead In Gas Is Voided" *New York Times*, January 30, 1975, pg. 22.

"Ethyl Corp., a Highflier Until the 1970s, Keeps Reeling From Environmental Jabs" By Vasil Pappass, *The Wall Street Journal*, October 2, 1979, pg. 48.

Kovarik, Bill *Charles F. Kettering and the 1921 Discovery of Tetraethyl Lead In the Context of Technical Alternatives*
Originally presented to the Society of Automotive Engineers Fuels & Lubricants Conference, Baltimore, Md. 1994 and revised in 1999.
http://www.radford.edu/~wkovariki/papers/kettering.html

"The Secret History of Lead" [Kitman, Jamie Lincoln]
*The Nation.* March 20, 2000.
http://www.thenation.com/doc/20000320/kitman

Markowitz, Gerald and Rosner, David, *Deceit and Denial: The Deadly Politics of Industrial Pollution.*
Berkeley, California: University of California Press ©2002.

"Arnold Says Standard Oil Gave Nazis Rubber Process" by Frank L. Kluckhorn *New York Times*, March 27, 1942, pg. I.

"Sharp Words Mark Standard Oil Case" Trussell, C.P., *New York Times*, August 22, 1942, pg. 26.

Hager, Thomas *The Alchemy of Air*
New York: Harmony Books ©2008.

"Nuclear Energy And The Fossil Fuels" by M. King Hubbert. Presented before the Spring Meeting of the Southern District, Division of Petroleum, American Petroleum Institute in San Antonio, Texas March 7-8-9, 1956.

**The conference where I interviewed Kenneth Deffeyes was** Nobel Conference 43- Heating up: The Energy Debate, October 2-3, 2007 at Gustavus Adolphus College, St. Peter, Minnesota.

Deffeyes, Kenneth S. *Beyond Oil: The View From Hubbert's Peak* New York: Hill and Wang ©2005.

McPhee, John Annals of the Former World New York: Farrar, Straus, and Giroux ©2000.

"Crude Oil: Uncertainty About Future Oil Supply Makes it Important to Develop a Strategy for Addressing a Peak and Decline in Oil Production" United States Government Accountability Office (GAO) GAO-07-283, February, 2007.

Neil Golightly's comments were made at "New Mobility: The Emerging Transportation Economy" conference sponsored by Sustainable Mobility and Accessibility Research and Transformation (SMART) at the University of Michigan, Ann Arbor, June 11-12, 2008.

"At Sea: Shell's Radical Rig" *Forbes*, Volume 182, Number 11, November 24, 2008. pg. 72.

"Difficult Oil" *Responsible Energy: The Shell Sustainability Report 2007* Royal Dutch Shell. Pg. 11.

"Thunder Horse: No Ordinary Project" BP America Website. Accessed January 22, 2009. http://www.bp.com/genericarticle.do?categoryId=9004519 &contentId=7009088

"Oil shale stuck between rock and wild place" by Michael Riley, *The Denver Post*, August 17, 2008 http://www.denverpost.com/news/ci_10220108?source=pop_section_news

"Oil Shale Pushed as Domestic Oil Source, but many Doubts Remain" by Kent Garber, *U.S. News & World Report*, November 3, 2008 http://www.usnews.com/articles/news/national/2008/11/03/oil-shale-pushed-as-domestic-oil-source-but-many-doubts-remain.

"In Waning Hours, Bush Administration Fortifies Oil Shale Industry" by Jad Mouawad, *New York Times*, November 18, 2008 http://greeninc.blogs.nytimes.com/2008/11/18/in-waning-hours-bush-administration-fortifies-oil-shale-industry.

Ashworth, William *Ogallala Blue: Water And Life On The High Plains* Vermont: The Countryman Press ©2006

"Little city is at center of a great debate" by Dan Egan. *Milwaukee Journal Sentinel*, December 6, 2008 http://www.jsonline.com/news/wisconsin/35664859.html

"Unconventional Crude: Canada's synthetic-fuels boom" by Elizabeth Kolbert, *The New Yorker*, November 12, 2007. pg. 46.

"Cheap oil, but at what cost?" by Howard Witt. *Chicago Tribune*, November 26, 2008.

**Iraq holds more than 115 billion barrels of oil...** Energy Information Agency (EIA) http://www.eia.doe.gov/cabs/Iraq/Full.html

### Chapter 3

**Carnot Cycle and engine efficiency,** Bosch Automotive Handbook 4th Edition, 1996.

"Advanced Technologies & Energy Efficiency" *U.S. Department of Energy* http://www.fueleconomy.gov/feg/atv.shtml. Accessed: 3/16/2008

"Swarming to public transit, cheaper gas" by Noah Bierman, *The Boston Globe* May 18, 2008. http://www.boston.com/news/local/articles/2008/05/18/swarming_to_public_transit_cheaper_gas.

"As Gas Prices Go Down, Driving Goes Up" by Clifford Krauss, *New York Times*, October 30, 2008.

"Evidence suggests commuters are abandoning transit habit," by Steve Hymon and Ruben Vives *Los Angeles Times*, November 20, 2008.

"Blood and Oil: Vehicle Characteristics in Relation to Fatality Risk and Fuel Economy" by Leon S. Robertson, *American Journal of Public Health*, 96,11, November 2006, pg. 1906.

**History of the Lohner-Porsche**, Porsche Cars North America Press Release, Los Angeles Auto Show, November 14, 2007.

**Partnership for a New Generation of Vehicles**, reference web site at www.pngv.org

"1999 Technology of the Year," by Kevin Clemens, *Automobile Magazine*, January, 2000.

"Chinese hybrid car is charging into weak market," by Don Lee, *Los Angeles Times*, December 13, 2008.
http://www.latimes.com/business/printedition/la-fi-chinacar13-2008dec13,0,6988333.story

"The Car of the Future—but at What Cost?" by Steven Mufson, *Washington Post*, November 25, 2008, pg. A01.

"The Economics of Hybrids" by Mike Spector, *The Wall Street Journal*, October 29, 2007 pg. R5.

**TABLE 1** was generated using industry data obtained through http://www.subaru.com/tools/comparator/index.jsp?from=topNav

Deberitz, Jürgen *Lithium: Production and application of a fascinating and versatile element*. Munich, Germany: sv corporate media GmbH ©2006.

"Rare Earth Elements- Critical Resources for High Technology" [Peter H. Stauffer, James W. Hedrick, Gretta J. Orris] United States Geological Survey 087-02, November 20, 2002.

http://pubs.usgs.gov/fs/2002/fs087-02.

"China gambit paying off for Goldman Sachs," by Cathy Chan and Adrian Cox, *Bloomberg*, October 24, 2006.

"Molycorp closes on purchase of Mountain Pass rare earth mining ops," *Antara News*, November 2, 2008.
http://www.antara.co.id/en/print/?i=1224119942.

**Chapter 4**

"Trumpeter Swans Favor Monticello For Winter Digs" by Beth Gauper. *St. Paul Pioneer Press,* March 6, 2005.
http://www.bethgauper.com/articles/20050306_monticello.hmtl

The Trumpeter Swan Society
www.trumpeterswansociety.org

Information on the Boiling Water Reactor (BWR) at Monticello, MN provided by Xcel Energy.

"France Moves Ahead With Nuclear Waste Project" by David Kestenbaum. *National Public Radio*, November 7, 2008
http://www.npr.org/templates/story/story.php?dtoryId=12837958

"Coal Production and Number of Mines by State, County, and Mine Type 2007" *Energy Information Administration (EIA)*
http://www.eia.doe.gov/cneaf/coal/page/acr/table2.html
Accessed on 11/11/2008

"2007 Background of U.S. Coal Industry" *U.S. Department of Commerce, Office of Energy and Environmental Industries.*

"U.S. Coal Supply and Demand: 2006 Review" by Fred Freme. *U.S. Energy Information Administration.*

"U.S. Coal Supply and Demand: 2007 Review" by Fred Freme. *U.S. Energy Information Administration.*

"U.S. Coal Exports 2006-2007" *U.S. Energy Information Administration*
http://www.eia.doe.gov/cneaf/col/quarterly/html/t7p01p1.html
Accessed 4/13/2008

Reece, Erik, *Lost Mountain*
New York: Riverhead Books ©2006.

Goodell, Jeff *Big Coal: The Dirty Secret Behind America's Energy Future*
Boston: Mariner/ Houghton Mifflin Company ©2007.

Address of Hon. Mary Kaptur of Ohio in the U.S. House of Representatives
on June 20, 2006 on Mine safety and Honoring the Miners of Harlan County

"Surface Mining Control and Reclamation Act of 1977: Public Law 95-87"
*U.S. Department of the Interior*
http://www.osmre.gov/topic/SMCRA/publiclaw95-87.shtm

Information on the Allan S. King Coal-Fired power plant in Oak Park
Heights, MN provided by Xcel Energy.

"Spill of coal ash blankets countryside," *St. Petersburg Times*, December 25,
2008 pg. 15A.

"A Summary and Comparison of Bird Mortality from Anthropogenic Causes
with an Emphasis on Collisions" [Erickson, Wallace P, Johnson, Gregory
D., Young, David P. Jr.] USDA Forest Service Gen. Tech Rep. PSW-GTR-
191.2005 pg. 1029.

"History of the Electric Power Industry" *Edison Electric Institute*
http://www.eei.org/industry_issues/industry_overview_and_statistics/history/
index.htm
Accessed on 7/17/2008

"Annual Report on U.S. Wind Power Installation, Cost, and Performance
Trends: 2007" [Wiser, Ryan, Bolinger, Mark], *U.S. Department of Energy*,
May 2008.

"Wind Energy Bumps into Power Grid Limits" by Mathew L. Wald. *New
York Times*, August 27, 2008

"Report Says Sun and Wind Power Could Threaten Nation's Electric Grid" by Mathew L. Wald. *New York Times*, November 10, 2008.

"T. Boone Pickens lowers spending for alternative energy plan" *Los Angeles Times*, November 12, 2008.

Interview with T. Boone Pickens took place at the Alternative Fuels & Vehicles National Conference and Expo in Las Vegas, NV on May 13, 2008.

"Profitable climate solutions: Correcting the sign error" by Amory Lovins. *Energy & Environmental Science,* November 11, 2008. http://www.rsc.org/delivery/_ArticleLinking/DisplayHTMLArticleforfree. cfm?JournalCode=EE&Year=2009&ManuscriptID=b814525n&Iss=Advanc e_Article

"Nissan Plans Electric Car in U.S. by '10" by Bill Vlasic, *New York Times*, May 13, 2008.

"Paradigm shift gives new momentum to electric cars" by Malachy Tuohy, *International Herald Tribune*, November 26, 2008.

Tesla Motors
www.teslamotors.com

Information on fast battery charging comes from a presentation on Hybrid Vehicles by Michael Tamor, Ford Motor Company, sponsored by the Center For the Study of Complex Systems at the University of Michigan, Ann Arbor, on 10/23/2007.

## Chapter 5

Steger, Will and Bowermaster, Jon, *Crossing Antarctica* New York: Laurael/Dell ©1991.

IPCC, 2007: Summary for Policymakers. In: *Climate Change 2007: The Physical Science Basis. Contribution of Working Group I to the Fourth Assessment Report of the Intergovernmental Panel on Climate Change* [Solomon, S., D. Qin, M. Manning,

Z. Chen, M. Marquis, K.B. Averyt, M.Tignor and H.L. Miller (eds.)]. Cambridge University Press, Cambridge, United Kingdom and New York, NY, USA.

"Scientific Assessment of the Effects of Global Climate Change on the United States" *A Report of the Committee on Environment and Natural Resources, National Science and Technology Council*, May 2008

"Understanding and Responding to Climate Change: 2008 Edition" *National Academy of Science*

**The conference where I interviewed James Hansen was** Nobel Conference 43- Heating up: The Energy Debate, October 2-3, 2007 at Gustavus Adolphus College, St. Peter, Minnesota.

"Target Atmospheric $CO_2$: Where Should Humanity Aim?" [Hansen, James, Sato, Makiko, Kharecha, Pushker, Beerling, David, Berner, Robert, Masson-Delmonte, Valerie, Pagani, Mark, Raymo, Maureen, Royer, Dana L., Zachos, James C.] *The Open Atmospheric Science Journal*, 2008, 2, pg. 217-231

"Study warns of environmental crisis" by Stephannie Furtak, *Yale Daily News*, November 14, 2008. http://www.yaledailynews.com/articles/printarticle/26487

"Nature's Carbon balance confirmed," BBC News, April 28, 2008 http://news.bbc.co.uk/go/pr/fr/-/2/hi/science/nature/7363600.stm Accessed: 4/30/2008

"Contributions of past and present human generations to committed warming caused by carbon dioxide" by Pierre Friedlingstein and Susan Solomon. *Proceedings of The National Academy of Science of the USA*, vol. 102, no.31 pg. 10832-10836, August 2, 2005.

Stern, Nicholas, *The Stern Review on the Economics of Climate Change* London: HM Treasury ©2006

"Warming Called Threat to Global Economy" by Juliet Eilperin, *Washington Post*, October 31, 2006, pg. A18.

**The conference where I interviewed Steven Chu was** Nobel Conference 43- Heating up: The Energy Debate, October 2-3, 2007 at Gustavus Adolphus College, St. Peter, Minnesota.

**Information on IGCC** obtained through the National Energy Technology Laboratory of the U.S. Department of Energy.
http://www.netl.doe.gov/technologies/coalpower/gasification/index.html

Information of FutureGen was obtained through the FutureGen Industrial Alliance
http://www.futuregenalliance.org/
"Carbon Dioxide Capture and Geologic Storage: A core element of a global energy technology strategy to address climate change" [Dooley, JJ, Dahowski, RT, Davidson, CL, Wise. MA, Gupta, N, Kim, SH, Malone, EL] *Battelle Memorial Institute*, April 2006.

"An Evaluation of Cap-And-Trade Programs For Reducing U.S. Carbon Emissions" *The Congress of the United States, Congressional Budget Office*, June, 2001

"The fool's gold of carbon trading" by Jonathan Leake, *The Sunday Times*, November 30, 2008.

☐Temporary La Niña☐s cooling effect does not stall global warming☐ *World Meteorological Organization* Info Note No. 44, April 4, 2008
http://www.wmo.ch/pages/mediacentre/infonotes/info_44_en.html

**Chapter 6**

**Information on Genetically Modified Corn** can be found at *Union of Concerned Scientists*. 2007. http://www.ucsusa.org/food_and_agriculture/science_and_impacts/impacts_genetic_engineering/environmental-effects-of.html
and
U.S. Grain Council, www.grains.org

"Ethanol plant's water usage raises some concerns" by Jim Paul *USA Today*, June 19, 2006
http://www.usatoday.com/tech/science/2006-06-19-ethanol-water_x.htm

"Water supply can't meet thirst for new industry" by Greg Gordon, *Minneapolis Star Tribune*, December 26, 2005.

"Reassessing Hypoxia Forecasts for the Gulf of Mexico" [Scavia, Donald, Donnelly, Kristina A.] *Environmental Science and Technology, American Chemical Society.* October 12, 2007.

"Alcohol As Fuel For Automobiles" *New York Times*, February 12, 1907, pg. 6.

"More Alcohol Wanted" By Harry A. Mount *New York Times*, February 13, 1921, pg. X9.

Leslie, Eugene H. *Motor Fuels: Their Production and Technology* New York: Chemical Catalog Company ©1923.

"Brazil seeks to cut gasoline payments" *New York Times*, January 11, 1931, pg. 60.

"Motor-Fuel Blend Decried By Oil-Men" *New York Times*, April 16, 1933, pg. N11.

"Interests Battle On Gasoline Blend" *New York Times*, April 15, 1936, pg. 18.

"Brazil Tries Mixing Alcohol From Sugar With Gasoline to Reduce Its Oil Imports" by William Hieronymus *Wall Street Journal*, November 28, 1977, pg. 30.

"A New Look at Alcohol Fuels", by Jack Anderson and Les Whitten, *The Washington Post*, August 9, 1977, pg. B13.

"Value to U.S. Doubted" by Marshall Schuon, *New York Times*, June 9, 1979, pg. 32.

"Energy Policy Act of 2005" *Environmental Protection Agency*, Public Law 109-58, August 8, 2005.

HR6: *Energy Independence and Security Act of 2007* http://www.govtrack. us/congress/bill.xpd?bill=h110-6

"Ethanol Fuels: Energy Balance, Economics, and Environmental Impacts are Negative" [Pimentel, David] *Natural Resources Research*, Volume 12, Number 2, June 2003.

"Ethanol Can Contribute to Energy and Environmental Goals" [Farrell, Alexander E., Plevin, Richard J., Turner, Brian T., Jones, Andrew D., O'Hare, Michael, Kammen, Daniel M.] *Science Magazine*, Volume 311, January 27, 2006, pg. 506-508.

"Thinking clearly about biofuels: ending the irrelevant 'net energy' debate and developing better performance metrics for alternative fuels" [Dale, Bruce E.] *Biofuels, Bioproducts & Biorefining*, 1:14-17, 2007.

"Implied Objectives of U.S. Biofuel Subsidies" [Rubin, Ofir D., Carriquiry, Miguel, Hayes, Dermot J.] *Center for Agricultural and Rural Development, Iowa State University,* Working paper 08-WP 459, February, 2008. http://www.card.iastate.edu/publications/DBS/PDFFiles/08wp459.pdf

Report DOE/EIA-0383(2009) *Energy Information Administration* (Early Release) December 2008.

"Consumer Price Index" *Bureau of Labor Statistics* http://www.bls.gov/news.release/cpi.nr0.htm

"Food and Fuel Compete for land" by Andrew Martin, *New York Times*, December 18. 2007.

"As global food costs rise, are biofuels to blame?" by Mark Clayton, *Christian Science Monitor*, January 28, 2008.

**Commodity, marketing, and transport pricing can be found at** Agricultural Market Services, U.S. Department of Agriculture http://www.ams.usda.gov

"Emerging Biofuels: Outlook on Effects on U.S. Grain, Oilseed, and Livestock Markets" [Tokgoz, Simia, Elobeid, Amani, Fabiosa, Jacinto, Hayes, Dermot J., Babcock, Bruce A., Yu,, Tun-Hsiang (Edward), Dong, Fengxia, Hart, Chad E., Beghin, John C.] *Center for Agriculture and Rural*

*Development*, Iowa State University. Staff Report 07-SR101, May 2007.

## Chapter 7

"Enzymatic Hydrolysis Technology Background" *U.S. Department of Energy*
http://www1.eere.energy.gov/biomass/printable_versions/technology_
background.html
Accessed: 12/02/2008.

"Cellulase: a perspective" [Eveleigh, D.E.] *Philosophical Transactions of the Royal Society of London*, A321, 435-447 (1987).

"Mycological Obituary: Elwyn T. Reese" Inoculum: *Newsletter of the Mycological Society of America*, Vol. 45(1), April, 1994, pg. 21.

"The new alchemy: turning trash into fuel" by John J. Fialka, *The Wall Street Journal*, November 2, 1999.

"GM Takes a Stake in Ethanol maker" by David Welch, *Business Week*, January 13, 2008.

"General Motors finances ethanol maker Coskata" by James R, Healey, *USA Today*, January 13, 2008.

"Coskata Inc. Selects Madison, Pa for Commercial Demonstration facility to produce Next-Generation Ethanol" Coskata Inc. Press Release, April 25, 2008.

"U.S. Sugar Looks Sweeter With Coskata Second-Gen Ethanol Plant" by Chris Morrison *BNET Industries*, November 19, 2008.
http://industry.bnet.com/energy/1000391/us-sugar-looks-sweeter-with-coskata-second-gen-ethanol-plant.html

"DOE Selects Six Cellulosic Ethanol Plants for up to $385 Million in Federal Funding" *U.S. Department of Energy, Office of Public Affairs*, February 28, 2007.

"Biofuel crops increase carbon emissions" by Alan Zarembo *Los Angeles Times*, February 8, 2008.

"Studies Deem Biofuels a Greenhouse Threat" by Elisabeth Rosenthal *New York Times*, February 8, 2008.

"Land Clearing and Biofuel Carbon Debt" [Fargione, Joseph, Hill, Jason, Tilman, David, Polasky, Steven, Hawthorne, Peter] *Science*, Vol. 319, February 29, 2008, pg. 1235.

"Use of U.S. Croplands for Biofuels Increases Greenhouse Gases Through Emissions from land-Use Change" [Searchinger, Timothy, Heimlich, Ralph, Houghton, R.A., Dong, Fengxia, Elobeid, Amani, Fabiosa, Jacinto, Tokgoz, Simla, Hayes, Dermot, Yu, Tun-Hsiang] *Science*, Vol. 319, February 29, 2008, pg. 1238

"Tropical Biofuels Getting Less and Less Green" by Eli Kintisch, *Science*, July 9, 2008.
http://science now.sciencemag.org/cgi/content/full/2008/709/1

"Clearing forests for biofuels hurts climate: study" *Reuters*, December 1, 2008.
http://www.reauters.com/articlePrint?articleID=USTRE4B04CA20081201
Accessed: 12/2/2008

"Hope or Hype" by Mark Neuzil, *Momentum*, Institute on the Environment, University of Minnesota, Fall 08-1.1 pg. 17.

"Now That's Green" by Kevin Clemens, *European Car*, Volume 40, Number 3, March, 2009.

"Biomass As Feedstock For A Bioenergy And Bioproducts Industry:The Technical Feasibility Of A Billion-ton Annual Supply" *USDA and DOE*, April, 2005.

"A National Laboratory Market and Technology Assessment of the 30x30 Scenario" *National Renewable Energy Laboratory* (NREL) Technical Report NREL/TP-510-40942, January, 2007.

"The Short History of Natural Gas Vehicles" *Random History*
http://www.randomhistory.com/2008/09/08_ngv.html
Accessed: 12/10/2008

"The abundant fossil fuel you've never heard of" by Jeremy Kutner, *Christian Science Monitor,* December 3, 2008.

"Oil from Coal— To meet the Nation's Need" by Bernard Jaffe, *New York Times*, September 12, 1948, pg. SM17.

"RAND study warns of liquid coal problems" by Ken Ward Jr. *Charleston Gazette*, November 5, 2008.
http://wvgazette.com/News/200811040756
Accessed: 11/5/2008.

"BMW Hydrogen 7" *BMW USA* Press Information
http://www.bmwusa.com/Standard/Content/Uniquely/FutureTechnologies/
Hydrogen.aspx?enc=DTVVlzsxJb0GJb9oWmD0WA==
"The Truth About Hydrogen" by Jeff Wise, *Popular Mechanics*, November, 2006.

"For a more Sustainable future" *Ford Motor Company* 2006/7 Sustainability Report.

Larry Burns (GM) keynote address at the Alternative Fuels & Vehicles National Conference and Expo in Las Vegas, NV on May 13, 2008.

"Ballard ready to give up on fuel cell car business" by Wendy Stueck, *Globe and Mail*, November 6, 2007.

"Honda CR-Z Hybrid and FCX Clarity Fuel Cell Vehicle Introduce Detroit to Next-Generation Green Cars" *American Honda Motor Company* Press Release, January 13, 2008.

## Chapter 8

"A Brief History of Twin Cities Transit" Minnesota Streetcar Museum
http://www.trolleyride.org/History/Narrative/TC_Transit.html

Levittown Historical Society
http://www.levittownhistoricalsociety.org/

"Total Midyear World Population" *Negative Population Growth* Facts and

Figures.
http://www.npg.org/facts/world_pop_year.htm

"2007 Production Statistic" *International Organization of Motor Vehicle Manufacturers*
http://oica.net/category/production-statistics/

"As China Roars, Pollution Reaches Deadly Extremes" by Joseph Kahn and Jim Yardley, *New York Times*, August 26, 2007.

"China's Cars, Accelerating A Global Demand for Fuel", by Arianna Eunjung Chu, *Washington Post*, July 28, 2008, pg. A01.

Carson, Rachel *Silent Spring*
Boston: Houghton Mifflin ©1962.

Schumacher, E.F. *Small is Beautiful*
London: Harper & Row ©1973

"M. Hubbert King on the Nature of Growth" Testifying before a House of Representatives subcommittee on the regulation of the national growth rate of energy usage. June 5, 1974.

"Deep Ecology Movement" *Foundation for Deep Ecology*
http://www.deepecology.org/movement.htm
McKibben, Bill *Deep Economy*
New York: Times Books ©2007.

"New Mobility: The Next Generation of Sustainable Urban Transportation" by Susan Zielinski *National Academy of Engineering*
http://www.nae.edu/nae/bridgecom.nsf/weblinks/MKEZ-6WHPJK?OpenDocument

"Pioneering New Mobility in Cape Town" by Katie Fry Hester and Susan Zielinski, Information sheet from SMART, University of Michigan.

"Emission Facts: Greenhouse Gas Emissions from a Typical Passenger Vehicle" *U.S. Environmental Protection Agency* EPA420-F-05-004 February 2005.

International Transport Forum 2008- Research Findings, Leipzig 2008- http://www.internationaltransportforum.org/Topics/pdf/ResearchFindings2008.pdf

"National Research Council Special Report 290- Potential Impacts of Climate Change on U.S. Transportation"- ISBN 0-309-11905-7, 2008

"Compendium of Physical Activities: an update of activity codes and MET Intensities," Ainsworth, Haskell, Whitt, Irwin, Swartz, Strath, O'Brien, Bassett, Jr., Schmitz, Emplaincourt, Jacobs, Jr. and Leon. *Medicine & Science in Sports & Exercise.* 32 (9): S498-S516

Carbon Dioxide Information Analysis Center- *Department of Energy* http://cdiac.esd.ornl.gov/pns/faq.html

"USDA 2001-2002- Agricultural Fact Book" *USDA* 2001-2002. www.usda.gov/factbook/chapter2.htm

"Monitoring the Nation's Health December Newsletter," *Center for Disease Control and Prevention* (2007). http://www.cdc.gov/nchs/pressroom/data/MNH_1207.htm

"Diet, Energy and Global Warming," Eshel, Martin (2006). *Earth Interactions* 10:1-17 http://geosci.uchicago.edu/~gidon/papers/nutri/nutriEI.pdf

"Driving vs. Walking: Cows, Climate Change, and Choice," Cohen and Heberger, April 2008, *Pacific Institute* www.pacinst.org

*ABC News* February 13, 2005

"Emission Facts: Average Carbon Dioxide Emissions Resulting from gasoline and Diesel Fuel" *Environmental Protection Agency* (February 2005) EPA420-F-05-001

"DOT 84-08" *Department of Transportation* June 18, 2008, http://www.dot.gov/affairs/dot8408.htm

"DOT Traffic Volume Trends" *Department of Transportation*
http://www.fhwa.dot.gov/ohim/tvtw/tvtpage.htm

"Greenhouse Gas Impacts of Expended Renewable and Alternative Fuels
Use" *Environmental Protection Agency* EPA420-F-07-035, April 2007

"Plug-in Hybrid Cars: Chart of CO2 Emissions Ranked by Power Source"
by Michael Graham Richard, *Tree Hugger*, April 15, 2008 http://www.
treehugger.com/files/2008/04/plug-in-hybrid-cars-co2-emissions-electricity-
energy.php

"Does Rail Transit Save Energy or Reduce Greenhouse Gas Emissions?"
O'Toole, *Cato Institute*, April 14, 2008.
http://www.cato.org/pubs/pas/pa-615.pdf


**Chapter 9**

Fisher, Jerry M. *The Pacesetter: The Untold Story of Carl G. Fisher*
California: Lost Coast Press ©1998,

"Autos: A Bailout Could Have a Green Twist" by Stacy Trombino, *Business
Week*, November 14, 2008.

"While Detroit Slept" by Thomas L. Friedman, *New York Times*, December
10, 2008.

Putnam, Robert D. *Bowling Alone*
New York: Simon & Schuster ©2000.

# INDEX